THE PERILS
OF
PROSPERITY
1914–32

The Perils o.

THE CHICAGO HISTORY OF AMERICAN CIVILIZATION

Daniel J. Boorstin, EDITOR

Prosperity, 1914-32

By William E. Leuchtenburg

 THE UNIVERSITY OF CHICAGO PRESS

CHICAGO & LONDON

THE UNIVERSITY OF CHICAGO PRESS, CHICAGO 60637
The University of Chicago Press, Ltd., London W. C. 1

Editor's Preface

The years between America's entrance into World War I and the end of postwar prosperity, which Mr. Leuchtenburg covers in this volume, have been peculiarly attractive to historical moralists and to critics of American civilization. The idealism of Woodrow Wilson and our failure to follow his lead into the League of Nations have become symbols for the continuing weaknesses of American diplomacy and for our refusal to accept responsibilities as a world power. Especially for European observers, the prosperity of our "Jazz Age" has seemed to illustrate "American materialism" at its worst. Most Americans, although finding it hard not to envy an age which held its liquor so well and had so much fun, shake their heads and defensively try to explain the period away. Glad to put its excesses outside the main stream of our history, we have called those years a national jag—a time when the American people took a vacation from sober traditional virtues. We have liked to think that the era proved next to nothing about our true national character. We have readily believed that its only legacies were a hangover and an instructive catalogue of the Deadly Sins.

In this volume, Mr. Leuchtenburg has placed the era in the full context of American history. He is neither defensive nor moralistic. With the advantage of being too young to lose objectivity through his own recollections, he reconstructs the story and the spirit of the age from its documents. He rediscovers people we mistakenly thought we knew, and he shows us that what we remember of Harding, Coolidge, and Hoover is not their character but their reputation. He stirs our sympathy for opinionated and bewildered men by letting them speak for themselves and by giving us a sense of the turmoil in which they lived.

The age itself, Mr. Leuchtenburg reminds us, cannot be taken in isolation from its past and future. He finds movements in the period which reach back to the nineteenth century: the rise of the city, the change from handicraft to assembly lines, the ascent to the world stage. He sees the beginnings of institutions which would produce the New Deal and with it the changed attitude toward government that has stayed with us ever since. For him the age was not a frolic, in which a people stepped out of character, but a climax of passions long brewing. He reminds us of the gulf which separates horse-and-buggy America from the new age of Franklin Roosevelt, but he also shows us how the crossing of that gulf was itself a major event in American history.

In these ways he admirably fulfils the aims of the Chicago History of American Civilization. The series contains two kinds of books: a *chronological* group, of which this volume is one, which will provide a coherent narrative of American history from its beginning to the present day, and a *topical* group, which will deal with the history of varied and significant aspects of American life. Immediately preceding this volume in the chronological group is Samuel P. Hays's *The Response to Industrialism, 1885–1914*. Dexter Perkins' *The New*

Editor's Preface

Age of Franklin Roosevelt, 1932–45 takes up the story where Mr. Leuchtenburg leaves off.

DANIEL J. BOORSTIN

Table of Contents

Prologue

In 1914 the United States was not so far from the early years of the republic. There were men still living whose fathers had known Jefferson and John Adams and had been acquainted with Longfellow. In prairie towns women remembered the day Ralph Waldo Emerson had alighted from the train to talk to the local Chautauqua. There were thousands of men still alive who had fought under Stonewall Jackson at Chancellorsville or had stood with George Thomas at Chickamauga, even a few veterans who had marched with Winfield Scott on the Halls of Montezuma. A small company of loyal Democrats who voted for Woodrow Wilson in 1912 had cast their first votes for Martin Van Buren or James K. Polk. Negroes walked the streets of Savannah and Charleston who had been born in slavery.

In railroad towns strung along the Burlington or the Great Northern, men sat in the sun who had fought the Nez Percés or the Sioux, who had scouted with Kit Carson and traded with Jim Bridger. In the Nevada hills, men with picks and burros still prospected for gold and silver; the last great strike had been made just eleven years before. Much of the land west of the Missouri was yet to be homesteaded. Arizona and New Mexico had been states for only two years. On the edge of modern, prosperous western towns, tribes of Indians still pitched their tents.

Only eighteen years later, when 1932 rolled around, it seemed an eon since the days of the nineteenth century. The task of industrialization had been essentially completed. Machines had replaced the old artisans; there were few coopers, blacksmiths, or cobblers left. The livery stable had been torn down to make way for the filling station. Technology had revolutionized the farm. In 1918, there were 80,000 tractors; in 1929, 850,000. The Old West had disappeared; ranchers were even concerned for a time lest they lose their cowhands to movie westerns. The empire builders like James J. Hill were gone.

The metropolis had shattered the supremacy of the small town, and life seemed infinitely more impersonal. It was proverbial that the apartment-house dweller did not know his neighbor. The tradition of personal journalism was all but ended; no one any longer knew who edited the magazine or newspaper. The depression destroyed the Chautauqua, but it could scarcely have survived the competition of the radio and the movies in any event. "Now the players do not come to the towns," wrote Sherwood Anderson in 1932. "They are in Los Angeles. We see but the shadows of players. We listen to the shadows of voices. Even the politicians do not come to us now. They stay in the city and talk to us on the radio."

Grayed by bureaucracy, life had lost a good deal of its earlier pungency. Little was left of the tradition of the self-made man. The aspiring attorney no longer read law in the office; even the businessman was more and more trained in professional business schools. The social worker ministered to the town

Prologue

drunkard. No one listened to the village atheist. The school-master held a diploma from Teachers College.

In 1914, the progressive movement was at its height. Americans believed that by adopting institutional changes—the direct primary, the short ballot, the recall—political life might be made over. There was no scourge that would not eventually yield to reason and goodness, they thought. When the reformers crusaded—against the city machine, the sweatshop employer, the traction magnate—they could identify the enemies they were fighting. In 1932, Americans no longer had the same sense of confidence either in themselves or in the efficacy of reform. They no longer believed evil would be so easily routed. They were not always even sure what "evil" was, or how to recognize their enemies.

In the American town of 1914, class lines, though not frozen, were unmistakable. Each town had its old families who fixed the social standards. Moral standards were set by the church and by the family. Parents were confident enforcers of the moral code. By 1932, much of the sense of authority was gone. Save in rural islands, the church had lost its hold. "We haven't enough religion among us," one man grumbled, "to get up a good church fight." Parents were no longer certain they knew how to raise their children. The old arbiters—the Newport aristocracy, the town gentry—were ignored.

As Newport mansions and Fifth Avenue homes were dismantled, social authority was diffused. If it passed anywhere at all, it passed to Hollywood. The excesses of the movie capital reflected the bafflement of a country faced by the problem of how to measure success and find stability when there was no longer a recognized class to provide leadership. Although boxing bouts had once been staged on offshore barges to avoid the police, by 1932 it had become a mark of social acceptance to hold a ringside seat at a championship fight. The old restaurants like Shanley's and Rector's vanished, and places like Texas Guinan's night spot took their place.

In retrospect, the years before World War I seemed like a lost Arcadia. Men remembered county fairs and church socials, spelling bees and sleigh rides, the excitement of the circus train or the wild dash of firehorses from the station house, the cool smell of an ice-cream parlor and the warm fragrance of roasted chestnuts. They recalled the sound of peanut whistles and the hurdy-gurdy, the clang of the trolley, the cry of the carnival pitchman, the oompah of the military band on a summer evening, the clatter of victorias and sulkies, the shouts of children playing blindman's buff and run-sheep-run. They remembered people: the paper boy with his off-key whistle, the brawny iceman sauntering up the walk with his five-cent cake of ice, the Negro stable boys, the printers and devils in the newspaper offices, Mark Twain on the streets of Hartford in a cream-white suit. They recollected general stores: the bolts of calico and muslin, the jars of cinnamon and gunpowder tea, bins of dried peaches and cornmeal, kegs of mackerel, canisters of striped candy. From the vantage point of 1932, it seemed as though they had danced endlessly at tango teas and strummed mandolins every evening.

Each age seems to the next an era of matchless innocence and simplicity. By 1932, the prewar years had taken on a luminescence that they did not wholly have at the time. Perhaps this was because the reminiscences were written mostly by the sons of the secure and relatively prosperous middle class. Actually, in the great cities before the war lived people who knew nothing of elm-lined streets, midsummer lawn parties, or gay cotillions. When the Children's Bureau, founded in 1912, began to examine American society, it discovered that a quarter of a million babies were dying each year. The United States had the highest maternal death rate of any "civilized" country in the world. Even in the best of times, millions lived in brutal poverty.

In 1914 the United States was far from being a bucolic premachine culture. For more than a century, textile mills had drawn workers from Merrimac farms to the looms. Well before the Civil War, iron forges and foundries had dotted the countryside. Since the war, especially since the 1880's, America had been industrializing at a rapid pace, and with industrialization had come a raft of problems—city slums, factory reform, unassimilated immigrants, and class animosity. Since the great railway strikes of 1877, America had known considerable industrial violence. In 1914 in Ludlow, Colorado, militiamen and mine guards had machine-gunned a tent colony of strikers, burning to death a number of women and children. Although America was still, in many ways, remarkably provincial, the tradition of isolation from foreign affairs had been eroded by the imperialist surge of the 1890's and the Spanish-American war.

Yet America had still not been made over by the machine in 1914. Technology had not invaded the home. Only a small percentage of families even owned telephones. Technology was not awesome—it suggested Josephine and the flying machine, the Wrights' frail crate, the Singer sewing machine, and the Victrola. The scientific heroes of the age, Thomas Edison and Luther Burbank, could be compared to early inventors like Benjamin Franklin and Robert Fulton. Fulton, in fact, had been honored at a gigantic celebration five years before. Automobiles were still mired in rural roads, and RFD mail carriers even had to ford streams. Just a few years before, Teddy Roosevelt, after taking a short automobile jaunt, had been commended for his "characteristic courage."

It was a happily secure world. Each town was pretty much self-dependent for its society and amusements, and so were the people in it. The world they experienced was comprehensible. The people they saw were the people they knew. Men spoke without embarrassment of their patriotism and their love of the flag; celebrated Memorial Day and the "oldtime Fourth"; and could still declaim Webster's reply to Hayne. With the Atlantic secured by British friendship and British power, it seemed in 1914 that the United States could have all the advantages of prosperity and power and none of the disadvantages.

But it was impossible for Americans to keep their Arcady. By 1914 the course of industrialization and urbanization had gone too far. In 1909 Taft rode to the Capitol inauguration in a horse and carriage, in 1913 Wilson traveled in an automobile. The assault on the decorum of nineteenth-century America was already far advanced before the 1920's. In 1907, girls had sung, "I'd Rather Two-Step Than Waltz, Bill," but by 1914, ragtime had already replaced the two-step. Hollywood was well along the road "from the long chase to the chaise longue." As early as the 1890's, Stephen Crane, Frank Norris, and Theodore Dreiser had been writing in a naturalistic vein. Beneath the complacency of the age lay a grave disquiet. "We are unsettled to the very roots of our being," wrote Walter Lippmann in 1914. "There isn't a human relation, whether of parent and child, husband and wife, worker and employer, that doesn't move in a strange situation."

Even for the middle class, 1914 scarcely represented Paradise

Prologue

Lost. Lives were much more sharply circumscribed than they were to be in 1932. While people remembered the happy tradition of tolerance of the eccentric, they forgot the capacity of the small town for imposing conformity. The rigid morality of the time produced a great deal of cant and not a little cruelty. Over the life of all classes, especially in the areas of rural Protestantism, hung the pall of Puritanism, "the haunting fear," as Mencken wrote, "that someone, somewhere, may be happy."

The years from 1914 to 1932 were a time of questioning. The thrust of the period was toward a single-standard society, which broke down the old cleavages of sex and social status. Intellectuals led the assault on the groups which had traditionally exercised moral authority, but the "revolution in morals" would have taken place without them. The nation had lost its fear of the wrath of God and its faith in the nineteenth-century moral standards the churches had supported. It no longer had the same reverence for the old mores, and it was determined to free itself from the harsh imperatives of religious asceticism.

During these same years, the supremacy of rural, small-town America was being challenged by the rise of the city to the dominant position in American life. The city represented a challenge for economic power: the determination of finance capitalism to regain the political pre-eminence it had forfeited in the Progressive era. The city threatened to disrupt class stability through the tumultuous drive by unskilled labor to form mighty industrial unions. The city imperilled the hierarchy of social status through the clamor of new immigrant groups for social acceptance. Most of all, the older America was alarmed by the mores of the metropolis. The city represented everything—Europe, Wall Street, religious skepticism, political radicalism, sophistication, intellectual arrogance—which prewar America most feared.

The assault on the authority of the older America would have created terrible problems in the best of times. The experience of World War I made matters much worse. It would have been better, observed Oswald Garrison Villard, if the lives of the soldiers had been taken "in cold blood on Broadway." The war and its aftermath killed much of the humanistic, cosmopolitan spirit of 1914. It reinforced the conviction that evil came from outside America and from alien sources within, and evil became identified with the groups demanding change. The war destroyed much of the traditional confidence in the ability of American society to assimilate all manner of men. By the time the country had gone through the bruising experience of the war, the League fight, and the Red Scare, it lost most of its desire to face squarely the challenge to the old order.

At the very moment when the country was confronting this assault on traditional standards, the United States was plunged into the responsibilities of becoming the world's greatest power. Never did a nation accept authority more reluctantly. Unlike Elizabethan England after the Armada, the United States experienced no thrill in new-found power. The country did not want to abandon its isolation, and the disruption of Europe by the war did not make involvement in Continental politics any more inviting. "If I had influence at the United States Treasury," wrote John Maynard Keynes, "I would not lend a penny to a single one of the present governments of Europe." Even more important, a century of tranquillity had taught the country that it was safe from the threat of foreign invasion and that it need have no concern with the disorders of Europe.

By the end of the Harding era, some of the wounds of wartime politics had healed, and the country could turn to the more exciting spectacle of the boom economy. Prosperity held the promise not merely of personal gain but of eliminating poverty, spreading knowledge, making American society more urbane, and resolving class bitterness. The country was infused with a benevolent materialism.

But prosperity held perils of its own. It invested enormous political and social power in a business class with little tradition of social leadership. It placed economic pre-eminence in the hands of the one country in the world least prepared to guide world trade. It made money the measure of man. High above New York's Columbus Circle, a huge electric sign blinked: "You should have $10,000 at the age of 30; $25,000 at the age of 40; $50,000 at 50." Prosperity fostered a shallow view of the universe, a desiccated religion typified by the vulgar Aimee Semple McPherson, billed as "the world's most pulchritudinous evangelist." It undermined facets of the American character which had developed under an economy of scarcity; in particular, it encouraged an anxious concern for social approbation. Certain that prosperity would endure forever, the architects of the New Era assumed that they had achieved a far more equable division of wealth, a sounder economy, and greater prescience than, in fact, they had. They ignored the rotten beams in the economic structure. In 1929, everything toppled.

The failures of the period are easier to see than its achievements, but the achievements were, in the long run, more important. It was an age not merely of a war between urban and rural values but also of a coming together of the city and the country. Although Al Smith sharpened the conflict between the metropolis and the small town in the 1928 campaign, he also made urbanism seem, to millions of Americans, more likable and less threatening than they had feared it would be. He quickened the education of the American people in the acceptance of urban values, particularly of the values of ethnic groups different from the ones which had hitherto been dominant in American life.

It was an age of shameful persecution of minorities, a time when white-hooded men rode into the night to impose their will on victims of a different race or religion. But it was a time of social gain too. Many people became more outspoken in their commitment to democracy, and democracy had for them a deeper content than it had had before. When Smith was assailed as a Catholic in the 1928 campaign, non-Catholics answered the canards. When Henry Ford's *Dearborn Independent* launched a campaign of anti-Semitism in 1920—among other inanities, it alleged that Benedict Arnold had committed treason as representative of a "Jewish front"—121 distinguished non-Jews, including President Wilson, former President Taft, Archbishop Hayes, and William Jennings Bryan, signed a letter of protest to Ford.

Through the decade, the United States moved quietly away from the rigid isolationism of 1920. By 1930, the United States had participated in more than forty League conferences, and by the following year, there were five permanent American officials in Geneva. Senator Borah charged, with some truth, that the country was entering the League by the back door. The Wilsonian crusade produced a small corps of men— Wilson's Secretary of War, Newton Baker, for example—who

had a sense of religious consecration to the cause of internationalism. "The acceptance of a strange and perverse fate
called upon me who loved the life of youth to come to your
houses and ask you to give me your sons that I might send
them into those deadly places," Baker said. "I swore an obligation to the dead that in season and out, by day and by night,
in church, in political meeting, in the market-place, I intended
to lift up my voice always and ever until their sacrifices were
really perfected." Some of Wilson's chief Republican critics
—notably Elihu Root and Nicholas Murray Butler—swung
around to defend Geneva and The Hague in Wilsonian terms.
Although the internationalists achieved little tangible in the
1920's, they planted the seeds of the cosmopolitanism of a later
era.

The period brought everything that had been festering in
the prewar years into the open. Much of it was ugly, but it had
been no less ugly when it was concealed. For the first time, the
United States came face to face with the swift pace of economic change, technological innovation, and the rapidly rising
standard of living. For the first time, it was confronted with
the need to fashion instruments and attitudes appropriate to an
economy of abundance. It was forced to do so at a time of
terribly rapid change (Stieglitz remarked that there was a new
generation every five years). It had to bridge the enormous
gap between the boyhood of Booth Tarkington's *Penrod*
(1914) and James T. Farrell's *Young Lonigan* (1932). The
generation of 1914–32 did not invent the problems with which
it had to deal—it would have preferred to ignore them. Its
success was less than complete, but this was the first serious
attempt of Americans to make their peace with the twentieth
century.

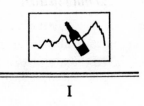

I

Armageddon

In the autumn of 1815 the "Northumberland," bearing the captive emperor Napoleon Bonaparte, dropped anchor before Saint Helena Island and opened a century of peace in western Europe. During that century, democracy and the rights of man won their greatest triumphs. Universal suffrage and public education, scientific marvels and social reforms, manifested a belief in the perfectibility of mankind. Localized wars there were—bloody enough in the case of the American Civil War and the Franco-Prussian struggle—yet war itself appeared more and more to be an anachronism, a dying institution. "It looks as though this were going to be the age of treaties rather than the age of wars," declared a leader of American peace forces in 1912, "the century of reason rather than the century of force."

In the early years of the twentieth century the menace of war grew—"incidents" in Africa, fighting in the Balkans—but not the general war that men had come to fear; and because it did not come, it lost its power to frighten. In 1913 Dr. David Starr Jordan, director of the World Peace Foundation, observed: "What shall we say of the Great War of Europe, ever threatening, ever impending, and which never comes? We shall say that it will never come. Humanly speaking, it is impossible." Even the assassination of Archduke Franz Ferdinand, heir to the Austro-Hungarian throne, by a young Bosnian terrorist in June, 1914, did not seem to mean war. "Never since Christ was born in the Manger," wrote a Maine newspaperman as late as July 30, "was the outlook for the universal brotherhood of man brighter than it is today."

Through the summer of 1914, Americans watched the growing war crisis almost with indifference. When, after weeks of gestures and countergestures, Britain sent her ultimatum to Germany, Secretary of Agriculture Houston recorded, "I had a feeling that the end of things had come. . . . I stopped in my tracks, dazed and horror-stricken." To the very last hour, war seemed unbelievable; when it came, it struck with a stunning sense of finality.

The only reasonable explanation was that Europe had gone berserk. The European powers, declared the *New York Times*, "have reverted to the condition of savage tribes roaming the forests and falling upon each other in a fury of blood and carnage to achieve the ambitious designs of chieftains clad in skins and drunk with mead." If the war had any rational cause at all, Americans thought, it could be found in the imperialist lust for markets. "Do you want to know the cause of the war?" asked Henry Ford. "It is capitalism, greed, the dirty hunger for dollars." "Take away the capitalist," Ford asserted, "and you will sweep war from the earth." Americans rejoiced in their isolation from Old World lunacy; and, after the initial sense of horror, their chief feeling was one of gratitude that they were not involved. "We never appreciated so keenly as now," wrote an Indiana editor, "the foresight exercised by our forefathers in emigrating from Europe."

President Woodrow Wilson urged a course of complete neutrality: he even asked movie audiences not to cheer or to hiss either side. The war, he said, was one "with which we have nothing to do, whose causes cannot touch us." Wilson cautioned the American people to be "impartial in thought as well as in action," but the impossibility of this soon became obvious. German-Americans and Irish-American Anglophobes cheered on the German cause. To many of the progressives, Britain suggested monarchy, privileged classes, and their ancient enemy Lombard Street (seat of international financiers). Germany (the Wisconsin reformers' model for a generation) suggested social insurance, the university scientist, and municipal reform. But sympathy for the Central Powers was on the whole a minority feeling. Overwhelmingly, American sentiment went out to the Allies.

Men who as schoolboys had read Gray and Tennyson, who knew Wordsworth's lake country as though they had tramped it themselves, who had been stirred by stories of Sir Francis Drake and Lord Nelson, could not be indifferent to the English cause. Nor did any nation evoke a greater sentimental attachment than France, the country of Lafayette, the land which had come to the aid of the Colonists in their struggle for independence.

At the same time, Americans had nervously eyed German militarism ever since the accession of Kaiser Wilhelm II in 1888. When Germany invaded Belgium in the early days of the war, Americans were outraged not only by the invasion of a neutral nation but by Chancellor Bethmann-Hollweg's tactless remark that the treaty with Belgium was "just a scrap of paper." The Machiavellianism, the glorification of brute force by the Germans, seemed amply proven by events like the sack of Louvain and, although in later years their influence was greatly exaggerated, by atrocity tales like those of the crucified Canadian and the Belgian babies with their hands severed. The execution of Nurse Edith Cavell, the destruction of the Cathedral of Rheims, and the mass deportation of French and Belgian civilians to forced labor completed the picture of a Prussian militarism which in its deliberate *schrecklichkeit* menaced Western civilization. Nevertheless, despite the indignation over Belgium, the United States had no thought of intervening. Even the bellicose Theodore Roosevelt, who would soon be the leader of the war hawks in America, wrote: "Of course it would be folly to jump into the gulf ourselves to no good purpose; and very probably nothing that we could have done would have helped Belgium."

As the struggle in Europe settled down to a war of attrition between great land armies, it quickly became clear that victory would go to the nation which could maintain control of the seas. Britain, the great naval power of the world, lost no time in taking advantage of its strategic position. In November, 1914, England mined the North Sea, seized American vessels carrying noncontraband goods to neutral nations, and forced all merchant ships to thread a narrow channel under British control. The Allies attempted nothing less than a gigantic blockade of the Central Powers; if they could prevent neutral merchantmen, in particular American ships, from carrying vital materials to Germany, they could force the Central Powers to sue for peace.

The United States could have taken a strong line with Britain, for Britain did not dare provoke a serious quarrel with her chief source of supply while she was involved in a desperate war. President Wilson, however, was unwilling, at a time when the Germans had overrun Belgium, to deprive Britain of her naval superiority. With England under such pressure, he felt a strong stand by the United States against Britain would be an unneutral act. Moreover, Wilson could not help but be influenced in his definition of "neutrality" by his own sympathies for the British cause, however much he tried to control them. Wilson had modeled his career on the example of English statesmen, he was an extravagant admirer of British government, and he actually courted his second wife by reading passages from Bagehot and Burke.

Wilson's closest advisers were firmly committed to the Allies. Robert Lansing, first Counselor and then Secretary of State, deliberately delayed the resolution of disputes in order to avoid a showdown with Britain. By May, 1915, Lansing was convinced that American democracy could not survive in a world dominated by German power. Wilson's alter ego, Colonel Edward House, was scarcely less pro-Ally, while, whenever notes of protest were sent to London, the strongly pro-British ambassador Walter Hines Page watered them down. On one occasion, Page took an American protest to Sir Edward Grey and said: "I have now read the despatch, but I do not agree with it; let us consider how it should be answered!" The result was the same as if the United States itself had embargoed all trade with Germany. Commerce with Germany and Austria fell from $169 million in 1914 to $1 million in 1916.

The outbreak of war in Europe at first produced a serious economic recession in this country, but by the spring of 1915 Allied war orders were stoking American industry and opening up new markets for farm products. Boom times came to the United States as trade with the Allies jumped from $825 million in 1914 to $3,214 million in 1916. Before the war was many months old, the Allied cause and American prosperity became inextricably intertwined. When Allied funds quickly became exhausted, the United States confronted the alternatives of permitting the Allies to borrow funds from American bankers or of allowing purchases to fall off sharply, with the probable consequence of a serious depression. At the outset of the war, Secretary of State William Jennings Bryan had warned that money was "the worst of all contrabands because it commands everything else," and Wilson, anxious about the country's gold reserve, had banned American loans and let it appear that he shared Bryan's concern. In March, 1915, however, Wilson and even Bryan relented and permitted the House of Morgan to extend a large credit to France. By the time the United States entered the war, the Allies had borrowed over $2 billion.

In February, 1915, Germany struck back at the Allied blockade by declaring a war zone around the British Isles and announcing that German submarines would destroy all enemy vessels in the area. Neutral ships in the war zone would be in danger, the Germans warned, since the British often flew neutral flags. Wilson responded to the German declaration in the strongest terms through a State Department dictum to Berlin that the Kaiser's government would be held strictly accountable for loss of American life or damage to American vessels. Under this pressure, the Germans were eventually forced to back down from their veiled threat to sink American ships. Not until 1917 would German-American relations be troubled by a menace to American lives and property on *American* ships. Instead, diplomats were faced with a new problem: the right of Americans to sail on the ships of belligerent nations.

The Germans did not yet have enough submarines to do serious damage to British commerce; yet even a few submarines could strike terror by attacking passenger ships. In March, a German U-boat ambushed a British liner and caused the death of one American aboard. Americans, however, continued to travel on British liners, which carried munitions into the war zone, and Wilson brushed off attempts to ban such travel. On May 7, 1915, came the inevitable tragedy. The queen of the Cunard fleet, the "Lusitania," unarmed but carrying a small amount of munitions, was torpedoed off the Irish coast; eighteen minutes later it sank with a loss of 1,198 lives, 128 of them American.

The United States was horrified by the sinking. Yet few Americans wanted war, and, with the country divided, Wilson was determined to avoid a rupture with Germany. "There is such a thing as a man being too proud to fight," the President said, to the disgust of Theodore Roosevelt and the bellicose nationalists. "There is such a thing as a nation being so right that it does not need to convince others by force that it is right." Nonetheless, Wilson sent three vigorous notes to Germany. In June, Germany, fearing war with the United States, ordered submarine commanders to spare all large passenger liners, including those of the enemy, but in August a German U-boat commander violated orders and sank a British White Star Liner, the "Arabic," with the loss of two American lives. When Wilson sent another strong protest, Germany replied with assurances that the "Arabic" incident would not be repeated, that no unresisting passenger ship would be sunk without warning or without care for the safety of passengers and crew.

The submarine wrought havoc with Wilson's neutrality policy and ultimately brought the United States into the war. It was an accepted principle of international law that no naval vessel would destroy an enemy merchantman without first giving warning and providing for the safety of passenger and crew. This was reasonable enough when merchant vessels were defenseless, but in the late summer of 1915 the British started arming merchantmen and ordering them to attack; a single shot could destroy a fragile submarine. A U-boat commander could not distinguish an armed from an unarmed vessel, and Britain and Italy were arming even their passenger liners. Wilson himself recognized the difficulty for a time. "It is hardly fair," he wrote Colonel House in October, 1915, "to ask submarine commanders to give warning by summons if, when they approach as near as they must for that purpose, they are to be fired upon."

On February 10, 1916, the Germans, not unreasonably, announced they would sink all armed merchantmen. Once the issue was forced, Wilson took a stern line. When Democratic congressional leaders called on him at the White House to protest going to war for the right of Americans to travel on armed ships, Wilson declared that Germany would be held strictly accountable. When another group of House Democratic leaders asked him what would happen if the Germans sank an armed vessel on which Americans were traveling, Wilson told them he would break relations with Germany and that this might well mean war.

In adopting this course with regard to armed merchantmen, Wilson was taking an inconsistent, an unrealistic, and, in view of his acquiescence in Allied transgressions, an unneutral line. Yet the Allied and the German maritime policies were not strictly comparable. Although the legality of the British system was uncertain, the British were able, because of their almost absolute control of the seas, to exercise controls in an orderly manner. If Britain seized American ships, the United States always had recourse to law and could obtain an indemnity; nothing would restore the loss of life from the ships Germany sank. Wilson felt justified in protesting mildly against seizure but issuing ultimatums about sinkings. Moreover, granting that passenger liners sometimes carried munitions and that they were after a time armed, the German policy of sinking passenger ships was intolerable. The U-boat ⁺hat deliberately fired on the "Lusitania" did not fear attack, for the "Lusitania" was unarmed; it was not concerned with the cargo, for the amount of ammunition aboard was insignificant. The Germans were using terror as a weapon. They ruthlessly took the lives of noncombatants and they exulted over their acts. Decades later, one has a sense of horror at the fate of the passengers. At the time, in a world not yet hardened to Lidice and Belsen, the German campaign of terror seemed unbelievably barbaric.

After Wilson's second "Lusitania" note, Secretary of State Bryan, fearing it might provoke war, resigned and was succeeded by the strongly pro-Allied Robert Lansing. Out of office, Bryan took the leadership of the peace forces in America. Convinced that Wilson was risking war for the right of a few Americans to travel on belligerent vessels in a war area, Bryan headed a movement to prohibit Americans from sailing on such ships. "Germany has a right to prevent contraband going to the Allies," Bryan had written Wilson, "and a ship carrying contraband should not rely upon passengers to protect her from attack—it would be like putting women and children in front of an army." When Germany announced it would sink all armed merchantmen, strong support developed in Congress behind resolutions introduced by Senator Gore of Oklahoma and Representative McLemore of Texas, supported by Bryan, to warn Americans not to travel on belligerent ships destined for war zones. In the House, the sentiment was 2–1 in back of the resolutions, but President Wilson brought such enormous pressure to bear against them that they were sidetracked in March. "Once accept a single abatement of right," wrote Wilson sternly, "and many other humiliations would certainly follow."

In that same month, March, 1916, a U-boat torpedoed an unarmed French channel steamer, the "Sussex," with heavy loss of life; no Americans were killed, but several were seriously wounded. This clear violation of the German promises made after the "Arabic" incident created a diplomatic crisis. Wilson appeared before Congress on April 19 to read an ultimatum to Germany that unless it abandoned unrestricted submarine warfare against all vessels, even armed belligerents, the United States would sever diplomatic relations. The Kaiser, convinced he did not yet have enough submarines to risk war, decided to appease Wilson. Germany replied on May 4, 1916, that her submarines would no longer sink merchantmen without warning and without humanitarian precautions, so long as they did not resist. But, the Germans added, this so-called "Sussex pledge" was conditioned on the United States persuading the Allies to give up their blockade of Germany. If the United States did not, Germany would retain freedom of action.

Wilson chose to ignore the German conditions and to accept the pledge. He thereby achieved a great (however temporary) diplomatic triumph. The main threat of war—the German submarine—was removed. At the same time, Wilson had adopted such a strong line that if Germany resumed submarine warfare, which, given the continuation of the British blockade, she was likely to do, the United States would almost certainly be plunged into war. The decision for peace or war was taken out of the hands of the United States and given to Germany.

For nine months after the "Sussex pledge" not only did relations with Germany greatly improve but American diplomats were mainly troubled by the British. American public opinion, incensed by the ruthless suppression of the Irish rebellion of April 24, 1916, particularly at the execution of Sir Roger Casement, was angered still further by British intensification of economic warfare. The British opened American mail, dealt cavalierly with American diplomatic protests, and blacklisted American firms suspected of trading with Germany. By July, 1916, President Wilson was confiding to Colonel House: "I am, I must admit, about at the end of my patience with Great Britain and the Allies." By the autumn of 1916 it appeared that the United States might be drifting toward an open break with Great Britain.

As the 1916 Presidential election approached, Wilson's Republican critics made a strong bid to defeat him by arguing that in his attempt to preserve peace he had sacrificed national honor. In their effort to dislodge Wilson, the Republicans had the support of the head of the Progressive party, Theodore Roosevelt, who viewed Wilson as a "demagogue, adroit, tricky, false, without one spark of loftiness in him, without a touch of the heroic in his cold, selfish and timid soul." When the Republicans nominated Charles Evans Hughes for the presidency (Hughes had distinguished himself first as governor of New York and then as Supreme Court Justice), Roosevelt secured the Progressive nomination for him as well.

One of the ironies of the 1916 campaign is that the Republicans attacked the President for a lack of concern with preparedness and Americanism at the very time when Wilson was under fire from radicals and reformers precisely because they thought he had become so chauvinistic. When Martin Glynn, former governor of New York, prepared his keynote address for the Democratic convention in June, Wilson instructed him to emphasize Americanism and the flag, and Glynn dutifully did so. The delegates, however, sat unresponsively as he went through his spread-eagle remarks. Glynn also felt called on to give some defense for Wilson's series of diplomatic notes, which the Republicans had scored as un-American timidity, and he cited a number of historical precedents for Wilson's actions. Fearing he would tire his audience with further examples, Glynn started to pass on to another subject, but delegates rose from their seats and shouted, "No! No! Go on!" An old campaign war horse, Glynn rose to the occasion. Each time he cited an example from the past when, provoked to the point of war, a President sent a diplomatic note instead, the crowd would shout, "What did we do? What did we do?" And Glynn would shout back, "We didn't go to war! We didn't go to war!"

The developments at the Democratic convention caught Wilson by surprise. On the very day of Glynn's speech, Wilson had led a preparedness parade in Washington with a flag draped over his shoulder. He felt exceedingly uneasy about the new Democratic slogan. ("I can't keep the country out of war," Wilson protested to Secretary of the Navy Daniels. "They talk of me as though I were a god. Any little German lieutenant can put us into the war at any time by some calculated outrage.") Despite his doubts, Wilson made good use of the peace appeal by charging Republicans with being a war party and by implying that, if he were elected, he would keep the country out of war. On the combined appeals of peace, prosperity, and progressivism, Wilson eked out a victory. The passion for peace proved so strong that Hughes was frequently forced to softpedal his attacks on Wilson's foreign policy, while Roosevelt's belligerent nationalism was a handicap rather than an asset. The Republicans, noted the *Saturday Evening Post* after the election, "woefully misread the public mind. They thought it was truculently heroic, and writhing under a sense of national disgrace, when, in fact, it was merely sensible. . . ."

Wilson's victory in 1916 was almost universally interpreted as a mandate for peace. As peace sentiment in America reached an astonishingly high pitch, Wilson made a bold attempt to bring the war to an end. All through the war, Colonel House had crisscrossed Europe in search of a formula for peace. Early in 1916, House and Sir Edward Grey, the British Foreign Secretary, drafted a memorandum providing that Wilson, on hearing from the Allies when the time was opportune, would call a peace conference. If the Germans refused to attend such a parley or if they would not agree to reasonable terms, the United States would "probably" enter the war on the side of the Allies. Wilson's adamant stand against Germany in regard to armed merchantmen early in 1916 stemmed mainly from a desire to maintain his usefulness as a mediator by not antagonizing the Allies. In May, 1916, all the President's careful plans were blown sky high when the Allies decided not to pursue farther the program outlined in the House-Grey agreement. Wilson's ultimatum of April, 1916, had given Britain and France reason to believe that a break between Germany and the United States was imminent; once America intervened, they had high hopes of winning a total victory over Germany. Moreover, the Allies were unwilling to risk a peace conference at a time when Germany held Belgium, northern France, and much of eastern Europe, without a firm pledge from the United States to fight unless Germany evacuated these areas.

Wilson, irked by the Allied rebuff, now decided on independent mediation without prior consultation with the Allies. To make clear his independence from the chancelleries of London and Paris, Wilson adopted a severe line with the Allies. He won legislation from Congress in September, 1916, to permit him to deny clearance and harbor facilities to nations that discriminated against American commerce and to use force to carry out these powers. He got the Federal Reserve Board to caution American bankers to use care in financing the Allied war trade. When Germany was derelict in upholding the "Sussex pledge"—in two cases, which Berlin held were "mistakes," American lives were lost—the President disregarded the provocations.

Wilson had decided on a bold change of policy to free himself from the tangle of maritime rights. He wanted greater maneuverability than a foreign policy geared to German submarine attacks offered. In the last eight months of 1916, Wilson said almost nothing about freedom of the seas, his chief concern since 1914, and stressed instead the impact of the war on democratic ideals and the future of Western civilization. The only way to avoid American involvement in the war, the President concluded, was direct American mediation, even at the cost of surrendering the tradition of American isolation from Europe's quarrels. In a speech in Omaha in October, 1916, Wilson counseled: "When you are asked, 'Aren't you willing to fight?' reply, yes, you are waiting for something worth fighting for; you are not looking around for petty quarrels, but you are looking about for that sort of quarrel within whose intricacies are written all the texts of the rights of man; you are looking for some cause . . . in which it seems a glory to shed human blood, if it be necessary, so that all the common compacts of liberty may be sealed with the blood of free men."

On December 18, 1916, Wilson sent identical diplomatic notes to the belligerent capitals asking them to state their war aims and to indicate upon what terms they would be willing to end the war. Since Germany, for reasons of her own, had made a peace feeler six days before, Wilson's message was received with dismay in Allied circles. Sir Henry Wilson fulminated, "That ass President Wilson has barged in and asked all belligerents for their terms." Lord Northcliffe told Page, "Everybody is mad as hell." If Germany desired a reasonable peace, Wilson had given her the opportunity. But the Germans were interested in a peace conference only as a device to split the Allies. At the very least, Germany was determined to control Belgium. "Albert shall keep his Belgium, since he too is King by Divine Right," the Kaiser advised Prince von Bülow in the autumn of 1916. "Though, of course, I imagine our future relationship as rather that of the Egyptian Khedive to the King of England." The Germans, whose dreams of glory included acquisition of the Belgian Congo, a large indemnity from France and England, and the end of British naval supremacy, aimed at nothing less than the destruction of Allied power.

On January 31, 1917, the German ambassador, Count von Bernstorff, informed the State Department that on the following day Germany would resume unrestricted submarine warfare. U-boats would sink all ships, passenger and merchant, neutral and belligerent, armed or unarmed, in the war zone. With the British blockade squeezing off supplies and with the war deadlocked, Germany staked everything on one great effort. She knew that the result would almost certainly be war with the United States, but she reasoned that the submarine campaign would end the war before the United States could give any more aid than it was already giving as a neutral. Wilson promptly broke off diplomatic relations with Germany.

American ships, fearing submarine attack, clung to port, refusing to sail unless they were armed. As wheat and cotton piled up on Atlantic piers, railroads were forced to embargo shipments to the seacoast. If Wilson accepted the German submarine policy, he would have to permit a blockade of American ports by the German navy; with ships rusting at their piers, factories, in the absence of markets, would throw men out of work and farmers would suddenly be plunged into a devastating depression. We had permitted the Allies to cut off our trade with Germany; could we afford to permit Germany to cut off our trade with the Allies as well? Yet Wilson refused to ask Congress for authority to arm ships. When on February 23 cabinet officers urged him to do so, he attacked them for attempting to revive the code duello. Two days later, however, Wilson changed his mind; from Ambassador Page he had received a dispatch that made him angry clear through.

Page's dispatch enclosed a message which the British Secret Service had intercepted and decoded from the Under Secretary of the German Ministry of Foreign Affairs, Alfred Zimmermann, to the German minister to Mexico. The Zimmermann telegram read: "We intend to begin on the first of February unrestricted submarine warfare. We shall endeavor in spite of this to keep the United States of America neutral. In the event of this not succeeding, we make Mexico a proposal of alliance on the following basis: make war together, make peace together, generous financial support and an understanding on our part that Mexico is to reconquer her lost territory in Texas, New Mexico, and Arizona." Japan was also to be invited by Mexico to join in the plan.

On February 26, 1917, Wilson asked Congress for authority to arm American merchantmen and to carry on an undeclared naval war. When a group of eleven senators led by Robert La Follette of Wisconsin filibustered the bill to death, the President, after attacking his opponents as a "little group of wilful men" who "had rendered the great government of the United States helpless and contemptible," went ahead and armed the vessels on the authority of an ancient statute of 1797. In March the first American merchantmen left port with orders to shoot on sight.

Still there was no war. Wilson had the clearest grasp of what war would mean. (Page had written him of the "shells and acres of bloated human bodies, careless of sun or rain, giving off stench.") The terrible campaign of the Somme in 1916 had cost the Germans some 500,000 men, the British 400,000, the French 200,000, and Wilson shrank from throwing American lives into the same inferno. Moreover, Wilson wished to avoid war because, he told Secretary Lansing, it was necessary that the United States keep itself intact so as to maintain the dominance of "white" civilization. At a cabinet meeting in February, Wilson declared, according to Secretary Houston, that if "in order to keep the white race or part of it strong to meet the yellow race—Japan, for instance, in alliance with Russia, dominating China—it was wise to do nothing, he would do nothing and would submit to . . . any imputation of weakness or cowardice." Late in February, when U-boat marauders had been roving the seas for days, the President was still opposed to war. Wilson could not sleep. His face was ashen. He was racked with doubt.

Yet he had reached the point of no return. A few hours before Wilson asked Congress to arm merchantmen, a German submarine torpedoed without warning the Cunard liner "Laconia" with the loss of twelve lives, including those of two American women. On March 12 an unarmed American merchant vessel was sunk without warning; on March 18 U-boats sank three more unarmed merchantmen with heavy loss of life. When this news came, the last member of Wilson's cabinet to hold out for peace capitulated and advocated an American declaration of war. Wilson himself, incensed by the Zimmermann note and angered by the sinkings, was given a new reason for war by the Russian Revolution, which by removing the last despot among the Allies made the war at last seem a clear-cut fight between democracy and autocracy.

On April 2, 1917, on a black, wet, Washington evening, Wilson went before Congress to declare that a state of war already existed with Germany. He had decided on war; yet he would make it a holy war, a war of service to mankind. No other kind of war was tolerable. It would be a struggle of democracy against autocracy, for it was only autocrats who could sanction such fiendish acts as the U-boat commanders had committed. "The world must be made safe for democracy," Wilson proclaimed. "Its peace must be planted upon the tested foundations of political liberty." Congress burst into applause, and men rushed forward to congratulate him. "My message today was a message of death for our young men," the white-faced Wilson remarked afterward to his secretary. "How strange it seems to applaud that."

In both houses of Congress a small band of progressives spoke out against war, convinced that the country was entering it at the behest of financial interests. "We are going into war," declared Senator George Norris of Nebraska, "upon the command of gold." But they were drowned out by the cry for war. Two days after Wilson's message, the Senate voted war 82–6, and early on Good Friday morning the House adopted the war resolution 373–50. On April 7 the *New York Tribune* headlined the end of the long months of fretful neutrality: "AMERICA IN ARMAGEDDON."

Why did the United States enter World War I? In later years millions of Americans became convinced that America was led into war by a conspiracy of bankers and munitions makers or was hoodwinked by British propaganda, but neither Wall Street nor Reuters (the British news service) played a decisive role. The United States entered the war because it saw no alternative when faced with unrestricted submarine warfare. Wilson's critics have argued that it was his quixotic insistence on neutral rights that provoked the Germans to the point where they had no choice other than to unleash the submarine and precipitate war. It is an argument which, although mistaken, has considerable substance. Wilson treated World

Armageddon

War I as though he were dealing with the War of 1812, ignoring the way in which the submarine had completely altered the nature of armed conflict. He contended that an American citizen had the right to travel on an armed ship, including ships which carried munitions, and had the right to look to his own country for protection. But the citizen in fact had none of these rights under international law and still less under cold common sense.

Wilson conducted his foreign policy by rules of war which neither Germany nor Britain respected. Neither country wanted war with America, but either would have gone to war with America rather than face defeat. Neither pursued her course out of respect for American principles of neutral rights. Both took calculated risks as to whether violating American rights at the cost of American intervention would or would not be a wise policy. The Dutch treated armed merchantmen as warships and interned them. If the United States had done the same, the British would have stopped arming merchantmen, and the Germans could have afforded to (and might have been coerced to) obey rules of safety.

When the United States submitted to the British blockade and, in effect, blockaded Germany herself, when the United States at the same time served as the Allied base of supplies, the submarine became indispensable to Germany. When Wilson attempted to dictate the terms on which Germany could wage war, terms which would have resulted in German defeat, war between Germany and the United States became almost inevitable. Like the hero of a Greek tragedy, Wilson spun his own fate by holding Germany to strict accountability, and he pushed the nation toward war by a merciless logic.

If war had come as a result of Wilson's ultimatum of April,

1916, the responsibility for war would have rested almost wholly on the President. But to censure Wilson for America's entrance into war in April, 1917—as revisionist historians have done—is to overlook completely the important developments in the year following Wilson's ultimatum. Convinced that a drastic change of direction in foreign policy was needed, Wilson shifted to a position of almost absolute impartiality toward the Allies and the Central Powers. At the same time, he attempted to bring the war to an end before European civilization was damaged beyond repair. It was too late. Neither the Allies nor Germany could afford to wage such a devastating war any longer. Yet, so terrible had been the loss of life, neither side felt it could justify ending the war on any terms save total victory.

Of Wilson's neutrality in the autumn of 1916 there can be no question. If the Germans had not sabotaged Wilson's peace moves, the President might have used economic pressure to compel the Allies to modify their methods of warfare. If the Germans had been content merely to resume submarine attacks on armed merchantmen in 1917, Wilson, despite his earlier statements to the contrary, would almost certainly have acquiesced. But the Kaiser, his appetite whetted by the promises of his military and naval advisers, insisted on unrestricted U-boat warfare against all vessels, neutral as well as belligerent.

The German decision of 1917 gives a perspective to Wilson's neutrality policies that was not available at the time. It seems likely that Germany would have unleashed its submarines the moment it had enough built to make such a tactic feasible. It would have done so irrespective of American policy. Once Germany declared unrestricted warfare on all vessels, the United States would have been forced, as the price of peace, either to suffer without retaliation heavy loss of life at sea or to end its trade with Europe. An embargo on American commerce would have been even less practicable in 1914 than it had been during the Napoleonic wars. Once the Germans had enough U-boats, they could not have been stopped from declaring unrestricted warfare by anything less than a strong show of American force—and American force was not great enough in these years to be effective—or by total American collaboration. World War I was a revolutionary effort to change the distribution of power in Europe. Since Germany believed, probably correctly, that it could not overthrow Allied supremacy without destroying American commerce, it is not clear that there was any policy open to the United States which would not ultimately have led to American intervention.

Apart from the issue of neutral rights, it is impossible, even at this distance, to know whether American entry was a wise decision, for we do not know what the consequences would have been if the United States had not entered. With power balanced on the Continent and the Atlantic controlled by Great Britain, the United States had been able to avoid huge armament expenditures, heavy taxation, a large standing army, peacetime conscription, and expeditions to fight localized wars. A German victory—and without American entrance a German victory was a distinct possibility—presented certain threats. It is by no means clear that a Germany which dominated both the Continent and the Atlantic would have been as benign as Britain had been and continued to be. Over all this conjecture hangs our later knowledge of the menace of Nazi power. The Germany of the Kaiser was certainly not the Germany of Hitler; yet there were enough elements of later German nationalism in the Hohenzollern Empire to give one pause. One thing was certain: if the Allies won, American interests would be safe. No one could say for certain then or now what would happen if Germany won the war.

All this, of course, is largely historical hindsight. Although a few men like the career diplomat Lewis Einstein and Secretary Lansing thought in terms of the menace of German power to the Atlantic System, they were in a minority. Lansing in fact kept his views to himself and argued for action against Germany on quite different grounds. Whatever the merits of the case, the United States did not go to war for reasons of self-preservation. Wilson himself did not feel that Germany menaced American security, while Roosevelt's bellicosity was more the product of an adolescent derring-do than of an understanding of the realities of power.

American entrance into the war cannot be seen apart from the American sense of mission. The United States believed that American moral idealism could be extended outward, that American Christian democratic ideals could and should be universally applied. This sense of national mission was combined with a new consciousness of national power. The United States was aggressively peaceful. Admiral Mahan had compared the duty of America to repress evil abroad with that of the rich to wipe out slums; this view carried with it the assumption of unique American virtue, which had the ironic effect of making it the duty of "peace-loving" Americans to resort to killing to impose virtue abroad. The culmination of a long political tradition of emphasis on sacrifice and decisive moral combat, the war was embraced as that final struggle where the righteous would do battle for the Lord.

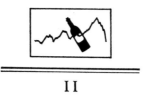

II

Innocents Abroad

Today World War I has a kind of musical comedy flavor: it suggests George M. Cohan and lines of jaunty Empire soldiers singing, "It's a long way to Tipperary"; it brings to mind men dressed in American Legion uniforms and selling red poppies or reminiscing about the "Mademoiselle from Armentieres"—almost anything but the bloody, pointless warfare of the trenches and what it did to bring centuries of Western civilization to an abrupt stopping place. "Events," wrote Winston Churchill in 1929, "passed very largely outside the scope of conscious choice. Governments and individuals conformed to the rhythm of the tragedy, and swayed and staggered forward in helpless violence, slaughtering and squandering on ever-increasing scales, till injuries were wrought to the structure of human society which a century will not efface, and which may conceivably prove fatal to the present civilization."

The United States entered the war at a critical time for the military fortunes of the Allies. In the spring of 1917, a French offensive on the Aisne had failed, certain French politicians and bankers were talking of peace, and ten French divisions had mutinied. In the autumn of 1917, Italy almost collapsed after the Austrian victory at Caporetto, and the Russian front vanished when the Bolshevik Revolution in November led to the negotiation of a separate peace that freed the German army on the Eastern Front for an assault on the west. Token American forces were landed in Europe as early as the summer of 1917, but no major unit of the American army saw action until October, 1917, near Verdun. By March, 1918, there were 300,000 Yanks in France; by November, more than two million, 1,400,000 of whom saw action.

In March, 1918, before American troops could have any important effect, Germany launched an offensive which drove the British back in the Somme valley; in late May, they turned against the French, captured 40,000 prisoners in a week, and reached the Marne fifty miles from Paris. In June, green but reckless American units helped hurl German troops back across the Marne at Chateau-Thierry and cleared Belleau Wood. Militarily unimportant, the appearance of fresh American troops, who had not been unnerved by years of battle, gave a great psychological lift to Allied morale. On July 15, the Germans began their last great drive for Paris, the Second Battle of the Marne, which engaged 85,000 American soldiers. Three days later, the Germans were finished. "On the 18th," wrote German Chancellor Hertling, "even the most optimistic among us knew that all was lost. The history of the world was played out in three days." The German Seventh Army, wrote its chief of staff, "achieved brilliant initial successes, with the exception of the one division on our right wing. This encountered American units! Here only did the Seventh Army . . . confront serious difficulties."

Innocents Abroad

On July 18, permitting neither his own troops nor the enemy's to rest, Marshal Foch ordered American and French Colonial troops to counterattack. In July and August, British and French troops played the major role in the Allied offensive, supported by hundreds of thousands of American soldiers in the destruction of the Aisne-Marne flank. In September, in the brief struggle at St. Mihiel, where more than half a million American troops wiped out the weak German salient and captured 16,000 prisoners, and in the bitter 47 days of the Meuse-Argonne battle, the assaults were primarily the work of American forces. Under General Pershing, American forces, now fighting as independent units, drove the Germans out of the Argonne Forest. The Meuse-Argonne battle engaged 1,200,000 American troops at a cost of 120,000 casualties; more Americans lost their lives in the Argonne than in all the rest of the battles combined. Together with British and French victories on the northern and central fronts, the American successes in the southern sector broke the Hindenburg Line and brought a triumphant end to the war.

Forty-eight thousand Americans were killed in action, 2,900 were listed as missing, and 56,000 died of disease—a considerable loss of life, yet less than the major European powers lost in a single battle like Verdun. Germany lost 1,800,000 men in the war, Russia 1,700,000, France 1,385,000, Austria-Hungary 1,200,000, and Britain 947,000. The United States "won the war" only in the sense that, after four years of combat in which Britain and France had given infinitely more in blood and treasure, American troops afforded the Allies a preponderance of power. General Ludendorff, who commanded the Western Front for Germany, greatly underestimated the capacity of Allied troops to hold their lines until the United

States was able to achieve the miracle of training and equipping two million troops and landing them in France.

Without naval support, the military success would have been impossible. The Germans calculated that if they could sink 600,000 tons of shipping each month, they could force Britain to ask for terms in six months. In February they sank 540,000 tons; in April, as the days grew longer, they sank 881,-000. On May 4 the first American destroyers, six of them, reached Ireland. At the urging of Admiral Sims and Secretary Daniels, the British relented in their opposition to the convoy system, and by July American destroyers were convoying merchantmen. By December losses to submarines had been cut in half, and by the spring of 1918 the U-boat was no longer a major menace, in part because the British accepted an American proposal to lay a mine barrage in the North Sea. Freed of this danger, British and American transports were able to move the two million American troops to Europe; and only two transports, both British, were sunk during the eastern voyage.

On the home front the war reached incredible proportions. Men who would once have balked at spending thousands soon learned to talk casually of spending millions. Secretary of the Treasury William McAdoo propped himself up in bed at night with a yellow writing pad on his knees to work out the financing of the war. "The noughts attached to the many millions were so boisterous and prolific," he recalled, "that, at times, they would run clear over the edge of the paper." "Sure we paid," replied Charles G. Dawes when his fellow Republicans were unfairly censuring Democratic officials after the war. "We would have paid horse prices for sheep if sheep could have pulled artillery to the front. . . . Damn it all, the business of an army is to win the war, not to quibble around with a lot of cheap buying. Hell and Maria, we weren't trying to keep a set of books, we were trying to win the war!" Despite the abandon with which money was spent, the war was conducted without major scandal, and, in the closing months, with increasing efficiency.

In the first year of the war inexperienced officials badly bungled the job of administering the economy, and important areas of production never did get straightened out. Production of heavy guns got into high gear only after the war had ended. American plants produced almost no tanks. American aviators flew British and French planes, and most of the artillery pieces American soldiers fired in Europe were supplied by the French. Most serious was the failure of shipbuilding. In the early weeks of the war General Goethals pointed out that "birds were still nesting in the trees from which the great wooden fleet was to be made." At the end of the war many of the birds were still nesting there. The first vessel from the largest government shipyard (at Hog Island, near Philadelphia) was not delivered until the war was over; the total American production from all yards was negligible. Only by buying and seizing German and Dutch ships and American ships built in private yards did the Shipping Board meet the desperate need for merchantmen and transports.

By early 1918, as railroad transportation was close to breaking down and soldiers at camp lacked adequate clothing and shelter, the country approached a national crisis. Stung by congressional criticism, Wilson summoned Bernard Baruch, a Wall Street speculator, to head the War Industries Board, which exercised sweeping authority over priorities and allocations. The board had dictatorial powers; it could determine what materials manufacturers could use and what they could or could not make. It issued the most minute regulations: elevator operators were told how many stops they could make, and traveling salesmen were limited to two trunks. Operating as economic dictator of the American economy, Baruch did a superb job of unsnarling red tape and bringing the mobilization to high efficiency.

The war marked the first large-scale government control of the American economy. Under a form of war socialism not unlike that which had been found necessary by European governments, federal agencies directed every major sector of the economy. The Fuel Administration, under Harry A. Garfield, doled out coal and oil supplies, introduced the European innovation of daylight saving time, and closed down unessential factories one day a week; the Emergency Fleet Corporation directed shipbuilding; the War Trade Board licensed foreign trade; the Railroad Administration operated the nation's railways as a single system. The National War Labor Board guaranteed collective bargaining, mediated labor disputes, and even commandeered an arms plant; and the government took over telephone and telegraph companies, warehouses, terminals, express companies, and sleeping-car companies.

On April 27, 1917, Ambassador Page warned Wilson that Britain did not have enough food to feed the civilian population of the British Isles for more than six to eight weeks. Under the adroit leadership of Food Administrator Herbert Hoover the entire nation was alerted to the need to conserve food. Restaurants served shark steak and whale meat, and bakers devised coarse breads to save wheat. ("Do not permit your child," wrote *Life*, "to take a bite or two from an apple and throw the rest away; nowadays even children must be taught to be patriotic to the core.") Hoover entered the grain market to purchase and distribute wheat, and he pegged hog prices so high that farmers doubled production. He bought the entire Cuban and American sugar crops and ordered grocers to limit each individual to two pounds a month. The Hoover program was an outstanding success; under it, the United States was able to ship three times as much food to the Allied countries as it had before the war.

An army of businessmen came to Washington to work in hot cubicles in temporary buildings at the challenging job of administering the greatest government operation in the history of the country. Working side by side with the business leaders was a new class of public administrators. These men, who had come on the national scene in the early years of the century, now got their first real chance to demonstrate their capacity to manage the economy. There was, Randolph Bourne observed acidly, a "peculiar congeniality between the war and these men. It is as if the war and they had been waiting for each other."

This wartime experience created both a class of businessmen, like Gerard Swope of General Electric, who favored the wartime practice of government-business co-operation, and a group of administrators who rejected the Victorian competitive ideal for the goal of a planned economy. John Dewey was struck in 1918 by "the social possibilities of war," the direction of the economy for public ends rather than for private profit. When in 1933 a new government came to power in the midst of a major crisis, it would know no way to mobilize the country save by invoking the experience of World War I, the only occasion when modern America had acted as a nation. As a result, the early New Deal would draw less on populism or progressivism than on the war mobilization, and the NRA would be drafted and administered by men—Baruch, Hugh Johnson, Swope, Leo Wolman, and many others—who had gained their first governmental experience in wartime Washington and cherished their memory of it through the 1920's.

The war confirmed the triumph of large-scale industrial organization. Forced for the first time to wage a modern war, the nation found that Jacksonian rhetoric about the virtues of the small entrepreneur was obsolete. The war itself not only created thousands of new millionaires, as any modern war does, but speeded both popular acceptance and acceptance in the business world of the virtues of large-scale, amalgamated, oligopolistic industries. At the end of the war, business was determined to retain as far as possible the wartime system of operating outside the antitrust laws, and the war experience accelerated the merger movement and the trade-association movement of the 1920's.

The war ended the casual voluntarism of the nineteenth century in the passage, over bitter protests, of the Selective Service Act. (Champ Clark, Democratic Speaker of the House, protested that "in the estimation of Missourians, there is precious little difference between a conscript and a convict.") Although there had been a draft in the Civil War, it was undertaken in the middle of the war as an emergency measure. It provided for the alternative of purchasing a substitute, and it was enforced with great difficulty. In World War I, save for the "Green Corn Rebellion" of tenant farmers, Indians, and Negroes in two Oklahoma counties, the draft was enforced with the quiet efficiency with which a powerful twentieth-century state goes about its business of turning lives to public ends.

Innocents Abroad

The wartime draft was only one of a number of measures which indicated for, the first time that an efficient state had been developing in the years of the Progressive era, changing the romantic, voluntaristic world of the Spanish-American War to the systematic routine of World War I. In 1916 America still thought to a great degree in terms of nineteenth-century values of decentralization, competition, equality, agrarian supremacy, and the primacy of the small town. By 1920 the triumph of the twentieth century—centralized, industrialized, secularized, urbanized—while by no means complete, could clearly be foreseen. Although a conflict between old and new values would rage throughout the 1920's, a major change in the temper of American society had occurred.

The American people entered the war with a discernible lack of enthusiasm. Even after the Zimmermann wire of February, 1917, and the sinkings the next month, most Americans probably still opposed the war. When it came, and young recruits were marched off to railroad depots in every town in the country, millions of Americans were bewildered by the suddenness with which war had followed the peace mandate of November, 1916, and they had no clear idea why the country was fighting. In areas where German-Americans or Irish-Americans or peaceminded Scandinavians were dominant, the war was greeted with indifference or sullen hostility. The Socialists were outspokenly opposed. On April 9, 1917, they adopted a resolution, later approved in a party referendum by a vote of 21,000 to 350, which proclaimed: "We brand the declaration of war by our government as a crime against the people of the United States." In the 1917 municipal elections, Socialist candidates received 22 per cent of the vote in New York City, 34 per cent in Chicago (where they had received

43

less than 4 per cent a year before), and 44 per cent in Dayton.

To combat popular opposition to the war, Wilson set up a Committee on Public Information, under George Creel. To arouse support for the war, the Creel Committee whipped up hatred of Germany and all things German, and in many communities the response of vigilante leaders went far beyond what Creel or Wilson had intended. The war, as Ludwig Lewisohn observed, was fought with a "peculiarly unmotivated ferocity." Aroused to fury at an enemy 3,000 miles distant whom they could not strike directly, civilians sought enemies within. Flying squads invaded farmhouses to force farmers to buy a quota of bonds, and if a farmer refused to buy at least the amount fixed by a private committee, they nailed a yellow placard to his house or splashed his home with yellow paint. Men suspected of disloyalty were forced to kneel to kiss the flag. Supposedly responsible Red Cross leaders warned that German-Americans had infiltrated the Red Cross to put ground glass in bandages; while in humorless patriotic zeal sauerkraut was renamed "liberty cabbage," and Fritz Kreisler was driven from the concert stage.

There appears in wartime, observed Walter Lippmann, a Gresham's law of the emotions whereby leadership passes from statesmanship to virulent jingoism. At first directed at German-Americans and alleged spies, the crusade for conformity quickly focused on any criticism of the war from any source. "Woe be to the man," warned Wilson, "that seeks to stand in our way in this day of high resolution when every principle we hold dearest is to be vindicated and made secure." "He who is not with us, absolutely and without reserve of any kind, is against us, and should be treated as an alien enemy," declared Theodore Roosevelt. "Our bitter experience should teach us for a generation . . . to crush under our heel every movement that smacks in the smallest degree of playing the German game." With such instruction from the nation's leaders, fanatics who, in Santayana's phrase, redoubled their effort when they had forgotten their aim, got out of hand and soon lost all sense of discretion.

In Chicago when Burton Rascoe printed selections from *Areopagitica* under the by-line "John Milton," he was deluged with letters denouncing Milton as an agent of Prussian *kultur*. An issue of the *Nation* was banned from the mails because it contained an article that criticized Samuel Gompers for co-operating in the labor policies of the administration. Under the Espionage Act of 1917 and the Sedition law of 1918, more than 1,500 persons were arrested; the Socialist leader Eugene Debs was one of the group sentenced to prison. A Federal judge in Texas declared that La Follette and five other senators should be stood up against an adobe wall and shot. President Nicholas Murray Butler of Columbia University, speaking of La Follette, told the American Bankers Association that "you might just as well put poison in the food of every American boy that goes to his transport as to permit that man to talk as he does." Inevitably, on some occasions words gave way to action; in Butte the crippled IWW leader Frank Little was dragged from bed by a band of masked men and hanged from a railway trestle.

The war offered an outlet for the messianic zeal of the Progressive era without jeopardizing the structure of American society. It gave a sense of national unity, partly real, partly imposed, to quiet the concerns about rifts of class and party and race that haunted the last years of the era. It was this sense of psychic release from baffling internal problems that

L. P. Jacks had in mind when he wrote of "the peacefulness of being at war." "The mass of the worried middle classes," observed Randolph Bourne, the keenest critic of the war, "riddled by the campaign against American failings, which at times extended almost to a skepticism of the American State itself, were only too glad to sink back to a glorification of the State ideal, to feel about them in war the old protecting arms, to return to the old primitive sense of the omnipotence of the State, its matchless virtue, honor, and beauty, driving away all the foul old doubts and dismays."

Wilson transmuted the war into a religious crusade, in which he invoked the old theme of the church militant and the more modern one of the secular religion of democracy. Secretary of War Newton Baker wrote of America's "high and holy mission"; Secretary Lane spoke of "the world of Christ" coming face to face with the world of force; while a government pamphleteer noted the conviction of the American people that the "war across the sea was no mere conflict between dynasties, but a stupendous civil war of all the world." The war, declared the Creel Committee, was "a Crusade not merely to re-win the tomb of Christ, but to bring back to earth the rule of right, the peace, goodwill to men and gentleness he taught."

Wilson and his intellectual supporters, such as John Dewey, felt that this "most terrible and disastrous of all wars" could be countenanced only by declaring it the harbinger of eternal peace. This presumption was fantastic in the light of what was actually happening in Europe in 1917: the breakdown of the whole nineteenth-century order that had made possible a longer peace than Europe had ever known and a wider spread of democracy than the world had ever seen. Extravagant Wilsonian expectations only intensified the disillusionment that came with peace. The American people began the war with a single purpose—to defeat Germany. But during the next few months they were promised a millenium, and when the ultimate disenchantment followed, they turned away from any idea of world responsibility. They were convinced that they had been betrayed into a pointless sacrifice. Moreover, when the League of Nations was rejected, the Wilsonians blamed the American people, thus creating a serious breach between internationalist leaders and the public.

The utopian spirit of the war took concrete form in Wilson's proposal of a postwar federation of nations, in itself not a utopian scheme but one which, from the first, was freighted with utopian aspirations. "It is the hour and the day," Max Eastman had written as early as February, 1915, "for President Wilson to take the first step towards international federation. He has it in his hands to make his administration a momentous event in planetary history—a thing not for historians, indeed, but for biologists to tell of. . . ." The idea of a parliament of man, of a world organization to abolish the scourge of war, had excited the imagination of poets and statesmen for centuries; it had elicited considerable interest in Europe, particularly in England, before and during the war; but it was not until Woodrow Wilson formulated his belief in a postwar league of nations that the idea began to become a reality.

In May, 1916, Wilson publicly espoused American membership in a postwar association, and on January 22, 1917, in an address to the Senate, he not only reaffirmed his support of American participation in a league of nations but for the first time sketched the terms of peace in which he believed. It was to be a "peace without victory," a "peace among equals," not a peace of indemnities and annexations. A year later, on January 8, 1918, to counteract Bolshevik arguments that the war was merely an imperialist struggle, Wilson went before Congress to deliver his famous Fourteen Points address, to explain to the world the kind of peace for which the United States and its allies were fighting. He called for the abolition of secret diplomacy, for freedom of the seas, the self-determination of nations, the removal of economic barriers among nations, the reduction of armaments, and the adjustment of colonial claims in the interest of the inhabitants of the colonies as well as the powers concerned. Most important was Point 14: "a general association of nations . . . affording mutual guarantees of political independence and territorial integrity to great and small states alike."

At first contemptuous of the Fourteen Points, Germany had been driven by October, 1918, to begin negotiations with Wilson for peace on the basis of them. Thinking Wilson would be an easy mark, General Ludendorff planned to use him to give Germany a breathing spell before resuming fighting, but Wilson proved a tough negotiator. He demanded that the Germans evacuate Belgium and France and guarantee they would not continue hostilities. To the true representatives of the German people, Wilson added, the terms of the Fourteen Points were available, but to the "military masters of the monarchical autocrats of Germany," the only terms were unconditional surrender. Partly in response to Wilson's suggestion that a republic would win better terms than an imperial monarchy, the German people rebelled, forcing the Kaiser to abdicate and flee to Holland on November 9, 1918. Although Ludendorff's maneuver had been foiled, Wilson's negotiations had one disastrous consequence. By insisting on negotiating only with democratic representatives, Wilson rescued the German military caste from the obloquy of surrender, and he provided the basis for the myth, which Hitler was to exploit, that Germany lost the war not through military defeat but through a "stab in the back" by democratic politicians.

Before Wilson could conclude the terms of peace, he had to meet Allied objections to negotiating with Germany on the basis of the Fourteen Points. The Allies, who had concluded a number of secret treaties carving up the choicer portions of the German Empire, were determined to wring from Germany as much as they could to compensate for a bloody, costly war. When Colonel House suggested that, if the Allies persisted in a vindictive policy, America might make a separate peace, the Allies yielded, but on two conditions: that Germany would have to pay reparations for damages to civilians, and that the Allies would individually reserve sovereignty of action on the principle of freedom of the seas. "War would not be war if there were freedom of the seas," Premier Clemenceau of France explained. On this basis, the armistice was signed on November 11, 1918 in a railroad car in Compiègne Forest.

The war for democracy had ended in triumph, and the way was now cleared for the creation of the great postwar federation of nations. "Every ancient right of princes or castes or classes to dispose of the wills of other men is on the table for liquidation," wrote the editors of the *New Republic* in November, 1918. "At this instant of history, democracy is supreme."

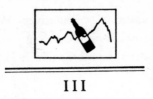

III

The Fourteenth Point

Woodrow Wilson was the Victorian statesman incarnate. At sixteen he hung a portrait of Gladstone over his desk—he called him "the greatest statesman that ever lived"—and he spent a lifetime trying to emulate the Englishman. The Fourteen Points were essentially the credo of English liberalism, and Wilson approached the Paris conference with a program —political democracy, self-determination, free trade—which spoke the language of Cobden and Bright. The Peace Conference would test the ability of nineteenth-century liberalism to survive in a twentieth-century world.

Like a British Prime Minister, Wilson viewed his own party as an alliance of men of the same ideological persuasion, with himself as head of a party government. Fearing that his position at the conference would be seriously jeopardized if his party was repudiated in the November, 1918, congressional elections, Wilson on October 25 issued an appeal to the voters: "If you have approved of my leadership and wish me to continue to be your unembarrassed spokesman in affairs at home and abroad, I earnestly beg that you will express yourselves unmistakably to that effect by returning a Democratic majority to both the Senate and the House of Representatives." Despite Wilson's appeal (his critics said because of it), the Republicans captured both houses of Congress. Although the election turned less on Wilson's message than on domestic issues like the price of wheat and wool, it was taken as a repudiation of Wilson, and it badly damaged his bargaining position in Paris. It appeared to European statesmen that Wilson, on the eve of the conference, had sought and lost a vote of confidence.

Foreign commentators on the American party system have all come to a single conclusion: there is no difference between the parties on principle or program. Whatever merit this observation has, and it has less merit than men like Lord Bryce believed, it held no water at all in the fight over the League of Nations. Wilson was bitterly hated by the two most influential spokesmen for the Republican party, Theodore Roosevelt and Senator Henry Cabot Lodge of Massachusetts. Both had shown considerable interest in the idea of a League at one time, but essentially they believed in balance-of-power politics and were contemptuous of Wilson's idealism. Moreover, however favorably they might have been disposed to the idea of a League in the abstract, they would have nothing to do with a Wilson League. They had even less intention of permitting the Democratic party to go to the polls in 1920 claiming credit both for having waged a victorious war and for having created a League of Nations. In their distrust of the proposal of the League, in their hatred of Wilson, in their concern for the fortunes of the Republican party, they would stop at nothing, even if they completely undermined Wilson's position and played into the hands of European nationalists.

The Perils of Prosperity, 1914–32

On November 27, 1918, Theodore Roosevelt issued a statement which was duly noted in the capitals of Europe: "Our allies and our enemies and Mr. Wilson himself should all understand that Mr. Wilson has no authority whatever to speak for the American people at this time. His leadership has just been emphatically repudiated by them. The newly elected Congress comes far nearer than Mr. Wilson to having a right to speak the purposes of the American people at this moment. Mr. Wilson and his Fourteen Points and his four supplementary points and his five complementary points and all his utterances every which way have ceased to have any shadow of right to be accepted as expressive of the will of the American people."

Two weeks after the election, Wilson made the surprising announcement that he would break precedent by going personally to Paris to head the American peace delegation. To accompany him on the delegation, Wilson named Secretary of State Lansing, Colonel House, General Tasker Bliss, and Henry White, an able career diplomat. Of the group, not a single man was from the Senate, and the only Republican, White, was not a major figure in the party. Wilson was buying trouble by these appointments, since he would one day have to get the treaty through a Republican-controlled Senate. But he saw no other alternative. He felt he could not name Lodge, the obvious choice, since Lodge had long been a bitter foe, and to name any other Senate Republican would be an affront to Lodge. It is no less true that Wilson's decision revealed a fatal flaw of character; he could not work with men of his own stature, and he detested day-by-day jockeying for position. Wilson preferred the enunciation of high principles to the intimate, personal associations of political maneuvering.

The Fourteenth Point

Wilson felt he had to go to Paris, because he rather than any of the Allied leaders was the true spokesman for the people of Europe who yearned for eternal peace. When he arrived in Europe, he was at the height of his prestige, the leader of a country which had brought an apparently endless war to a triumphant end, the prophet who declared that never again would men have to wage war. Wherever he went, he was greeted with wild acclaim, acclaim beyond that ever before accorded to a democratic political figure. The enthusiastic crowds convinced Wilson all the more that he was the representative of the people of Europe, indeed of the world, and that with their support behind him he could force their leaders to accept a "peace without victory." This was a fundamental error. The masses who adored Wilson also hated the Germans and were determined to gain both revenge and recompense for the war. On the very day Wilson reached Paris, British voters gave David Lloyd George a vote of confidence in an election notable for the government's promise to squeeze Germany "until the pips squeak." Wilson's real problem lay less with the leaders, many of whom (like Lloyd George) had considerable sympathy with his aims, than with the people, who forced the leaders into extreme positions.

The Peace Conference at Paris opened on January 12, 1919, with twenty-seven countries represented, in an atmosphere of seething unrest. "I am doubtful," Lloyd George later told Parliament, "whether any body of men with a difficult task have worked under greater difficulties—stones crackling on the roof and crashing through windows, and sometimes wild men screaming through the keyholes." Since no effective treaty could be drafted by delegates from twenty-seven nations meeting at one time, the conference turned the chief task over to a Council of Ten which quickly gave way to a Council of Four: Wilson, David Lloyd George of Great Britain, Georges Clemenceau of France, and, although he was often absent, Vittorio Orlando of Italy. The eloquent Orlando was concerned only with problems affecting Italy; the energetic Lloyd George, while anxious to preserve British power, had a larger view of the world situation.

The chief debates at the conference took the form of a prolonged duel between Wilson and Clemenceau. Wilson's great strength at Paris stemmed from his understanding that the world could ill afford another war of the dimensions of World War I and that balance-of-power politics would almost certainly prove inadequate to prevent another war. He also understood that a vindictive peace would never last, that it would breed new wars, that it would create a feeling of irredentism in Germany. His great weakness was that he had little understanding of power—either economic power or political power—and he thought in terms of abstractions. Wilson's abstractness, wrote Walter Weyl, "is part of a curiously a priori metaphysical idealism. His world stands firmly on its head. Ideas do not rest upon facts but facts on ideas. . . . He seems to see the world in abstractions. To him railroad cars are not railroad cars but a gray general thing called Transportation; people are not men and women, corporeal, gross, very human beings, but Humanity—Humanity very much in the abstract."

Clemenceau, a fierce partisan who had won the sobriquet of "The Tiger," was now seventy-eight years old. He sat at the conference table, a black skull cap on his wrinkled head, with burning memories of the past—of the Franco-Prussian War, of the humiliation at Sedan, of the siege of Paris, during which people had been forced to eat cats to stay alive, of that second invasion of 1914, of the bodies piled high at Verdun, of the ruthlessness of the Germans as they retreated. He had one interest, France, and one concern, that Germany must never march again. If Wilson could give him that, they could agree, but Clemenceau had nothing but contempt for the words of idealism or for drafts of leagues. He wanted either the promise of American armed power or the destruction of the sources of German strength. For the rest, he cared nothing. "God gave us the Ten Commandments, and we broke them," Clemenceau allegedly declared. "Wilson gives us the Fourteen Points. We shall see."

Pilloried as a fool trapped by the wily diplomats of Europe (John Maynard Keynes called him a "blind and deaf Don Quixote"), Wilson was in fact an adroit negotiator. He succeeded in preventing a distribution of colonial spoils on crude imperialist lines and instead obtained adoption of the mandate system (primarily the contribution of Jan Smuts of South Africa). He held to the principle of self-determination in blocking the Italian claim to the Yugoslav port of Fiume and in opposing French proposals for a buffer state west of the Rhine or permanent French occupation of the territory. When the conference deadlocked, Wilson threatened to return home, and the French were forced to compromise on occupation of the Rhineland for a maximum of fifteen years and of the Saar for the same period, with a plebiscite at the end of that time to determine whether the Saarlanders wanted to belong to France or Germany. In return, Wilson agreed to a treaty promising armed aid if France were the victim of an "unprovoked" attack by Germany, although both Wilson and Clemenceau must have known that the Senate would never agree to such a pact. Even though the Versailles treaty did not conform wholly to the principle of self-determination, never in the history of Europe were so few people left under foreign domination. Winston Churchill estimated that after the new boundary lines of 1919 were drawn, less than 3 per cent of the people of Europe would have preferred to live in another country.

Wilson's most spectacular triumph had come when the Conference on January 25, 1919, voted to incorporate the League of Nations as an integral part of the treaty. It was the high point of the negotiations, but once more Wilson was undercut by Republican critics at home. On March 5, 1919, Henry Cabot Lodge introduced a Republican round robin, signed by 39 senators or senators-elect, more than enough to defeat the treaty, declaring that "the constitution of the League of Nations in the form now proposed to the peace conference should not be accepted by the United States." Furthermore, the round robin stated, no League proposal should be considered until the peace had been concluded. That night, Wilson, who had returned for a brief visit to America, struck back at his critics at an enthusiastic rally in New York. "When that treaty comes back," he announced, "gentlemen on this side will find the covenant not only in it, but so many threads of the treaty tied to the covenant that you cannot dissect the covenant from the treaty without destroying the whole vital structure."

But Lodge made his point. When Wilson returned to Paris, he was forced to renegotiate in order to place some of the Republican demands in the League Covenant. Wilson gained specific recognition for the Monroe Doctrine and inserted a two-year "escape" clause providing for the withdrawal of member nations from the League. In return for these concessions to Wilson, the other members of the Big Four required concessions also, and Wilson's hand was weakened. "You come over here," one delegate shouted, "and dictate what we should do and what we should not do, and yet you do not let us have our say as to what you propose doing over there!"

Attacked by partisan nationalists at home, faced by an alliance of European nationalists at Paris, Wilson was forced to make a series of concessions which abandoned, wholly or in part, many of his cherished principles. Although he believed in open covenants openly arrived at, the treaty was drafted behind closed doors. Although he believed in the self-determination of nations, he consented to turn over the Austrian Tyrol to Italy, to put Germans under Polish rule in Silesia and the Corridor, and to allow Japan to take over the German sphere of influence in Shantung. Although he advocated a peace among equals, he agreed that Germany would have to pay an immediate indemnity of $5 billion, sign a blank check for future reparations, surrender vast amounts of coal- and iron-rich territory, lose much of her merchant marine, and be stripped of her entire overseas empire. Although he had expressed doubt about the causes of the war, the treaty pinned the "war guilt" on Germany. The treaty made no mention of freedom of the seas and did nothing to break down economic barriers, in part because, as Wilson confessed on one occasion, he was "not much interested in the economic subjects."

The League of Nations met a warm response in the United States. In the summer of 1919, the vast majority of the American people favored American entrance into the League; the proposal received the indorsement of thirty-three governors of both parties. If the League were not approved, wrote an

Ohio newspaper, "God pity us all, for there will be war from now to kingdom come." The chief opposition came from a group of about fourteen Republican and four Democratic irreconcilables led by Senator William Borah of Idaho, who vowed war to the death on the "unholy thing with the holy name." "If the Savior of man," asserted the intractable Borah, "would revisit the earth and declare for a League of Nations, I would be opposed to it." Fearing the emasculation of American nationality, former Senator Albert Beveridge of Indiana denounced the League as the work of "amiable old male grannies who, over their afternoon tea, are planning to denationalize America and denationalize the Nation's manhood." German-Americans execrated the treaty as a merciless *Diktat*, Italian-Americans were infuriated by Wilson's opposition to seizure of Fiume by Italy, and Irish-Americans insisted that the League was a British conspiracy. Progressives were horrified by the severity of the treaty; the terms of the pact, wrote LaFollette, were "enough to chill the heart of the world."

Powerful as these opponents were, the irreconcilables alone did not have enough votes to kill the treaty. More important was the band of "strong reservationists" led by Senator Lodge who wanted, at the very least, major revisions of the treaty, which the other powers would have to approve. Some of the strong reservationists would have been content with this; others merely used the demand for reservations as a cloak to conceal their outright opposition to the League. Among the strong reservationists, the Roosevelt-Lodge group played a critical role. In July, 1918, Beveridge wrote Roosevelt, "Wilson has hoisted the motley flag of internationalism. . . . That makes the issue, does it not? Straight Americanism for us." Roosevelt answered, "You understand exactly how we feel."

The Fourteenth Point

When Alice Roosevelt Longworth, Teddy's daughter, saw Wilson enter the White House on his return from Paris, she made the sign of the evil eye and cried: "A murrain on him, a murrain on him, a murrain on him!"

As chairman of the Senate Foreign Relations Committee, Lodge held a strategic redoubt. Although he professed to favor the treaty with reservations, Lodge packed the committee with senators who were opposed to it in any form. With public opinion against him, Lodge resorted to delaying tactics until opposition to the League could build up. He was not an isolationist; he was, if anything, more willing than Wilson to engage in European power politics. At the same time, he was a fierce Republican partisan who, with his eye on the 1920 election, was determined to prevent Borah from leading a bolt from the party and was unwilling to give Wilson the advantage of the League issue. Fancying himself a "scholar in politics," he resented Wilson's assumption of the same role. "I never expected to hate anyone in politics with the hatred I feel towards Wilson," Lodge wrote Roosevelt in 1915. Historians have not been able to agree on Lodge's motives in the League fight, but it is difficult to dispute Professor Garraty's conclusion that "in the last analysis, Lodge preferred a dead league to the one proposed by Wilson."

Faced by such formidable opposition, Wilson's only hope of victory was to combine Democratic approval of the League with that of the "mild reservationists," and to court the latter group among the Republicans. Unfortunately, he found it personally impossible to attempt to conciliate his opponents in the Senate; many of them, he felt, were men with "bungalow minds." When the Democratic floor leader, Senator Martin of Virginia, told Wilson that he was not sure that the treaty could win a two-thirds vote, the President was furious. "Martin!" he rasped, "Anyone who opposes me in that I'll crush!" He hated controversy, of which he had had his fill in Paris, and he rebelled against further compromise where he felt a matter of principle was involved. Instead of appealing to his foes in the Senate, Wilson, like a British Prime Minister, decided to go to the country.

Through the summer of 1919, while Lodge held intentionally fruitless hearings, opposition to the League mounted, as the spotlight focused on professional haters of England like Senator James Reed of Missouri, still nursing grievances over the Stamp Act, and on inane warnings that the League would be dominated by the Vatican or by the colored races of the world. While Wilson was in Paris, twenty-six Democratic members of the Massachusetts legislature cabled him to return home to reduce the high cost of living, "which we consider far more important than the League of Nations." Passenger ships docked with their cargoes of war-weary American soldiers, released from the nightmare of shell barrages and lice-ridden trenches, returning with tales of being fleeced by French storekeepers and condescended to by the British.

Exasperated by Lodge's delaying tactics, Wilson left Washington in early September to stump the country. Warned by his doctor that he was in no physical condition to undertake such a strenuous tour, Wilson, perhaps unconsciously seeking martyrdom, determined to go ahead anyway. As he crossed the Middle West, he met with indifferent success—in some places great enthusiasm, in others moderate interest—but when he reached the Far West, he was greeted with ovations, and his tour of California was nothing short of a triumphal procession, with great crowds voicing their approval of the

League. As he swung back east toward Washington, he stopped at Pueblo, Colorado, where he delivered one of the great speeches of his career. People wept openly as he talked of the graves of American soldiers in France and urged that Americans should never again have to die in foreign fields. That night, exhausted by the grueling schedule, Wilson was stricken with severe pain. Determined to go on nonetheless, he was only with great difficulty persuaded to cancel the remainder of his tour. Four days after returning to the White House, the President was found by Mrs. Wilson lying unconscious on the floor. He had suffered a stroke which paralyzed the left side of his body.

The speaking tour was a disaster. Despite his warm reception in the West, Wilson did not change a single Senate vote. More important, Wilson's illness deprived the League cause of its leader. For seven and a half months Wilson did not meet his cabinet. For the next year and a half, from October, 1919 to March, 1921, the country had no president; it was ruled by a regency headed by his wife. While the stroke did not becloud his mind, it changed Wilson's personality. He became more irritable; he lost his judgment; at times, he broke down in tears. With compromise essential to success, compromise became less possible than ever.

On November 6, 1919, Senator Lodge finally reported the treaty out of committee, appending to it a series of fourteen reservations. The most important of these declared that the United States, in accepting Article X (under which nations agreed to respect and preserve the territorial integrity and political and independence of all League members against external aggression), assumed no obligation to fulfill its requirements unless Congress so provided in the specific case. If this was Lodge's price for the treaty, the Senate Democrats were willing to pay it, but Wilson would have none of it. The President denounced the Lodge reservation as a "knife thrust at the heart of the treaty," because it removed any *moral* obligation on the part of the United States.

On November 19, 1919, a Senate motion to pass the treaty with the Lodge reservations failed by a vote of 39 for to 55 against. Under orders from Wilson, the Democrats voted against the motion, and they were joined in the opposition by the irreconcilables, who were against the treaty in any form. An attempt to pass the treaty without reservations failed 38–53, with only a single Republican voting in favor of the motion. The treaty, it should be noted, was not defeated because of the two-thirds rule; neither side could get even a majority.

When Congress reconvened in December, 1919, a groundswell of public opinion demanded a compromise to save the treaty. Neither Wilson nor Lodge would budge. When Senator Lodge met with Democrats to talk over a compromise, Senator Borah threatened to remove Lodge as majority leader, and Lodge broke off negotiations. Even without Borah's intervention, it is unlikely that Lodge would have yielded enough to make a compromise acceptable to Wilson. And Wilson was more adamant than ever. He warned that he would simply put the treaty in his pocket and end negotiations if the Senate passed it with the Lodge reservations.

Exasperated by Wilson's obstinacy, his party split. The most important Democratic newspapers announced they would now go along with the Lodge reservations if this was the only way America could enter the League, and a number of Democratic senators broke ranks. On March 19, 1920, the Senate voted for the second and last time on the treaty. This time twenty-one Democrats defied Wilson and voted for the treaty with the Lodge reservations, enough to yield a 49–35 majority but seven votes short of the necessary two-thirds. Twenty-three Democrats, acting at Wilson's request, had joined the Republican bitter-enders to defeat the treaty. "We can always depend on Mr. Wilson," Senator Brandegee observed cynically to Lodge. "He never has failed us."

Who killed the League? Professor Thomas A. Bailey has written: "In the final analysis the treaty was slain in the house of its friends rather than in the house of its enemies. In the final analysis it was not the two-thirds rule, or the 'irreconcilables,' or Lodge, or the 'strong' and 'mild reservationists,' but Wilson and his docile following who delivered the fatal stab. . . . This was the supreme act of infanticide. With his own sickly hands Wilson slew his own brain child. . . ."

If one accepts this judgment, one must think that Wilson was mistaken on two crucial points. Wilson believed that if he had accepted the reservations, one or more of the other nations would have refused to ratify the treaty. No one can say with finality whether this was so. Britain might have objected to the reservation which stated that the United States would not be bound by decisions where the British Empire cast six votes, as well as to the reservation added by Democratic Senator Gerry of Rhode Island placing the Senate on record in favor of Irish independence. Latin-American nations might have objected to the reservation on the Monroe Doctrine, Japan to Senate refusal to sanction the Shantung arrangement. On the whole, however, other powers would probably have preferred American ratification, even with such egregious reservations, to American absence from the League. In any event, it was worth a try.

More important was Wilson's objection to Lodge's reservation on Article X. Since, under any circumstances, the United States could not send troops without action by Congress, Wilson's strong protest appears rather tenuous at first glance. (So, it should be added, does Lodge's persistence.) Yet there was much sound sense in Wilson's refusal to accept a world organization which gave the illusion of security but did not actually gain it. Although most Americans favored the League, few understood the implications of collective security. The League fight became polarized as one between internationalists and isolationists, but the real issue was much more complex. Wilson himself understood that the League involved a sharp break with the American tradition of isolation. Many of the "internationalists," on the other hand, supported the League not as an assumption of new responsibilities but as a magical formula that would free the United States from the obligation of foreign wars. Like the abolitionists, these pro-League men had little sense of social order and they thought of the League not as a way to mass American, French, and British power (as well as a step toward an ultimate world order) but as an effort to remake the world entire. This was what Randolph Bourne meant in calling the League "a palpable apocalyptic myth, like the syndicalists' myth of the 'general strike.'"

The American people were being asked to guarantee the territorial integrity and existing political independence of all members of the League, and this was a good deal to swallow. The country had never really abandoned its isolationist assumptions, particularly the assumption that the United States unaided could maintain its national security. During the war these convictions were merely driven underground. It is astonishing that despite the tradition of isolation, despite Wilson's collapse, despite partisan bitterness and the animosity of ethnic groups, 85 per cent of the senators voting on November 19 were willing to accept the League in some form. Yet even if the country had entered the League, it is doubtful that Americans would have been willing to assume their full obligations. The United States had not been prepared by a threat to its own security for the kind of enterprise it was later to undertake in Korea. It had insufficient incentive for abandoning either isolation or absolute national sovereignty. It would take the chastening experience of the World War II, Hiroshima, and the Cold War to provide that incentive.

This is not to say that Wilson did not make serious blunders, although his responsibility for the failure to accept the League scarcely matched that of Lodge. As early as the spring of 1917, Wilson knew of the secret treaties; yet he did nothing to force the Allies to rescind them. At the time Wilson held all the aces; he could even have fought a wholly maritime war until he got the terms of peace he wanted. Yet out of some deepseated inability to face unpleasantness, Wilson ignored the fact of the treaties, and he proclaimed idealistic war aims as though the treaties did not exist. In the fight for the peace treaty in the Senate, Wilson was once more unable to battle for an effective compromise. It is his eternal fame that he achieved more than any other man had ever done in bringing the nations of the world into a parliament of man. For this reason, his own failings were deeply tragic for himself and for the world.

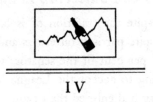

I V

Red Scare

In the year 1919, Senator McKellar of Tennessee advocated sending native-born American citizens with radical beliefs to a penal colony in Guam. South Carolina's James F. Byrnes asked for the intervention of the federal government to balk an uprising of Negroes that he declared Reds were planning in the South. Some New York schoolteachers were dismissed after a campaign to determine "Who's Red and Who's True Blue." General Leonard Wood, the Army Chief of Staff, noted his approval of a minister's call for the deportation of Bolshevists "in ships of stone with sails of lead, with the wrath of God for a breeze and with hell for their first port." "If I had my way with these ornery wild-eyed Socialists and I.W.W.'s," shouted the evangelist Billy Sunday, "I would stand them up before a firing squad and save space on our ships." In Indiana a jury deliberated two minutes before acquitting Frank Petroni, who had shot and killed a man for yelling, "To hell with the United States!" The great Red Scare of 1919 was underway.

Although there had been a fear of radicalism, particularly

of anarchism, before the war, and although radicals had been censured during the war as pro-German, the Red Scare did not really begin until the creation of the Communists' Third International in March, 1919. The Bolshevik Revolution of November, 1917, had awakened the fears of conservatives, but it was less the revolution itself than the spread of revolutionary principles to other countries which excited alarm. In March, 1919, Communist uprisings in Bavaria and Hungary whipped up fears that bolshevism might engulf the Western world. No one doubted that a revolution in the United States had a high place on the Communists' agenda. Karl Radek, the executive secretary of the Third International, boasted that money sent to Germany for the Spartacist uprising "was as nothing compared to the funds transmitted to New York for the purpose of spreading bolshevism in the United States."

The extremism of the Red Scare consisted not merely in exaggerating dangers but also in failing to distinguish between genuine revolutionaries and radicals of a peaceful persuasion, although before the war Socialists had been treated with a good deal of respect. Eugene Debs had even been something of a folk hero. The Socialists themselves were responsible for a good deal of the postwar confusion. The anti-war and uncompromisingly anticapitalist position of the Bolsheviks had an electrifying appeal to American radicals. Debs, who, as Daniel Bell has remarked, had "an almost compulsive desire to be 'left' of orthodox labor opinion," gave outright support to the Russian Revolution, although he was to sour on it in the last years of his life. Bolshevism was a success and hence an enormous challenge and stimulus to American radicals; for a time, Socialists of the most varied persuasions were pro-Bolshevik.

The Perils of Prosperity, 1914–32

Even before the Russian Revolution, Bolshevik leaders had come to the United States. At the end of 1916, Nikolai Bukharin arrived in New York, where he edited the journal of the Russian Socialist Federation; early in 1917, Leon Trotsky joined the staff of the same paper, in the back of a rank cellar at 77 St. Mark's Place. Foreign-language federations had always been a minority within the American Socialist party; but the Bolshevik Revolution brought a flood of new members into the Slavic groups by mid-1919. The foreign-language federations—enthusiastically pro-Bolshevik almost to a man—soon outnumbered the English-speaking groups in the Socialist party. In September, 1919, at a hall in Chicago which they renamed "Smolny" after the Soviet headquarters in Petrograd, the foreign-language federations organized the American Communist party. Only 7 per cent of the new party spoke or understood English.

At the same time, a left-wing faction within the Socialist party, led by native-born radicals, attempted to convert the party to the Bolshevik pattern of an immediate revolution guided by a small cadre of party workers. The most prominent member of the native-born left-wing faction was John Reed, an Oregonian who had been a cheerleader at Harvard. This romantic, who had followed war, strikes, and revolution from New Jersey to Mexico, ardently admired the Russian coup. He declared approvingly: "The Bolsheviki believe in democracy of the working class, and no democracy for anybody else." Reed, however, was unwilling to permit the radical movement in America to fall into the hands of foreign-language groups. In September, 1919, meeting at the same time as the foreign-language Communists, the Reed faction organized the Communist Labor party. The Communist Labor party was also overwhelmingly composed of members who did not know English, but its leaders—men like Reed and Ben Gitlow—were English-speaking. No question of ideology divided them; both parties, which ultimately were to merge as the Communist party, sought recognition by the Third International. Together, the two Communist parties numbered between 25,000 and 40,000; the Communists had about three times as many members as the Communist Labor party.

The Russian Revolution came at a time when American Socialists were demoralized; after a generation of agitation, they were weaker than they had been many years before. The Bolshevik coup not only promised a reversal of fortunes but suggested that radicals need not go through the painful process of educating a majority to their point of view. In May, 1917, there had been only 11,000 members of the Bolshevik party in all of Russia. Five months later, the Bolsheviks held power. Captivated by this pattern of success, many American radicals believed that a revolution in the United States was imminent, and some thought it would come in a matter of months. John Reed wrote Roger Baldwin, who had been sent to jail as a conscientious objector, that he would be freed from prison by the workers long before his sentence ended.

The belief in imminent revolution that stirred the Communists was only one aspect of a spirit of millenarianism which swept the United States and Europe immediately after the war. John Dos Passos recalled of the spring of 1919: "Any spring is a time of overturn, but then Lenin was alive, the Seattle general strike had seemed the beginning of the flood instead of the beginning of the ebb, Americans in Paris were groggy with theatre and painting and music; Picasso was to rebuild the eye, Stravinski was cramming the Russian steppes into our ears, currents of energy seemed breaking out everywhere as young guys climbed out of their uniforms, imperial America was all shiny with the new idea of the Ritz, in every direction the countries of the world stretched out starving and angry, ready for anything turbulent and new, whenever you went to the movies you saw Charlie Chaplin."

Organized labor had long been the despair of the radicals —Lenin dismissed Samuel Gompers, head of the AF of L, as merely an "agent of the bourgeoisie"—but in 1919 the millennial spirit caught up many of the old-line union leaders, some of whom had tasted national power for the first time during the war. If they were influenced by developments abroad, it was less the Russian Revolution than the Nottingham program of the British Labour party, with its demand for nationalization of basic industries, which caught their imagination. Of all the postwar proposals, the most important was the Plumb Plan: the railway brotherhoods, which had flourished under government operation of the lines during the war, advocated nationalization of the railroads. Despite the opposition of Gompers the AF of L endorsed the Plan, which congressional critics denounced as "a bold, bald, naked attempt to sovietize the railroads of the country."

If the Socialist support of bolshevism served to wipe out distinctions between various shades of radicalism, the growing militancy of organized labor in 1919 appeared to align labor unions with world-wide radicalism. Prices shot up in the spring of 1919 and continued to climb until the fall of 1920; the cost of living soared in 1920 to 105 per cent above the prewar level, which not only created a public sense of irritation on which the Red Scare could feed but also touched off

a wave of strikes by workers attempting to keep up with rising prices. Accustomed to orthodox union techniques, the
country was deeply shaken by the dramatic strikes of 1919.

When, on January 21, 1919, 35,000 Seattle shipyard workers struck for higher wages and shorter workdays, the Seattle
Central Labor Council, representing all organized labor in the
region, voted to conduct a general strike to support their
brothers. This decision was taken under the influence of James
Duncan, an outspoken opponent of conservative union methods and an admirer of the Russian Revolution. For five days
the city of Seattle was paralyzed; streetcars ceased to run,
schools closed their doors, business came to a standstill. The
general strike was crushed by Mayor Ole Hanson, who out-
rageously exaggerated the Red menace. The strike alienated
middle-class opinion and persuaded the country that a genuine
threat of revolution might be in prospect.

Many Americans had always associated radicalism with terrorism. They remembered Czolgosz (President McKinley's
assassin) and the Haymarket anarchists. In the spring of 1919
the popular stereotype began to take on substance. On
April 28 a small brown package arrived in Mayor Hanson's
office in Seattle; when opened, it was found to contain a
homemade bomb. On the following day a similar package
came to the home of former Senator Thomas W. Hardwick of
Georgia; when his maid opened it, it blew off her hands. The
next day a New York postal clerk, reading a newspaper account of the Hardwick bombing on the subway, remembered
having set aside sixteen similar parcels, bearing "Gimbel's"
stickers, for insufficient postage. He raced back to the post
office and located the packages before any damage was done;
postal authorities around the country, warned by New York,

71

intercepted eighteen more. The packages had been sent (obviously timed for May Day) to John D. Rockefeller, Postmaster-General Burleson, Judge Kenesaw Mountain Landis, and a group of other foes of organized labor and advocates of immigration restriction. In addition, packages had been sent to men who were apparently thought to be enemies of labor or of radicalism but who actually had liberal records: Senator Hardwick, Justice Holmes, Secretary of Labor William B. Wilson, and Frederic C. Howe, commissioner of immigration at Ellis Island and a warm friend of the immigrant.

On the evening of June 2 a new series of bombs exploded in eight different cities at the same hour. Once more, there was little logic to the bombings, which struck indiscriminately at minor officials and major figures. Most important was the bombing of Attorney-General A. Mitchell Palmer's home in Washington, D.C., which shattered the front of his house. The bomb-thrower himself was blown to pieces by the blast, but enough evidence was found to indicate that he was an Italian alien from Philadelphia and an anarchist.

The bombings of June 2 were obviously the result of a coordinated effort and had the semblance of a revolutionary plot, but it is extremely unlikely that Communists had anything to do with any of the bombings. The first set appears to have been the work of one or more deranged individuals, the second set the work of anarchists who were probably psychotic as well. In no way did the pattern of bombings fit into Communist strategy, and the way in which they were carried out suggested the actions not of professional revolutionaries but of ignorant and deluded men. At the same time, it is understandable that many Americans, already edgy over bolshevism and increased labor militancy, viewed the bombings as an organized conspiracy to capture control of the government by violence.

At this critical juncture, with the American middle class uncertain whether American workers were pledged to their own government or to some alien creed, the Boston police went on strike. Underpaid, overworked, with miserable working conditions, they had voted in the summer of 1919 to affiliate with the AF of L. Policemen in many American cities had taken such action without arousing public concern, but the decision of the Boston police was seen, in the hothouse atmosphere of 1919, as proof of labor radicalism, although the police were in no way involved in radical activity. Boston's Police Commissioner Curtis, a tactless, overbearing man with a long record of hostility to labor, brought the issue to a head on September 8, 1919, by firing nineteen policemen for union membership. Striking back the next day, the angry police decided by an overwhelming vote to walk off their jobs. Although the police had serious grievances and although they had been provoked by the commissioner, their decision to strike was a major blunder, for it left the city without protection and arrayed the middle class solidly against them.

Within twenty-four hours, violence broke out on the streets of Boston. Two men were killed in South Boston and another in Scollay Square. Shop windows were smashed on Summer Street and Washington Street, and passers-by helped themselves to shoes and neckties. The actual amount of damage done in the rioting and looting was small, but the country fastened on the image of thugs brazenly rolling dice on Boston Common in the shadow of the State House while the city was left defenseless against criminals. Public opinion strongly condemned the strike, President Wilson calling it "a crime against civilization."

Samuel Gompers urged the men to return to their jobs and let the issues of the strike be arbitrated, and the police unanimously agreed. But Commissioner Curtis, supported by the nation's press, was determined to punish the strikers; he declared that no policemen would be reinstated and that he would recruit an entirely new force. The next day, Governor Calvin Coolidge, who had done almost nothing during the strike, wired Gompers his refusal to arbitrate: "There is no right to strike against the public safety by anybody, anywhere, anytime." Overnight, Coolidge became a national hero.

Two days after the Boston police struck, steel workers issued a strike call for September 22, 1919. Of all areas of industry, steel had put up the stiffest resistance to organized labor; since the bloody Homestead strike of 1892 the AF of L had virtually abandoned efforts to organize the steel mills. With the confidence gained from its stronger position during the war, the federation decided on a new effort. A new kind of labor leadership was required, and that leadership was supplied by William Z. Foster, reared in a foul Philadelphia slum, who had gained his labor experience with the radical IWW in the mining and lumber camps of the West but who had left the IWW to organize industrial unions within the AF of L.

The grievances of the steelworkers were acute. Nearly half the men worked twelve hours a day, seven days a week, for an average wage of $28 a week; many of the workers lived in drab shacks of the most primitive sort. The industry was run by autocrats like Judge Elbert Gary, the head of U.S. Steel, and a fierce defender of the open shop. The strike began when Gary refused to recognize the union or even to meet such elementary demands as one day's rest in every seven; by the end of the week, 365,000 men were out. Although the country initially had considerable sympathy for the workers' demands, the steel companies, aided by Attorney-General Palmer, aroused public opinion against the strike by painting it as another radical outbreak. Since radicals had in fact played some part in the strike, particularly in Gary, the attempt to discredit it as a Red uprising gained credence. With public opinion against them, the strikers had little hope. After two months the workers returned without a single gain; the strike had cost twenty lives and over $100 million in wages.

While the steel strike was sputtering to an end, a new stoppage—the third major strike that fall—was called in the bituminous coal industry. The United Mine Workers had negotiated a no-strike agreement with the Fuel Administration in 1917, to expire in March, 1920; when the war ended, the union contended that the agreement ended too. Although anthracite miners had received wage raises, the soft-coal miners had received none. By the summer of 1919, as food prices zoomed upward, the miners were in almost open rebellion against their leaders, who were forced to yield to demands for a strike.

Despite the conservatism of the strike leader, John L. Lewis, and the opposition of the UMW to radical unionists, the mine owners, following the example of the steel operators, pinned the label of radicalism on the strike. The chief spokesman for the operators even charged that the strike was being financed by Moscow gold on direct orders from Lenin and Trotsky. Woodrow Wilson, partially recovered from his stroke but still a seriously ill man, denounced the proposed strike as "a grave moral and legal wrong." Cut off from the more liberal members of his cabinet, Wilson was persuaded by Attorney-General Palmer to take drastic action. Palmer, using powers under the wartime Lever Act, obtained a temporary injunction from Federal Judge Albert Anderson to halt the strike, although union leaders had supported the Lever Act only after a personal promise from Wilson that it would not be used against them. Moreover, since the Fuel Administration had stopped controlling coal prices, the workers felt Wilson was arguing that the war was over for the operators but not for them. With 394,000 men out of the mines, Lewis calmly perused Homer's *Iliad* while he waited for the owners to surrender. But when Judge Anderson issued a second, and permanent, injunction, Lewis declared, "We cannot fight the government," and he ordered the men back to work. Defying both Lewis and the court, the miners refused to return; the coal strike went on as though nothing had happened. It finally required a personal appeal from the President, accompanied by an offer of a substantial wage increase, to end the walkout.

By the autumn of 1919 millions of Americans had come to believe that the country was faced by the menace of revolution, although genuine revolutionaries constituted almost no threat of any kind and the great strikes were for the most part expressions of legitimate grievances. Political careerists, reactionary employer groups, and monomaniacal faddists stirred up new alarms and exploited the sense of panic, in part out of ignorance, in part to serve their own ends. An Anti-Saloon League official asserted that the bombing of Palmer's home "was inspired by Germans with wet tendencies," while the

Red Scare

head of New York's Lusk Committee declared, in all seriousness, that radicalism "was started here and elsewhere by paid agents of the Junker class in Germany as a part of their programme of industrial and military world conquest." Employer groups used the Red Scare to denounce the closed shop as "sovietism in disguise."

As the wave of strikes followed the bombings, the country urged the government to take action against the radicals. The spotlight suddenly shifted to Attorney-General A. Mitchell Palmer. A Quaker with a long record of support for progressive legislation, Palmer had been Wilson's floor manager in 1912. Regarded by many as the father of women's suffrage and the child labor law, a strong advocate of the League of Nations, Palmer was the prototype of the Wilsonian liberal. The Democratic party's contact man with labor in the 1916 campaign, Palmer was appointed Attorney-General partly because of his popularity with labor and the foreign-born. Yet no sooner had he been sworn into office in March, 1919, than he started a campaign against enemy aliens. After the June 2 bombings he hired William J. Flynn, reputedly an expert on anarchism, and asked for and received a $500,000 increase in his budget in order to combat radicalism. In August he set up an antiradical division in the Department of Justice under J. Edgar Hoover.

On November 7 the first of the Palmer raids began, with the arrest of 250 members of the Union of Russian Workers in a dozen cities; many were roughly handled, particularly in New York City, where they were beaten by the police. Most of the prisoners were released with "blackened eyes and lacerated scalps," the *New York Times* reported. Only 39 men were recommended for deportation. On December 21, 1919,

249 aliens, most of whom had no criminal record and had committed no criminal offense, were deported to Russia on an army transport, the "Buford." Although the country was worried about a Bolshevik conspiracy, few of the people deported were Communists; most of them were anarchists, including Emma Goldman and Alexander Berkman, and many of them were philosophical anarchists who had no intention of ever using violence.

Palmer turned next to the Communists. Working with an agent in the Labor Department, which had authority over deportations, Palmer in the last week of 1919 secured warrants for the arrest of more than 3,000 aliens who were members either of the Communist party or the Communist Labor party. On a single night in January, 1920, more than 4,000 alleged Communists were arrested in a dramatic coast-to-coast raid in 33 cities. If the persons arrested were citizens, they were turned over to state authorities for prosecution under antisyndicalist laws; if they were aliens, they were held for deportation.

Palmer invaded private homes, union headquarters, and meeting halls. People were held incommunicado, denied counsel, and subjected to kangaroo trials. In one city, prisoners were handcuffed, chained together, and marched through the streets. In New England, hundreds of people were arrested who had no connection with radicalism of any kind. In Detroit, 300 people were arrested on false charges, held for a week in jail, forced to sleep on the bare floor of a vile corridor, and denied food for 24 hours, only to be found innocent of any involvement in a revolutionary movement. Not for at least half a century, perhaps at no time in our history, had there been such a wholesale violation of civil liberties. The raids yielded almost nothing in the way of arms and small results in the way of dangerous revolutionaries. Although a few individuals (the steel baron Charles M. Schwab was one) protested against the raids, Palmer emerged from the episode a national hero.

The Red Scare ended almost as quickly as it began. The beginning of the end came in New York State. Directed by the irresponsible Lusk Committee, the antiradical campaign in New York reached its climax when the state legislature expelled five Socialist members of the Assembly, although the Socialist party was a legally recognized party and the members were innocent of any offense. Throughout the country, newspapers and public figures, including the *Chicago Tribune* and Senator Warren G. Harding of Ohio, denounced the action of the legislature. Most effective was Charles Evans Hughes, who not only reproached the legislature but offered the Socialists legal counsel. Although members of the legislature condemned Hughes as "disloyal" and "pro-German," the campaign against the radicals was dealt a heavy blow. Not only had a firm stand been taken on democratic principle, but the idea that the New York legislature felt threatened by five mild Socialists made the Red Scare appear more than a little ridiculous.

Early in 1920 an insurrection against Palmer in the Labor Department, led by Secretary of Labor Wilson and Assistant Secretary Louis Post, turned deportation proceedings in a saner direction. Aided by court decisions which held that men could not be deported on evidence illegally obtained, Post insisted on giving aliens proper counsel and the right to fair hearings. Convinced that Palmer had been violating civil liberties, Post cancelled action against dozens of aliens and by spring released nearly half of the men arrested in Palmer's

January raids. Palmer demanded that Post be fired for his "tender solicitude for social revolution," but when Post was hauled before a congressional committee, he made such an excellent presentation of his case that his critics were forced to back down. In the end, although 5,000 arrest warrants had been sworn out in late 1919, only a few more than 600 aliens were actually deported.

Finally, Palmer, seeking the 1920 presidential nomination, let his attempts to capitalize on the Red Scare get out of hand. In April he issued a series of warnings of a revolutionary plot which would be launched on May 1, 1920, as a step toward overthrowing the U.S. government. Buildings were placed under guard, public leaders were given police protection, state militias were called to the colors, and in New York City the entire police force of 11,000 men was put on 24-hour duty. May Day passed without a single outbreak of any kind. Not a shot was fired. Not a bomb exploded. As a result, the country, vexed at Palmer, concluded he had cried wolf once too often. Congress now turned to an investigation not of the radicals but of Palmer.

On September 16, 1920, at the lunch hour, a wagonload of bombs exploded on the corner of Broad and Wall Streets in New York, the heart of the financial center of the nation, killing 33 people, injuring over 200 more, and wrecking the building of the House of Morgan. None of the people killed was a financier; all were workers—clerks, stenographers, runners. Palmer declared that it was part of a Bolshevik conspiracy to overthrow the government; a year before, he would have had the nation behind him. This time, despite public horror at the deed, judgment was suspended, and the country took the event in stride, assuming, with logic, that the event

Red Scare

was probably the result of a group of demented anarchists and not a Communist plot.

By the end of 1920 the Red Scare was over. It was pushed to the back pages of the newspapers as the country turned to more absorbing topics like the Chicago Black Sox scandal, which involved bribery of big-league baseball players by gamblers. By 1920 the Communist wave had been turned back in Europe, and the nation, as it felt secure once more from external threats, came to realize that the internal danger had been vastly exaggerated too. The Red Scare appeared, together with the war and League issues, to be another instance of the political intensity of the Wilson regime. The election of Warren G. Harding, amiable but bumbling Republican presidential candidate in 1920, marked a desire for release from political turmoil and a chance to enjoy the pleasures of peace. His election meant not merely an end to internationalism and social reform but also an end to the Red Scare. "Too much," Harding declared, "has been said about Bolshevism in America."

The 1920's, despite their chauvinism and conservatism, were hostile to the spirit of the Red Scare; the decade was one when interest in politics was at its lowest ebb in half a century, and Palmer was defeated less by liberal opponents than by the hedonism of the age. (New York's Mayor Jimmy Walker declared in a debate on a censorship bill: "I have never yet heard of a girl being ruined by a book.") At the same time, the Red Scare left a bitter heritage of suspicion of aliens, distrust of organized labor, hostility to reformers, and insistence on political conformity, which created a smothering atmosphere for reform efforts in the 1920's.

One product of the Red Scare left a running sore. In May,

The Perils of Prosperity, 1914–32

1920, Nicola Sacco and Bartolomeo Vanzetti, two Italian aliens who were admitted anarchists, were arrested for a shoe-company robbery and the murder of a paymaster and his guard in South Braintree, Massachusetts. In July, 1921, Judge Webster Thayer sentenced them to death after a trial where, critics of the decision argued, the court was swayed less by the evidence than by the anarchist beliefs and Italian origins of the accused. Thayer himself was heard to refer to them as "those anarchist bastards." For the next six years, they remained in prison while legal experts like Felix Frankfurter punched holes in the case, judges and state officials heard and rejected appeals, and the fate of Sacco and Vanzetti became a matter of international concern. As the day of execution approached, French workers rioted in Lyons, Londoners marched on the American embassy, an American flag was burned in Casablanca, and the Uruguayan Chamber of Deputies formally requested President Coolidge to intervene. On August 23, 1927, their last appeal having been denied, Sacco and Vanzetti died in the electric chair.

Since all the forces of upper-class respectability—Judge Thayer, the governor, the president of Harvard, the best old families of the cradle of democracy—had a part in the affair, the execution of Sacco and Vanzetti appeared to be an act of class reprisal and made words about democracy and freedom seem merely cloaks for class interest. The novelist John Dos Passos, who had stood watch in the shadows of Charlestown Prison, expressed the belief of many intellectuals that the case had wiped out all middle ground and split the nation into two warring camps.

they have clubbed us off the streets   they are stronger
they are rich   they hire and fire the politicians the news-

Red Scare

papereditors the old judges the small men with reputations the
collegepresidents the wardheelers (listen businessmen collegepresidents   judges   America will not forget her betray-
ers). . . .

all right you have won   you will kill the brave men our
friends tonight

America our nation has been beaten by strangers who have
turned our language inside out who have taken the clean words
our fathers spoke and made them slimy and foul. . . .

all right we are two nations

No single act did more to turn liberal intellectuals to radicalism. "Don't you see the glory of this case," remarked a
character in Upton Sinclair's *Boston* (1928). "It kills off the
liberals." In the 1920's, although writers like Dos Passos and
Edna St. Vincent Millay were deeply involved in the Sacco-
Vanzetti case, intellectuals were too non-political for radicalism to make a great impact. "It was characteristic of the Jazz
Age," recorded Scott Fitzgerald, "that it had no interest in
politics at all." "Politics and voting," pontificated Gertrude
Stein, "do not make any difference." But in the 1930's, after
the crash of 1929 had split American society asunder, intellectuals enraged and sickened by the execution of Sacco and
Vanzetti would play an important role in radical politics. The
Red Scare of 1919, apparently ended by the fall of 1920,
would cast a long shadow over the politics of 1930's.

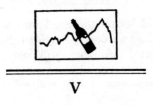

V

The Politics of Normalcy

By 1920 the nerves of the country had been rubbed raw by bitterness over the war, the debate on the League, the Red Scare, and the postwar inflation. In a word, the nation had had enough of Wilsonism. Wilson climaxed a long era of muckraking, of pointing out the evils of American society. The country yearned for release from the attacks of the reformers and the demands they made for altruism and self-sacrifice. "The moralist unquestionably secures wide popular support; but he also wearies his audience," pointed out Charles Seymour, "and many a voter has turned from Wilson in the spirit that led the Athenian to vote for the ostracism of Aristides, because he was tired of hearing him called " 'The Just.' " Wilson had become, in Mark Sullivan's words, "the symbol of the exaltation that had turned sour, personification of the rapture that had now become gall, sacrificial whipping boy for the present bitterness." Wilson was a pariah. His ideas were regarded as in some way desperately threatening the community and at the same time responsible for the evil that had befallen it.

The Politics of Normalcy

The reaction against Wilson threw the American party system out of balance. The professional politicians in the Republican party, confident of victory in 1920, did not have to name men of the stature of Roosevelt, Taft, or Hughes; they could bypass the strong-willed men and pick a weak party regular whom they could control. They could afford to ignore the three strong candidates for the Republican nomination—the former Army Chief of Staff General Leonard Wood, Governor Frank Lowden of Illinois, and isolationist Senator Hiram Johnson of California. Although little public attention was paid to Ohio's Senator Warren Harding, as early as February his manager, Harry Daugherty, had predicted that the three strong candidates would kill one another off and that Harding would get the nod from the Old Guard leaders who would dominate the convention. After the convention deadlocked, Daugherty forecast, the winner would be chosen by a gathering of "fifteen or twenty men, somewhat weary" at "about eleven minutes after two o'clock on Friday morning."

The Republican convention came close to following Daugherty's script. On Thursday, when the balloting began, the three leading candidates quickly established a deadlock, and Lodge recessed the convention until the next day. At a suite in the Blackstone Hotel that night, a group of party leaders, mostly senators, debated what to do; although not all agreed, the majority decided on Harding. "This man Harding is no world beater," they told reporters, "but we think he is the best of the bunch." At a little after two o'clock on Friday morning, Harding entered the "smoke-filled room" in the Blackstone and was asked for and gave assurances that nothing in his background would embarrass the Republican party. On the next day, after several ballots, he won the Republican nomination. "Well," said Harding, "we drew to a pair of deuces and filled."

The story of the "smoke-filled room" quickly became a legend; Harding's nomination was attributed to a cabal of senators who conspired to foist their candidate on the convention. Actually, his nomination was less the product of a conspiracy than of the fact that he embodied perfectly the conservatism of the delegates. President Nicholas Murray Butler of Columbia University later said that he had never seen such a shocking attempt to buy the presidency (Leonard Wood could apparently have had the nomination if he had been willing to give the oil interests three cabinet posts), and Editor William Allen White of the Emporia, Kansas, *Gazette* wrote: "I have never seen a convention—and I have watched most of them since McKinley's first nomination—so completely dominated by sinister predatory economic forces as was this." The convention was dominated by lobbyists for industrial and financial interests who knew what they wanted out of government, and were willing to pay for whatever privileges they got, but they did not have to force Harding on the delegates. Harding was the man the convention wanted. The times, said Connecticut's Senator Brandegee with a shrug, did not require "first-raters."

Like the Republican party after Theodore Roosevelt's death in 1919, the Democrats had been deprived of their strongest leader, by Wilson's physical incapacity. Wilson made matters still worse by giving strong indications that despite his illness and the no-third-term tradition he wanted the Democratic nomination in 1920 for himself. By his enigmatic role Wilson destroyed the political hopes of the one first-rate candidate the party had, his son-in-law, William Gibbs

McAdoo. (There was also an important faction, including Franklin K. Lane and Franklin D. Roosevelt, which wanted to give the Democratic nomination to Herbert Hoover. "Politically things do not look interesting," Lane wrote in December, 1919. "There are no big men in the line except Hoover.") Badly divided among several candidates, the Democratic convention took forty-four ballots to pick Governor James Cox of Ohio as the Democratic nominee; Franklin Roosevelt, who had been a popular Assistant Secretary of the Navy, was chosen as his running mate.

Wilson wanted the 1920 election to be a "solemn referendum" on the issue of the League, but it was a good deal less than that. The Democratic platform itself was a compromise with the isolationist wing of the Democratic party, while Cox, after making a forthright statement in favor of the League, later weakened. Republican internationalists confused matters still further. They worked out an elaborate rationale, drafted by Elihu Root, explaining that the Republican party had been for the League all along but that Wilson had killed it by refusing to accept the reservations. In part, they rationalized their support of the nationalistic Harding by arguing that once in office Harding would be an internationalist even if he had not been in the past. As Dr. Frank Crane dryly remarked, Harding was the first President to be elected "in the belief that he [would] not keep his promises."

Before the campaign even began, it was a foregone conclusion that Harding would win. If it were a prize fight, said Hiram Johnson in October, "the police would interfere on the grounds of brutality." By mid-October, odds on the election were 7–1 in favor of Harding, the highest electoral odds ever recorded. All the Republican party had to do was play it safe. (From his deathbed, Boies Penrose the Pennsylvania machine politician advised: "Keep Warren at home. Don't let him make any speeches. If he goes out on a tour somebody's sure to ask him questions, and Warren's just the sort of damned fool that will try to answer them.") By Election Day the odds had jumped to 10–1, but, obvious as it was that Harding would win by a handsome margin, no one anticipated the magnitude of his victory. Harding took 37 out of the 48 states, with 16 million votes to 9 million for Cox. With 61 per cent of the popular vote, Harding won a greater majority than any previous candidate, a margin even greater than Franklin Roosevelt was to win in 1936. Harding captured every borough in New York City and every county on the Pacific Coast. For the first time in history, Tennessee went Republican. As Joseph Tumulty said, "It wasn't a landslide; it was an earthquake."

The 1920 election was a national disavowal of the ideas for which Wilson had stood, and Cox was lost in the process. Harding won through a combination of opposites, people who thought the peace too harsh and people who thought it too lenient, people who thought Wilson had betrayed internationalism at Versailles and people who thought he had forfeited national integrity, workers who held him responsible for the high cost of living and businessmen who damned him for coddling workers. Most Americans resented government intervention in the economy, especially wartime regimentation, but farmers were angry because Wilson withdrew price supports from wheat in the spring of 1920 and because, when a farm depression struck that summer, he did not restore them.

The Democrats themselves were badly divided. Western

The Politics of Normalcy

Democrats were convinced that Wilson had favored southern cotton over western wheat, while drys were provoked because Cox was a wet. (Bryan declared, "My heart is in the grave with our cause.") Cox also had to contend with Irish-American ire at the League and German-American hostility to the war itself, although neither group seems to have voted for Harding in any unusual proportion. Many Americans believed that Wilson and the Democrats had broken a promise to keep the country out of war; even closer to the mark is Preston Slosson's observation that the average American felt that "while his government could perhaps not have avoided the war, the war ought somehow to have avoided America." Similarly, there was less resentment at the League than at the League issue. As Professor Freidel observes, "They had wearied of the subject without, in most cases, ever really grasping what all the noise was about."

Harding capitalized on an immense feeling of nostalgia for the years before the war, for the days when life was simpler. In a speech in May, 1920, in Boston, Harding caught the spirit of the country in urging a return to "not heroism, but healing, not nostrums but normalcy," thereby coining a word and defining a mood. The country, bemused by Wilsonian rhetoric, wanted to return to a reality which was concrete, which had the hardness and durability of matter. The election of 1920, declared the Republican vice-presidential candidate Calvin Coolidge, in one of his rare epigrams, was "the end of a period which has seemed to substitute words for things."

Harding had no qualification for being President except that he looked like one—which is, given the mythological role of the President in American culture, not an unimportant consideration. He was handsome, gray-haired, with a splendid figure, but as the head of a nation rising to pre-eminence as a world power, Harding was hopelessly miscast. A kindly man, honest and loyal, he was mentally slovenly. McAdoo observed of Harding's speeches that they "leave the impression of an army of pompous phrases moving over the landscape in search of an idea; sometimes these meandering words would actually capture a straggling thought and bear it triumphantly, a prisoner in their midst, until it died of servitude and overwork." Harding himself had a sense of the dignity of the White House and an almost pathetic understanding of his own inability to measure up to it. When Nicholas Murray Butler came to see him at the White House one day, Harding looked up and said with a sigh, "I knew that this job would be too much for me."

As a human being, Harding was warm and lovable; he had an almost limitless store of liking for and interest in other people. When Harding freed Eugene Debs from prison on Christmas day, 1921, he insisted that the Socialist leader call on him at once. "Well," said the jovial Harding, bounding toward him, "I have heard so damned much about you, Mr. Debs, that I am now very glad to meet you personally." A member of the Elks, the Odd Fellows, the Hoo Hoos, the Moose, and the Red Men, Harding brought to the White House both the virtues and the defects of his associations; but in the White House even his virtues were defects, for an uncritical friendly sociability, a virtue understandably cherished in small-town America, was to prove his undoing as President. Years before, his father had unknowingly presaged the disaster that awaited Harding in the White House: "It's a good thing you wasn't born a girl. Because you'd be in a family way all the time. You can't say No."

The Politics of Normalcy

In some ways akin to the administration of Grant, Harding's administration was one of government by crony. Like Grant, he surrounded himself with old friends. As Brigadier General and White House Physician, he named Old Doc Sawyer of Marion, Ohio. As Director of the Mint, Harding appointed a man who had been sheriff of Pickaway County, Ed Scobey. Rev. Heber H. Votaw, Harding's brother-in-law, former Seventh Day Adventist missionary to Burma, was selected as Superintendent of Federal Prisons, after Harding had removed the post from the civil service lists. As Comptroller of Currency, Harding installed a Marion lawyer who had spent no more than a few months as head of a small bank, Daniel Crissinger; Harding later appointed Crissinger, who had been a boyhood chum, to the top banking post in the nation, Governor of the Federal Reserve System. As head of the Veterans Bureau, Harding chose a chance acquaintance, Colonel Charles R. Forbes, whom he had met on a vacation in Honolulu. With his friends installed in public office, Harding, who felt uneasy with cabinet officers like Hughes and Hoover, managed to establish in the White House the same atmosphere of informal male conviviality that permeated the backroom of a Marion saloon. Alice Roosevelt Longworth found the White House study filled with the President's cronies, "the air heavy with tobacco smoke, trays with bottles containing every imaginable brand of whiskey, . . . cards and poker chips at hand—a general atmosphere of waistcoat unbuttoned, feet on desk, and spittoons alongside."

In an apartment in the Wardman Park hotel, Harry Daugherty, Harding's Attorney-General, lived with his intimate friend Jesse Smith, who was both housekeeper and confidant. It was Smith who presided over the headquarters of the Ohio

Gang at 1625 K Street. The little green house on K Street was part brothel, part speakeasy. Frequently the President's bootlegger, Mort Mortimer, would wheel his trucks laden with cases of liquor up to the door in broad daylight. But it was more than that. Here Daugherty's friends did a flourishing business selling immunity from prosecution, government appointments, liquor withdrawal permits, and pardons and paroles for criminals. Jesse Smith served as liaison between K Street and Daugherty's Justice Department, and for more than two years Smith and his confederates ate high on the hog. In a rough, off-key voice, Smith would rumble, "My God, how the money rolls in."

On May 23, 1923, in the Wardman Park apartment, Jesse Smith committed suicide. It was the beginning of the end for the Ohio Gang. Harding, deeply disturbed by Smith's death, received a series of warnings from Doc Sawyer and others of corruption in the Veterans Bureau under his friend Colonel Forbes. Harding at first refused to believe them, but by the time he left for a tour of the West, the President had a good idea of how deeply he had been betrayed. "My God, this is a hell of a job!" he told William Allen White before leaving. "I have no trouble with my enemies. . . . But my damned friends, my God-damn friends, White, they're the ones that keep me walking the floor nights!" Harding was spared most of the details of the scandals and the opprobrium that followed. On his western trip he was taken ill; his condition steadily worsened, and on August 2, 1923, Harding died of a cerebral embolism.

In the months after Harding's death, the corruption in his administration was gradually exposed. In response to protests from the American Legion and private contractors, an investigation was launched into the management of the Veterans Bureau; it revealed that Colonel Forbes had been operating a gigantic swindle which in less than two years cost the country more than $200 million. At a time when disabled veterans on hospital cots lacked bandages, bedding, and drugs, Forbes condemned carloads of these supplies and sold them off at a fraction of their cost in return for a rake-off. Similar frauds were perpetrated in the purchase of hospital sites and in the construction of hospitals. Forbes was fined $10,000 and sentenced to two years in Leavenworth penitentiary. His legal adviser, Charles Cramer, probably innocent, committed suicide.

At the urging of Robert La Follette, a Senate investigating committee headed by Senator Thomas Walsh of Montana probed for the details of government oil leases. The committee found that Secretary of the Interior Albert Fall, with authority given him by Harding and with the acquiescence of Secretary of the Navy Denby, had leased government oil reserves at Elk Hills, California, which had been set aside for the United States Navy, to Edward Doheny, the president of Pan-American Petroleum. At about the time they were leased, Doheny's son had given Fall a black bag containing $100,000 in exchange for an unsecured note. Fall also leased, without competitive bidding, the reserves at Teapot Dome, Wyoming, to Harry Sinclair. Sinclair's oil firm transferred $233,000 in Liberty bonds to Fall's son-in-law, and Fall himself received $85,000 in cash and a herd of blooded cattle for his ranch in New Mexico. Fall was fined $100,000 and sentenced to a year in prison, the first cabinet officer in history to go to jail. Denby, the unwitting agent of the deals, resigned from the cabinet.

The last of the Harding scandals led to Attorney-General Daugherty himself. In return for agreeing to sell priceless German chemical patents for a pittance, Harding's Alien Property Custodian, Thomas Miller, received $50,000 in bonds. Miller was convicted and sentenced to eighteen months in jail. Smith had deposited the bonds in an account which Daugherty controlled in the bank of Daugherty's brother in Washington Court House, Ohio. When in March, 1924, Daugherty was called before a Senate committee, he refused to submit to cross-examination, on the grounds that his personal relations with President and Mrs. Harding made it impossible. Daugherty's response further blackened the reputation of the Harding administration, for it indicated either that Harding or his family would be damaged by material in the bank records or that Daugherty was using Harding as a shield to defend himself. At this point Calvin Coolidge, who had succeeded Harding in the presidency and who had been laggard in not removing Daugherty much earlier, was aroused, and Daugherty was forced to resign.

The most striking feature of this corruption in government, the worst in at least half a century, was the public response to it. Instead of public indignation at Doheny and Fall, there was a barrage of abuse at the men who brought the corruption to light. The *New York Tribune* stigmatized Senators Walsh and Wheeler as "the Montana scandalmongers," the *New York Times* called them "assassins of character," and the *Post* labeled them "mudgunners." In part, this response was due to the fact that only the Veterans Bureau corruption came to light while Harding was alive. When he died, he was a beloved President, mourned throughout the nation. When the corruption of his administration was revealed, Coolidge was in the White House, and Coolidge was the symbol of pristine virtue.

Born on a Vermont farm which had been worked by Coolidges for five generations, he summoned up images of the democracy of New England town meetings. He had gone to a one-room schoolhouse and done chores on the farm over week ends. He spoke with a Yankee twang. A man with a pinched face, taciturn, unsmiling (Mrs. Longworth said that he must have been weaned on a pickle), morose, even mean-looking, a deeply lonely man, Coolidge was a perfect expression of Puritan asceticism. In years when American society was changing at a frightening pace and Americans sought security by incanting their continued allegiance to older virtues at the same time that they were abandoning them, Coolidge was the most usable national symbol the country could have hoped to find.

He had been sworn into office in the living room of the Plymouth, Vermont, farmhouse of his family, where his father as justice of the peace read the oath which Coolidge pronounced by the light of an oil lamp. The ceremonials of American democracy were taken care of, and this was what really mattered. The American people responded to Walsh and Wheeler as they did to the Wilsonian reformers; both seemed bent on pointing out that the American democratic creed cloaked evil and injustice, and the resentment of the people was aimed not so much at the wrongdoers as at the blasphemers. Coolidge came along at a fortuitous time, just when the democratic creed was in need of a new version of an old symbol; he suggested the rugged honesty of the New England hills, rural virtues, clean living, religious faith, public probity.

95

Coolidge served the needs of big business and the Old Guard even better than Harding had. Harding, although his administration was friendly to business interests, was primarily a politician, not an ideologue. Coolidge was a man of convictions who deliberately converted his administration into a "businessman's government" and the Republican party into a business party. In turn, business interests exploited Coolidge's idiosyncrasies to their own advantage. His seventeenth-century belief in frugality was used by Secretary of the Treasury Mellon to justify tax cuts, his taciturnity and inactivity in office served to demonstrate the insignificance of government. As the Washington newspaperman Clinton Gilbert shrewdly observed: "Conservatism since the war had taken on the mob psychology that we used to associate with popular movements, and progressivism had become hesitantly intellectual. Mr. Coolidge is the unconscious demagogue of conservatism."

Coolidge had the small-town man's awe of the successful big-city businessman. As Governor he had looked up to Senator Murray Crane, the Massachusetts paper tycoon; as President he looked to Andrew Mellon, head of the aluminum monopoly. In the State House he had been shepherded by Frank Stearns, the Boston department store executive later known as Lord Lingerie. When he entered the White House, Coolidge installed William Butler, a Massachusetts textile manufacturer, as head of the Republican party; at the 1924 convention, Henry Cabot Lodge sat unnoticed and unconsulted.

Coolidge's prescription for government was simple. All prosperity rested on business leadership. What was of "real importance to wage-earners," he wrote, "was not how they might conduct a quarrel with their employers but how the business of the country might be so organized as to insure steady employment at a fair rate of pay. If that were done there would be no occasion for a quarrel, and if it were not done a quarrel would do no good." Under the circumstances, the only function for a President was to give business its head, to see that the government interfered with business as little as possible. Calvin Coolidge, wrote Irving Stone, "aspired to become the least President the country had ever had; he attained his desire."

The 1920 election expressed the yearning for "normalcy," but it was the Old Guard, restored to power by Harding's triumph, who exploited the demand for normalcy to their own ends. "We have torn up Wilsonism by the roots," Lodge gloated. "I am not slow to take my own share of vindication which I find in the majorities." After twenty years of Roosevelt's attacks on malefactors of great wealth, Taft's trust-busting, and Wilson's reforms, the Old Guard was determined to call a halt to social welfare measures and to push legislation favorable to big business. Nor were businessmen who gave $8 million to the Republicans in 1920 shy about demanding a return on their investment. Yet despite landslide victories in presidential years, Old Guard Republicans were to find that although they could easily block progressive legislation, passing laws of their own was tough sledding. Stymied by progressives in Congress through much of the decade, the conservative Republican leadership had its greatest success in areas lying more directly under executive control, particularly in staffing government agencies, the courts, and regulatory commissions with conservative appointees.

Business interests succeeded in having Andrew Mellon named Secretary of the Treasury, although Harding had never heard of Mellon before he appointed him. A wealthy contributor to the Republican organization in Pennsylvania, Mellon was soon to have the droll title of "the greatest Secretary of the Treasury since Alexander Hamilton." Mellon immediately set out to cut government spending and reduce taxes on high incomes. In 1921 he got Congress to repeal the excess-profits tax, but a band of Senate progressives blocked his efforts to cut taxes on high incomes. In 1924 Mellon's new assault succeeded in cutting the maximum surtax on high incomes, but Congressional insurgents imposed the highest estate tax in American history, levied a new gift tax, and opened tax returns to full publicity. The bill was such a stunning victory for the progressives that Coolidge thought of vetoing it; in the end, furious at the insurgents, he signed it only with the greatest reluctance. When Mellon set out for a third time in 1926 to slash taxes, progressive forces in both houses had been demoralized by the Coolidge landslide, and he was finally able to have his way. The Revenue Act of 1926 wiped out the gift tax, cut the estate tax in half, and trimmed the maximum surtax from 40 to 20 per cent. When Mellon, who served as Secretary of the Treasury under all three Republican Presidents, got Congress in 1928 to reduce corporation and consumption taxes still further, he had rounded out a tax program which reversed almost completely the progressive tax policies of the Wilson years.

In the postwar years business launched a determined campaign to break unions where they existed and to maintain the open shop where they did not. In 1920, President Eugene Grace of Bethlehem Steel announced that even if 95 per cent of his workers belonged to a union, he would refuse to recognize it. The Harding administration gave covert and open support to the drive against the unions. In 1922, the Railroad Labor Board, with Wilson's appointees replaced by more conservative Harding men, ordered a wage slash that led to a walkout of 400,000 railroad shopmen. The Board promptly issued instructions to the railroads to set up company unions, as the Pennsylvania Railroad had already done, a practice which would deprive the strikers of seniority rights. When the shopmen stayed out, Attorney-General Daugherty obtained a sweeping injunction from Judge Wilkerson in Chicago which handcuffed their leaders and broke the strike. "So long and to the extent that I can speak for the government of the United States," Daugherty declared, "I will use the power of the government to prevent the labor unions of the country from destroying the open shop." Contrary to all precedent in periods of prosperity, union membership declined sharply in the 1920's.

During these same years, the Supreme Court handed down a series of decisions which staggered organized labor. In 1915 the Court upheld the yellow-dog contract (by which workers agree, as a condition of employment, not to join a union); in 1919 it approved an assessment of triple damages against the United Mine Workers under the Sherman Antitrust Act; in 1921 it declared illegal a boycott to force unionization and drastically limited picketing. In 1922 in the Coronado case, the Court denied labor the protection it thought it had received from the Clayton Act by permitting a union to be sued for damages under the antitrust laws.

At the same time, other Supreme Court rulings shackled almost every effort at social reform and virtually destroyed the movement for social legislation. In a 5–4 decision (*Hammer* v. *Dagenhart*, 1918), the Court declared the Child Labor Act of 1916 unconstitutional, on the grounds that Congress could not

The Perils of Prosperity, 1914–32

use its commerce power to regulate labor conditions. When Congress then passed a new law levying a prohibitive tax on products manufactured by children, the Court found that act also invalid (*Bailey* v. *Drexel Furniture Co.*, 1922). In 1923 (*Adkins* v. *Children's Hospital*) the Court declared unconstitutional a District of Columbia minimum wage law for women. By these decisions the Court made it impossible to pass the most primitive kind of social legislation to protect women and children, irrespective of whether the federal government or individual states enacted the laws.

The Republican Old Guard, which had little trouble in spiking labor and social reform efforts, found the farm interests a much more formidable foe. During World War I, encouraged both by the lure of profit and by the urging of the government that food would win the war, American farmers had plowed up the grasslands and marginal farmlands. With the tremendous wartime demand, prices of farm products soared to astronomic levels (cotton, which brought 13 cents a pound in 1913, jumped to 38 cents in 1919), and farmers enjoyed a heady prosperity. In 1920 farm prices crashed, wiping out some farmers, destroying wartime gains for others. By 1924, farm prices were moving upward again, but the farmer, unlike the manufacturer and the worker, never regained his wartime prosperity, in large part because he lost his foreign markets in the resurgence of economic nationalism abroad after the war.

Farmers looked back longingly to the golden era before the war, but most of them were actually better off than in the prewar days so far as return on their crops was concerned. Their problem was rather that they had to pay much more of their income for mortgage interest and taxes. Even more important, farmers wanted their share of the new appliances and luxuries the city dweller had—electricity, automobiles, and radios. What they resented was less their low income—the poverty of farmers in the 1920's has been exaggerated—but rather that they were not sharing the new urban prosperity. In 1919, they had 16 per cent of the national income; by 1929, only 9 per cent. The farmer felt that he was losing out, that the country was being industrialized at his expense. For the first time in the history of the United States, farm acreage decreased; between 1919 and 1924, 13 million acres were abandoned to brush. The farmer believed that American farms were the bases of the country's moral grandeur—one powerful farm leader spoke of "the shrines of American farm homes" —and he felt not only that he was in danger of being reduced to peasantry but that the agrarian way of life was being destroyed, often, ironically, by his own desire for profit. In the 1920's farming became increasingly a speculative business enterprise, signifying less and less a permanent tradition of attachment to the soil separate from the commercial world of the city. The farmer was convinced that he had reached a crossroads; only state intervention could save him from being passed by the city man and shunted to a side road.

In May, 1921, a group of western and southern senators led by William Kenyon of Iowa and Arthur Capper of Kansas met in the offices of the Farm Bureau Federation to organize the "farm bloc," which was to unite farm-district congressmen behind agricultural legislation. With members in both parties and in both houses of Congress, the farm bloc in the next two years drove through the Packers and Stockyards Act of 1921, which subjected rates of commission merchants and stockyards to public control and aimed at preserving competition among packers; the Grain Futures Act of 1921, which gave the Secretary of Agriculture control over grain exchanges; the Capper-Volstead Act of 1922, which exempted farm co-operatives from the antitrust laws; and the Agricultural Credits Act of 1923, which created twelve Intermediate Credit Banks to make loans to groups of farmers.

The farm legislation of the Harding administration would at one time have been regarded as a stupendous achievement, but by the 1920's farmers were no longer content with the old panaceas of government regulation and cheap credit. Under the leadership of George Peek, a farm-implements manufacturer who had been won to the idea of government intervention by his wartime experiences in Washington, farm interests pushed for what amounted to government price supports. Under the so-called McNary-Haugen plan, they sought to dump farm surplus abroad in order to raise farm prices in the United States. The Harding and Coolidge administrations, under the influence of Secretary of Commerce Herbert Hoover, fought fiercely against all attempts to raise farm prices through government intervention. When Congress passed the McNary-Haugen bill in 1927 and again in 1928, Coolidge killed the proposal by veto.

There was much to be said for Coolidge's vetoes. Since the farmer refused to accept production controls, McNary-Haugenism would have been a failure; increased surpluses and constricted world markets would have frustrated it. As a new instrument of economic nationalism, it would have invited reprisals and still further strangled international trade. At the same time it is true that McNary-Haugenism, for all its faults, was at least a serious effort to improve the lot of the farmer. Many of its ideas—the concept of parity (that is, of economic equality of agriculture with industry), of compulsory co-operation of farmers, and of government responsibility for farm income—would be central to the New Deal legislation of the 1930's. Correct in rejecting this particular proposal, Coolidge put nothing else in its place. Republican leaders in the 1920's dealt cavalierly or unintelligently with the farm problem; they spoke for the urban industrialist and had nothing of value to say to the beleaguered farmer. Two days after he vetoed one of the McNary-Haugen bills, Coolidge raised the tariff on pig iron 50 per cent; several days later the price of pig iron soared 50 cents a ton.

By the end of the Harding administration, the Republican party was firmly committed to single-interest government. By allying the government with business, the Republicans believed that they were benefiting the entire nation. Hamilton was the patron saint of the decade. The 1920's represent not the high tide of laissez faire but of Hamiltonianism, of a hierarchical concept of society with a deliberate pursuit by the government of policies most favorable to large business interests. No political party, no national administration, could conceivably have been more co-operative with business interests. "Never before, here or anywhere else," beamed the *Wall Street Journal*, "has a government been so completely fused with business." If, as Republican orators promised, this alliance succeeded in maintaining prosperity, the wisdom of single-interest politics would be proven. If it failed, a sharp reaction against single-interest politics would be inevitable. This, in essence, became the central theme of the politics of the 1920's: whether the business interest, given full support by a co-operative government, could maintain prosperity and develop social policies which would redound to the benefit not merely of itself but of the whole American people.

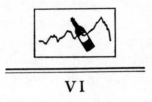

VI

The Reluctant Giant

American foreign policy in the 1920's was built on disillusionment with World War I—a dirty, unheroic war which few men remembered with any emotion save distaste. There had been earlier wars which, no matter how great the cost, the nation recalled with affection. This was a war it chose to forget. No one sang songs like "Rally Round the Flag" or attended romantic plays like "The Drummer Boy of Shiloh." It was not a war of gallant sorties and dashing cavalrymen; nothing brought home its impersonally unheroic quality more than the Unknown Soldier, the American doughboy whose very identity had been obliterated. The war left a determination in millions of Americans never to fight again; at no time in our history has the hold of pacifism been stronger than in the interlude between the first and second world wars. ("I can't explain it," said one of Dos Passos' soldiers, "but I'll never put a uniform on again.") Even more important, it left a deep cynicism about American participation in European affairs, a cynicism caught in the statement attributed to Lloyd George at Versailles: "Is it Upper or Lower Silesia that we are giving away?"

Sounding the old theme of American innocence and European wickedness, the United States arraigned Europe as perversely war-loving, decadent, politically unorthodox and economically chaotic, and for welshing on its debts. Before the United States would associate with European nations, they would have to "clean up and pay up." From its perch of insular security, relatively unscathed by the war, the United States lectured on disarmament to a war-shocked Europe that feared new invasions. With infuriating smugness, the United States failed to see that the whole structure of the peace, which Wilson and the Americans had helped construct, left a great power vacuum in central Europe—a vacuum that in time would invite a resurgent German militarism unless American power were exercised. By urging disarmament without assuming any political responsibilities, the United States was asking France to give up its only hope for security.

The ghost of the United States sat at every council table of Europe. By taking international responsibilities corresponding to the power it actually held, the United States might have given France the assurance it needed and at the same time have moderated French policies toward Germany, thereby strengthening democratic elements in the Weimar Republic. By rejecting the French security treaty, by stripping France of any hope of American aid in the event of a German invasion, the United States intensified a French nationalism which, particularly after France's occupation of the Ruhr in 1923, provided a convenient "foreign threat" with which Hitler could excite the German people. At the same time, by ignoring considerations of power and by a sentimental and legalistic attitude toward Germany, the United States helped upset the balance of power on the Continent.

In Harding's first message to Congress, he announced that the United States would have no connection with the League of Nations; in one of his last addresses, he declared that the League issue was as "dead as slavery." Harding not only refused to support even the health program of the League, but for months a State Department career officer did not even open the mail from Geneva. When in the Geneva protocol of 1924 the League attempted to set up a system of collective security defined more precisely than under its original Covenant, Secretary of State Charles Evans Hughes responded to the proposal in the harshest possible fashion. He accused the League of drafting a document which implied "a proposal of a concert against the United States," alleged that League sanctions against an aggressor might be "inimical to American trade," and warned that the United States would maintain the rights of neutrals. In essence, Hughes was saying that the United States would disrupt any attempt of the League to carry out a program of collective security through the use of sanctions.

Yet the United States could never achieve total isolation. Measured by American participation in the war and the brief interest in the League, the 1920's seem like an era of intense isolationism. Measured by prewar standards, American participation in world affairs was considerable. The spirit of Wilsonian internationalism never entirely died out, and, to internationalists like Newton Baker and Cordell Hull, Wilson remained a saintly guide. (As Wilson lay dying on the night of February 3, 1924, scores of people knelt in the snow outside his home in prayer.) More important, American power was so great that the United States found itself inevitably involved in world affairs, even though against its will. But American participation was of a singular sort. Convinced that power was in itself evil, the makers of American foreign policy concentrated on destroying instruments of power or getting nations to pledge that they would not use power. For a time successful, in the end the peace movement failed disastrously because, as Robert Osgood writes, "peace was seen as merely the avoidance of war rather than as a continuous process of political accommodation."

In one area of the world, the United States made no pretense of a policy of isolation. To the tradition of American non-involvement in foreign affairs, Latin America, and especially the Caribbean, had long been an exception. Where national security or extensive American economic interests were involved, American foreign policy could be militantly interventionist. When Harding took office, American troops in Nicaragua were upholding a minority regime, American naval officers were running Santo Domingo and Haiti, and relations with Mexico, bent on consolidating her revolution to the disadvantage of American investors, had reached the point of total breakdown. Harding declared that he would rather "make Mexico safe and set it aglow with the light of new-world righteousness, than menace the health of the republic in old-world contagion."

By 1924 the United States was running the financial policies of ten Latin-American nations. Harding landed marines in Honduras, and Coolidge carried American imperialism in the banana republics to its farthest point by conducting a private war in Nicaragua to support a Conservative regime against a Liberal uprising. Lashed by criticism from Republican progressives in Congress, Coolidge began to beat a retreat in the fall of 1927. He named Dwight Morrow ambassador to Mexico, and Morrow proved a brilliant choice. The ambassador won a settlement of the oil lands dispute, brought a halt to the anticlerical campaign, and, most important, by his friendly demeanor undid much of the damage his predecessors had wrought. By the end of the Republican era, relations with Latin America were better than they had been at any time in this century.

The world looked to the United States for leadership not merely because of its military potential but because it had become incomparably the greatest economic power in the world. By 1929 the national income of the United States was greater than that of Great Britain, Germany, France, Canada, Japan, and seventeen other nations combined. The war had produced a revolutionary change in the world economy. In 1914 the United States was a debtor nation; American citizens owed foreign investors three billion dollars. By the end of 1919 the United States was a creditor nation, with foreigners owing American investors nearly three billion dollars. In addition, the United States had loaned over ten billion dollars to foreign countries, mostly to carry on the war, in part for postwar reconstruction. These figures represent one of those great shifts in power that occurs but rarely in the history of nations.

For three hundred years the American people had been dependent on European capital. The American Revolution was in part a struggle between British lenders and American borrowers; in the nineteenth century it was the stream of European capital into the United States that built the American railway system. For three centuries the country had balanced its trade by exporting more than it imported, and the American economy was geared to creating an export surplus—largely of farm products like cotton and wheat—and selling it abroad. The shift in the war wiped out the basis for the export surplus and demanded a herculean effort to redredge the channels of world trade.

Britain had maintained its position as the creditor nation of the world by the drastic method of sacrificing its agriculture, in the repeal of the Corn Laws in 1846, and maintaining a policy of free trade. This expedient had unfortunate social results within Britain, but it was the only policy consonant with its position as a creditor nation. As the new creditor nation, the United States had little alternative save to adopt the British method. Yet no American government would have dreamed of sacrificing American agriculture. The administration would have given even less thought to banking the fires of American industry. It was the misfortune of the world and, ironically, a curse for the United States that the American economy was too well balanced to let the nation play the role of creditor. The new leading creditor nation of the world was a country for whom foreign transactions were, relatively speaking, an insignificant element in its economy. Under the circumstances, the boldest, most imaginative kind of leadership was required to prevent world trade from being paralyzed and to avert an economic disaster that would have terrible political and social consequences.

Instead, the United States under Harding and Coolidge made an exceptionally difficult situation far worse. If the United States was to function as a creditor nation, it had to import more than it exported. But the country moved in precisely the opposite direction. By an emergency tariff in 1921 and the Fordney-McCumber Tariff Act of 1922, the United

States drowned any hope that it would be more receptive to European goods. The Fordney-McCumber Tariff restored the high prewar rates of Payne-Aldrich and added a few new tolls of its own. (Harding dumbfounded one reporter by explaining, "We should adopt a protective tariff of such a character as will help the struggling industries of Europe to get on their feet.") By including farm products in the new tariff rates —from reindeer meat to acorns—high-tariff advocates quieted traditional farm opposition to protection.

As a gesture toward scientific rate-making, the act empowered the President to raise or lower rates by up to 50 per cent of the existing rate. Of the thirty-seven times they used this power, Harding and Coolidge raised rates thirty-two. The five rates which were lowered included tariffs on bobwhite quail and paintbrush handles. Simultaneously the government operated a great fleet of merchant ships at a heavy loss, thereby reducing still further the number of dollars sent abroad for foreign services. In 1930, neomercantilism (the attempt to export more than was imported, regardless of long-run effect) was carried as far as it could go with the adoption of the Hawley-Smoot Tariff; in the teeth of protests from thirty-four countries and over one thousand American economists, Congress stepped up tariff rates still higher. As the economists had warned, the new law throttled world trade and brought a wave of retaliation from other countries.

With a remarkable capacity for self-delusion, the United States insisted at the same time on collecting its "war debts" from Europe. Europeans pointed out that there was no way they could repay the United States save by sending goods and services, and they could not do that as long as the United States erected high tariff walls and refused to receive their goods. Nor would the United States admit that there was any connection between war debts and reparations, even though it was through receiving reparations payments that the Allied nations would be able to repay war debts. Not until a disaster occurred did the United States act. In 1923 Germany defaulted on its reparations payments, and French troops moved into the Ruhr. When the Germans countered with a policy of passive resistance, the resulting runaway inflation threatened to topple the whole postwar financial structure of Europe. At this point Secretary Hughes intervened to use American finance instead of French bayonets to maintain the peace of Europe. After the Dawes Plan of 1924, named for the American consultant Charles G. Dawes, the reparations-debts tangle was "cleared up." Germany paid reparations, and the former Allies paid their war debts. What actually happened was that America loaned money to Germany; Germany paid reparations to the Allies; and the Allies sent money to the United States to service their debts. It would have made equal sense for the United States to take the money out of one Treasury building and put it into another.

In the kind of thinking behind the Dawes Plan lay the heart of American financial policy in the 1920's. A creditor nation unwilling to absorb more imports than exports, its agriculture and industry clamoring for foreign markets, the United States maintained world trade by private investment of American dollars abroad. New York replaced London as the financial capital of the world. American capital was even used to build a London subway. Once its economic colonial status was ended by World War I, the United States swiftly started colonizing Europe with American plants and investments. American capital developed rubber plantations in the Dutch

East Indies, built American branch factories in Scandinavia, mined tin in Bolivia, and drilled oil wells in Iraq. During these same years, Europeans obtained dollars from the hordes of American tourists who stormed the Continent, and from immigrants to the United States who sent money to relatives across the sea. Moreover, so substantial was America's role in the world economy that, even with tariff barriers, the United States continued to import an impressive amount of goods. It was on this foundation of quicksand that American prosperity and world trade in the 1920's was built. By the loan of American dollars and by American investment abroad, European and other nations were able to buy American goods.

The whole system of finance—reparations and debts, the ability of American farmers to sell abroad, the economic health of European nations—depended on a continual willingness of the United States to lend money outside its borders. In the middle of 1928, American investment overseas started to fall off, probably because there were better opportunities at home, although partly in recognition of the dubious nature of many of the investments that had been made and that were proposed. When, after the crash of 1929, America also reduced its direct investments abroad and cut drastically its purchase of foreign goods, the underpinnings of the international economy were pulled out and the whole system collapsed.

In the Far East, Republican administrations in the 1920's demonstrated that excessive interest in Oriental problems, combined with a withdrawal from European affairs, which has characterized Republican foreign policy in the twentieth century. No sooner had the war ended when the peace of the world was threatened by a naval armaments race among the United States, Great Britain, and Japan, a race made still more disturbing by American uneasiness over the Anglo-Japanese alliance in the Pacific. On February 24, 1921, a week before Harding's inauguration, Senator Borah introduced a resolution calling for a tri-Power disarmament conference. Harding opposed the idea and exerted White House pressure against it, but the notion struck a responsive chord with a war-weary, economy-minded nation. Borah's proposal whisked through the Senate that spring without a dissenting vote and through the House with only four dissenting votes. In July the British, egged on by the Canadians who had little liking for the growing tensions between Britain and the United States, warned that they would take the initiative if Harding did not. Under pressure at home and abroad, Harding capitulated and invited nine European and Asiatic powers to take part in a conference to discuss disarmament and Far Eastern problems.

When the Washington Conference opened on November 12, 1921, the delegates settled back to listen to Secretary of State Charles Evans Hughes make the perfunctory remarks expected of presiding officers. As Hughes began his address, delegates nodded to acquaintances around the room and smothered yawns. Suddenly, Hughes electrified the audience by announcing that the only way to disarm was to disarm. He proposed a ten year "holiday" on the construction of capital ships, with tonnage for the United States, Great Britain, and Japan set at a 5–5–3 ratio. He not only offered to destroy thirty American battleships, already afloat or partially completed, but went on to tell Great Britain and Japan precisely what they would have to scrap. Hughes declared that Britain should stop construction on the four new "Hoods," and as Britain's Admiral Beatty leaned forward in his chair, Hughes went on to sink the "King George the Fifth" and others of the fleet. In a few minutes, Hughes annihilated 66 ships with a total tonnage of 1,878,043, including, as one English writer observed, more British battleships "than all the admirals of the world had destroyed in a cycle of centuries." It was an absolutely unique diplomatic episode. Hughes's speech was greeted by a "tornado of cheering" and delegates waved hats, yelled, and hugged one another.

Japan was reluctant to accept the short end of the ratio, which seemed both to endanger her security and to injure her national pride. In order to get Japan to yield, the United States was forced to agree not to fortify the Philippines, Samoa, Guam, and the other American Pacific possessions, save for Hawaii, and Britain was required to make a similar concession. Without fortifying her island outposts, there was little chance that the United States could menace Japan. Once these concessions were made, the conference reached agreement on the basis of the 5–5–3 ratio, with France and Italy each permitted one-third the capital-ship tonnage of the United States or Great Britain. For the first time in history, major powers had actually consented to disarm.

A Four Power Treaty between the United States, Britain, Japan, and France bound the signatories to respect each other's rights in the Pacific, to refer any future disputes in the region to a joint conference, and to consult in case of a threat from another power; most important, the treaty specifically ended the Anglo-Japanese alliance. Under Hughes's remarkable leadership, the conference went on to conclude a Nine Power Treaty which bound the states attending the conference to respect "the sovereignty, the independence, and the territorial and administrative integrity of China" and to uphold the Open Door. In the Nine Power Treaty, Hughes had

succeeded where Hay had failed in securing formal acceptance of the principle of the Open Door. As a result of the
conference, the conciliatory Japanese worked out a series of
other agreements to clear away tensions in the Far East. Japan
gave China sovereignty over Shantung, withdrew the most
noxious of her Twenty-one Demands, granted cable rights on
the island of Yap to the United States, and consented to leave
Siberia.

In later years, when Japan devastated the American fleet at
Pearl Harbor and overran the Philippines, Hughes was subjected to harsh criticism for surrendering American strategic
supremacy at the Washington Conference. He was accused of
having sunk more of the American fleet than the Japanese demolished at Pearl Harbor. This kind of criticism was wholly
unrealistic. The alternative was an arms race which the country would never have sanctioned. Not until 1938 did Congress
authorize a navy even up to the strength permitted by the
Washington Conference. Nor would the country have undertaken the huge expense required to fortify Guam and the
Philippines; on the very eve of Pearl Harbor, such a program
was strenuously resisted.

The conference succeeded in halting the construction of
capital ships and aircraft carriers, which was more than any
other disarmament conference had been able to do; it got rid
of the objectionable Anglo-Japanese alliance; it reduced tension in the Far East; and it provided a more hopeful atmosphere for peace throughout the world. Without halting the
arms race, there was little hope of a political settlement in the
Pacific. The conference added to the Japanese sense of security and helped keep the Japanese moderates in power for almost a decade. The treaty did nothing to lessen America's

impotence in the Far East, but no treaty could have done that.

It is true, nevertheless, that the American people held unrealistic assumptions about the Washington Conference. Behind the Washington treaties lay the idea of peace achieved by self-denying ordinances and, if the peace were broken, by the mobilization of international public opinion. It was as though a world war had never happened. The United States continued to hold excessive expectations in the Far East, overlooking the fact that Japan had come out of the war as one of the great world powers. With its chain of former German islands in the Pacific, Japan could endanger American communications from Hawaii to the Philippines. With the annihilation of German interests in the Pacific and the apparent withdrawal of Russia as a Pacific power, the war had turned the western Pacific into a Japanese lake. All the conference did was to freeze the status quo. Caught by the illusion of a democratic, united China open to American trade, the United States was continuing to buy trouble. It left Japanese power intact at the same time that, by legal instruments and public pronouncements, it committed itself to the cause of Chinese independence, to frustrating Japanese expansion, and to maintaining Pacific possessions which it was unwilling to defend.

At the Washington Conference, the United States attempted to prevent war by limiting arms and signing pledges of non-aggression. In the Kellogg-Briand Pact, America carried the idea of a "parchment peace"—a peace built on paper promises—to the ultimate limit of an agreement to abandon war entirely as an instrument of national policy. The idea of a treaty to outlaw war was the brain child of a civic-minded Chicago lawyer, Salmon Levinson, who won the support of Senator Borah and of a group of peace-foundation officials. It was an idea perfectly in tune with Borah's views of foreign affairs; generally regarded as an isolationist, Borah was, as Edgar Kemler has noted, actually a "vestigial internationalist" who looked to the power of public opinion and to the instrumentality of international law to maintain peace and secure justice.

In the early spring of 1927 Professor James T. Shotwell of Columbia University persuaded the French foreign minister Aristide Briand to announce that he was ready to enter into an agreement with the United States for the mutual outlawry of war. Briand was less interested in Shotwell's principles than he was in drawing the United States into the French system of alliances. Cool to the proposal, Secretary of State Kellogg, after a nine-month barrage of public opinion stirred up by Borah, relented and notified Briand he would negotiate a treaty to outlaw war, but only if it was extended to other powers. This was not at all what Briand had in mind (Assistant Secretary of State Castle noted jubilantly in his diary, "We have Monsieur Briand out on a limb"), but Briand had no choice other than to accept Kellogg's terms.

On August 27, 1928, the Pact of Paris (popularly known as the Kellogg-Briand Pact) was signed by the United States and fourteen other nations; it bound the signatory nations to renounce war as an instrument of national policy except in the case of self-defense. Most of the countries of the world eventually signed, although Britain included a reservation that it would not be restrained from going to war to defend its overseas empire, the United States reserved freedom of action under the Monroe Doctrine, and France announced that the pact would not apply to its obligations under previous treaties or under the League covenant. The Kellogg Pact, as Frank

Simonds observed, was "the high water mark of American endeavors for world peace which consisted in undertaking to combine the idea of political and military isolation with that of moral and material involvement."

When Republican President Herbert Hoover entered the White House on March 4, 1929, the atmosphere was one of universal hope for peace and prosperity. The United States was enjoying boom times, and American investment abroad had unsnarled the debts-reparations tangle and sparked a flourishing world trade. The moderates still held control of the Japanese government, and the United States, through the Washington Conference, had apparently worked out a modus vivendi with Japan. The major powers of the world had just agreed to renounce war as an instrument of national policy.

Within three years, the whole system of peace and prosperity would collapse. The stock-market crash of 1929 and the withdrawal of American investments from Europe brought world economic disaster. In September, 1931, Japanese armies would invade Manchuria, breaking pledges under the Nine Power Treaty and the Kellogg Pact, and it became painfully clear that the United States would do nothing about it. Pledges and treaties proved no substitute for the mobilization of force or for political solutions. Before Hoover left the White House, Adolf Hitler would come to power in Germany, convinced he had nothing to fear from nations which expected to block war and expansion through documents like the Kellogg Pact.

In retrospect, the folly of American foreign policy in the 1920's is easy to see, but it was not folly alone that produced the breakdown of peace and prosperity. Given the terrible disruption of European society by the war, and developments under the surface well before the war, even American entrance into the League might not have prevented the rise of fascism. In the Far East, it is questionable whether the United States could have blocked Japanese expansion save at the price of war. (Whether thwarting Japanese expansion was necessary to American security is, of course, a separate and more difficult question.) Granting that the tariff policies of these years were foolhardy—it is hard to account for the blindness of men of the perspicacity of Hughes on this score—no truly viable economic alternative presented itself.

Even if one could determine an ideal policy, one must place it in the framework of the possibilities of the times. In the fall of 1920 Sir Gilbert Murray scolded his fellow Englishmen for "expecting of America more than ought to be expected of any normal agglomeration of human beings." The shift of power to the United States came too quickly; it required a drastic change of attitude at a time when there was no apparent foreign menace to American security, and this was probably too much to expect. Different policies and more enlightened leadership might have diverted some of the worst consequences; it is not clear that they could have avoided the main part of them. The world in the 1920's spun tragically toward the disasters of the 1930's.

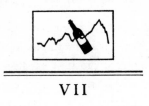

VII

Tired Radicals

In 1914 the progressive movement had reached its zenith. Two years before, the country had been aroused by a four-party contest in which the conservative Republican incumbent, William Howard Taft, had been overwhelmed by his progressive rivals; Woodrow Wilson, the Democratic spokesman for the New Freedom, had ousted Taft from the White House, while Teddy Roosevelt, the Progressive party candidate, had run a strong second. Even Taft, who in 1912 carried only two states in the Electoral College, had established a record as a reformer in office—particularly by a vigorous prosecution of trusts—that would have seemed unbelievable a short time before. Most startling of all, Eugene Debs, the Socialist candidate, had polled almost a million votes. Wilson in office had proceeded to carry out the mandate for the New Freedom, driving through Congress an impressive number of reforms. In 1914 progressivism was triumphant; six years later it was apparently dead as a doornail, buried under the Harding landslide. What killed progressivism?

The most obvious answer was that progressivism had been

killed by the war. In 1912, when social reform was at flood-tide, the chief leaders of the movement were Roosevelt, Wilson, La Follette, Bryan, and Debs. By 1920, these leaders and their followers were snarling enemies, hopelessly divided by the issues of the war. Bryan had resigned from Wilson's cabinet, to be met by a tirade of abuse from Wilson's supporters, and, although there was a temporary reconciliation in 1916, he was an outspoken opponent of Wilson's strategy on the League three years later. Roosevelt's supporters viewed Wilson and La Follette with the angry contempt usually reserved for traitors. Roosevelt himself had denounced La Follette as a "hun within our gates" and "the most sinister enemy of democracy in America." Wilson kept Debs in a federal prison, and Debs scornfully dismissed Wilson as "the most pathetic figure in the world."

Nothing reveals the damage the war did in splitting the ranks of the progressives so much as the progressive attitude toward La Follette. No man in America had done more to advance the cause of social reform than "Battle Bob." As governor of Wisconsin, he found the state a corporation barony and, working with a group of university professors, transformed it into the model social laboratory of the nation. Elected to the Senate in 1905, he quickly became the recognized leader of the progressive forces fighting for railroad legislation, conservation, and protection for labor. But once he came out in opposition to entrance in the war—he denounced it as a plot of profiteers and protested that "the poor who are called to rot in the trenches have no organized voice"—none of this counted. The muckraker Charles Edward Russell execrated him as a "traitor in disguise" who was doing "the dirty work of the Kaiser"; La Follette, he declared, was "a big yellow streak." During the war, La Follette's old allies, President Van Hise of the University of Wisconsin, John Commons, Richard Ely, and E. A. Ross signed a statement censuring him for disloyalty, while Ely wrote that La Follette had been "of more help to the Kaiser than a quarter of a million troops."

There had long been a close tie between progressivism and nationalism, particularly among the followers of Theodore Roosevelt who, not unlike Joseph Chamberlain in England or, to a degree, Bismarck in Germany, stood for a strong state with a sense both of social obligation and of imperial mission. After their defeat in 1912, Roosevelt and his followers emphasized the nationalist strain in progressivism, rebuking Wilson for failing to uphold national honor, first in Latin America, then in Europe. As leaders of the Progressive party concentrated their fire on Wilson's foreign policy, they became more and more chauvinistic and less and less interested in domestic reform. In December, 1914, the Progressives issued a statement which ignored the reform planks of their 1912 platform and centered on a demand for a higher protective tariff. In January, 1916, the Progressive National Committee denounced Wilson for failing "to deal adequately with the National honor and industrial welfare" and called for "a reawakening of our elder Americanism, of our belief in those things that our country and our flag stands for."

Roosevelt himself gave up on progressivism and turned to preparedness and war. He not only refused to run on the Progressive ticket in 1916 but urged both the Progressives and Republicans to nominate the bleakly conservative Henry Cabot Lodge as a man of "the broadest national spirit," who, Roosevelt told the stunned Progressives, was one of the "staunchest fighters for different measures of economic reform in the direction of justice." The Progressive platform of 1916 was indistinguishable from that of the Republicans, which, as the *New Republic* observed, was a "stupidly, defiantly and cynically reactionary document." When the Republicans nominated Hughes, the Progressives indorsed him too, on the grounds that only he could "serve the two vital causes of Americanism and Preparedness." The 1916 campaign marked the end of the Progressive party.

In 1912 the Progressives had been militant crusaders against reaction. As Roosevelt and the Progressives merged with the Republicans on nationalist grounds, they adopted the social ideology of the Old Guard too. In September, 1915, Roosevelt decried the "policy of harassing and jeopardizing business"; six months later he warned that commissions must stand "unflinchingly against any popular clamor which prevents the corporation from getting ample profit." Senator Beveridge, who had a distinguished record as a reformer and especially as a fighter for child labor laws, became a bitter foe of organized labor, attacked the income tax and called for a sales tax, and protested against "persecuting" businessmen. (The Indianapolis Associated Employers, Beveridge wrote enthusiastically, had been highly successful "in the suppression of strikes by force.") In 1918 Roosevelt urged the election to the Senate of four reactionaries, including Albert Fall of New Mexico. "To a peculiar degree," wrote Roosevelt, "Fall embodies the best American Spirit." Delighted by the victories of Fall and other deep-dyed conservatives, Roosevelt was dismayed only by the fact that George Norris and Robert La Follette were needed to form the new Republican majority in the Senate.

The fight over the League and the ugly events of 1919

dealt bruising blows to progressivism. In 1916, Wilson, as spokesman for the progressive wing of the Democratic party, won over a large section of the Progressives, disgusted with Roosevelt's indorsement of Lodge and attracted by Wilsonian reforms, as well as many Socialists and independent social reformers and intellectuals. By 1920, they had turned against Wilson, convinced that he had cynically betrayed democratic ideals at Versailles and that he had stamped out dissent at home. Heralded as the hope of the age, Wilson, in Amos Pinchot's words, put "his enemies in office and his friends in jail." Intellectuals who, as Joseph Freeman wrote, had a sense of "craft solidarity . . . with the professor in the White House," now felt distrustful of all exhorters, teachers, soothsayers, and statesmen. Leery of political messiahs, they approached politics with a new wariness. Herbert Croly spelled out the credo of the postwar liberal: "No more dashes into the political jungle. No more intervention without reservations, without understanding and without specific and intelligent political preparation."

In 1913 progressive intellectuals were giving the United States its first intelligent analysis of modern society and blueprinting an ebullient, buoyantly hopeful program of reform. By 1919 they were a disenchanted lot; discouraged by the war and the peace that followed, they had become, as Walter Weyl wrote, "tired radicals." "The chief distinguishing aspect of the Presidential campaign of 1920," wrote Herbert Croly in the *New Republic*, "is the eclipse of liberalism or progressivism as an effective force in American politics." Faced by the victory of political reaction and the disappointment of their hopes for a new international order, they felt an overwhelming sense of their own impotence. Society seemed infinitely less malleable than it once had; they were no longer certain of their ability to shape institutions to their own desires. The man "who aspired to overturn Society," wrote Weyl, "ends by fighting in a dull Board of Directors of a village library for the inclusion of certain books."

Having lost faith in progress, in the rationality and disinterestedness of man, and in the malleability of society, the intellectuals could no longer retain faith in the prewar political solutions. Croly turned from political problems to religious ones, from the problem of changing society to the quest for individual regeneration, and Walter Lippmann attempted to work out a naturalistic ethics. The disillusionment also strengthened the elitist strain in the progressive intellectuals. Since things had turned out so badly, men like Lippmann concluded not that their analyses were mistaken and their assumptions unrealistic but that the people had failed them. In *Public Opinion* (1922), Lippmann emphasized the irrationality of decision-making in politics and argued that men viewed reality in "stereotypes"; in *The Phantom Public* (1925), he attacked the idea that "the compounding of individual ignorances in masses of people can produce a continuous directing force in public affairs" and urged less power for the people and more for an elite class of experts. The former muckraker Lincoln Steffens gave up on parliamentary democracy entirely ("I can't see why everybody is so anxious to save this rotten civilization of ours") and became a warm admirer of Lenin and Mussolini. There was much more *élan* among the intellectuals who hoped to apply science to politics—John Dewey, Charles Beard, Thorstein Veblen—but they talked a good deal about method and not at all about concrete political proposals.

The war and its aftermath played a major part in the transition from the reform atmosphere of the prewar years to the conservative spirit of the 1920's, but too much can be charged to this alone. Much of the explanation of the change lies in the nature of progressivism itself. There was a considerable area of ideological agreement between prewar progressivism and the acquisitive aspirations of the Coolidge era. When Woodrow Wilson declared he was fighting for "the man on the make," when he cried, "just let some of the youngsters I know have a chance and they'll give these gentlemen points," he was talking the language of the businessman. Many of the progressives, especially the Wilsonians, had no trouble adapting themselves to the Coolidge era; such men as Newton Baker and Joe Tumulty surrendered their interest in social reform and found lucrative jobs with oil companies and private utilities in the 1920's. Businessmen, who formed the core of reform groups in many American cities, were excited by the possibilities of the "new" capitalism. As part of a new managerial class with professional aspirations, they made an easy transition from their prewar interest in "efficiency" in government to the postwar emphasis on scientific management and factory welfare programs. A middle-class movement hostile to interest-group politics, progressivism was shocked by the militancy of labor in 1919, and many progressives aligned themselves with property-conscious conservatives. The very men who voted for Wilson and Roosevelt in 1912 flocked to the polls to give landslide majorities to Harding and Coolidge.

Despite the loud clamor against the trusts, progressivism had always been less an economic movement than one of moral reform, and progressivism faded in the 1920's in part because it had succeeded too well. Women's suffrage had been a long-time goal, and prohibition and immigration restriction, while they do not seem "progressive" to a New Deal liberal, were important aims of the prewar progressives. A blend of economic and moral concerns, progressivism in the 1920's tended to concentrate almost wholly on these "moral" issues, although not without some uneasiness over what it had wrought. Prohibition, observes Richard Hofstadter, "was the skeleton at the feast, a grim reminder of the moral frenzy that so many wished to forget, a ludicrous caricature of the re-forming impulse, of the Yankee-Protestant notion that it is both possible and desirable to moralize private life through public action." When the immigration-restriction law passed the Senate in 1924, not a single progressive opposed it, and even men like George Norris voted in its favor.

Without a solid labor base, progressivism had little hope for success in the 1920's, but the "moral" issues diverted white, old-stock workers, the backbone of the AF of L craft unions, from economic issues. In 1924, when the Ku Klux Klan, a hooded order which was anti-Catholic, anti-Semitic, anti-Negro, and anti-foreigner, reached the height of popularity, William Allen White ran for governor of Kansas. He decided to be a candidate, he explained, because "the way the Catholics and Jews and colored people were persecuted by the Klan in Kansas was a dirty shame, and I couldn't rest under it." After his defeat he wrote, "Here was a funny thing: labor in the Middle West is shot through with the Ku-Klux Klan. It voted for Coolidge . . . because he was right on the Pope. I didn't get much of it because I was wrong on the Pope. . . . Certainly nothing has hit labor such a smash in my memory in politics as the Ku-Klux Klan. . . . It will be a decade be-fore labor recovers what it has lost by flirting with the Ku-Klux Klan."

The Perils of Prosperity, 1914–32

American radicalism was almost defunct in the 1920's. Prosecution during the war cut IWW membership in half; government raids in the Red Scare and defection of "Wobbly" leaders to the Communists decimated the remainder. The Palmer raids almost wiped out the Communists by cutting the membership of the two Communist parties at least four-fifths. (Ironically, by driving the Communists underground, the government strengthened the conspiratorial sense of the Slavic groups, who fancied themselves as being in the same position as the Bolsheviks under the Czar.) By 1920 there were only 8,000 to 15,000 Communists in the United States (the actual count is probably much closer to the lower figure), of whom only 1,000 to 2,000 were English-speaking. The Socialist party went rapidly downhill. In 1920 Eugene Debs, prisoner 9653 at the Atlanta federal penitentiary, won 900,000 votes on the Socialist ticket, but this was a much smaller percentage than he had received in 1912. In that banner year of socialism, the party had 118,000 members; ten years later, in 1922, it had only 11,000. In some states the Socialists virtually disappeared. In Oklahoma, the leading Socialist state in the country in 1914, where merchants had displayed the red flag in their store windows as a commercial expedient, the socialist party claimed only 14 members in 1924.

In the Great Plains states, the historic home of populism and Republican insurgency, progressivism continued to thrive. In 1915 the former Socialist A. C. Townley organized the Nonpartisan League in the heavily rural state of North Dakota. Finding the wheat farmers chafing under a government subservient to the millers of Minneapolis and St. Paul, Townley urged them to take the state away from the "sleek, smooth-tongued, bay-windowed fellows that looked well, talked well, lived well, lied well." In 1916 the League elected an obscure farmer to the governorship of North Dakota, and in the next few years it spread through the wheat belt from Minnesota to Washington. With a program that Thorstein Veblen labeled "agrarian syndicalism," the League in North Dakota created a state bank, a state grain elevator, a state flour mill, a compulsory hail insurance fund, and public low-cost housing for farmers and workers. In South Dakota the League added a state cement plant and a state-owned coal mine.

Elsewhere, however, the League was never able to match the success it had in the wheat area tapped by the Twin Cities. Harried as unpatriotic for its coolness or actual opposition to American participation in World War I, the League was crushed by a critical fall in farm prices in 1921. The state bank and many other state projects ran into financial difficulty, and the League discovered that so long as a state was dependent on Minneapolis or Chicago capital, it could not carry on socialistic experiments even within its borders. By 1922 the League was moribund.

Since the League's program was not narrowly agrarian, it was able to combine with trade unions in a farmer-labor political movement. In Minnesota it laid the foundations for an enduring tradition of farmer-labor unity, but outside the wheat belt farmers were more skeptical about farmer-labor cooperation. The more prosperous corn-belt farmers were more likely to view labor unions as enemies rather than allies. When Samuel Gompers called for farmer-labor unity in June, 1921, the farm journal editor Henry Wallace, later to be Franklin Roosevelt's Secretary of Agriculture, replied: "The fact is that the farmers are suffering more now from the leaders of labor than from the leaders of industry or finance." He lectured Gompers to urge union labor to reduce "exorbitantly high wages" as "an evidence of good faith."

In the face of all these handicaps, what is striking is not the weakness of progressivism but its strength. Through much of the period, the progressives in Congress held the balance of power, and were able to stave off conservative Republican attempts to enact special-interest legislation. In the early years, the progressives were even able to pass legislation of their own. The Esch-Cummins Act of 1920, although a compromise measure, placed railroads under virtually complete federal control, while the Water Power Act of 1920, although it proved ineffective, marked the beginning of federal regulation of electric utilities. In the Harding administration, farm interests won the greatest amount of legislation Congress had ever passed.

Most impressively, from 1921 to 1925 Senator George Norris almost single-handedly and by brilliant legislative legerdemain stopped the Harding and Coolidge administrations from turning the power site at Muscle Shoals in the Tennessee Valley over to private interests. By 1928 Norris had won enough congressional support to turn the tide and throw the private utilities on the defensive. Congress twice passed bills for an ambitious government development of the valley; frustrated both times by presidential vetoes, the campaign that would result in the creation of the Tennessee Valley Authority was, by the end of the Republican era, near success.

The progressives came back from their smashing defeat in 1920 to scare the daylights of the Old Guard in the 1922 elections. In 1920 the Wilson administration had suddenly reduced spending, ended loans to Europe, and raised taxes; the postwar boom was quickly punctured, prices broke violently, and

Tired Radicals

by 1921 the country faced a serious depression. In a single year, America's foreign trade was cut in half and farm prices plummeted. Desperate farmers, not knowing where to turn, used whatever weapon they could improvise. In the cotton belt, night riders burned cotton gins when owners failed to heed warnings not to buy cotton, and in a vain effort to push up prices masked riders in Kentucky cautioned farmers not to send their tobacco to market. In the 1922 elections, farmers resorted to the ballot; progressive Republicans upended Old Guard leaders in the midwestern farm states. In Iowa, irate farmers elected Smith Wildman Brookhart to the Senate; in Wisconsin, La Follette was returned with a 300,000-vote margin; in Minnesota, a Farmer-Labor candidate ousted Senator Frank Kellogg. Even in the East, the Harding forces met defeat. In the Old Guard stronghold of Pennsylvania, Gifford Pinchot, the leading conservationist of the Progressive era, defeated a reactionary candidate in the Republican gubernatorial primary. "Yesterday," said Senator Moses on hearing the news, "was a bad day for us Tories."

By 1923 midwestern progressives from the farm belt, desparing of both major parties, were talking of launching a national third party in 1924, and they had considerable support among a segment of middle-class intellectuals and reformers and from the Socialist party. The one stumbling block to a third-party move was the hesitancy of organized labor. The powerful railroad unions, infuriated by Harding's support of antilabor forces, had decided on political action against the Republicans. Rather than run a third ticket they preferred to support the Democrat, William McAdoo, who had won their favor by his operation of the railroads during the war. When, however, it was revealed that McAdoo had been employed as counsel by the oil tycoon, Edwin Doheny, at an annual retainer of $50,000, the unions threw over McAdoo, gave up on the Democratic party, and consented to support an independent ticket in 1924.

The Progressive convention of 1924 in Cleveland had much the same spirit of evangelical revivalism that had characterized the 1912 convention of the earlier Progressives. To the convention came veterans of old protest parties: General Jacob Coxey; the New Jersey editor John Streeter, who wore a flowing beard because he had taken an oath in the 1890's not to shave until populism was victorious; the spokesman for a newer urban progressivism, Fiorello La Guardia, who told the convention he had come "to let you know there are other streets and other attitudes in New York besides Wall Street. I speak for Avenue A and 116th Street, instead of Broad and Wall."

The Progressives named La Follette as their candidate for President and as their Vice-Presidential nominee chose Senator Burton K. Wheeler, the Montana Democrat whose probe had driven Harry Daugherty from the cabinet. The Progressive platform attacked monopoly, urged that Congress be given the power to override the Supreme Court, supported government ownership of railroads and, eventually, of water power resources, backed collective bargaining, and advocated the direct nomination and election of the President.

On June 24 the Democratic party assembled in Madison Square Garden for the famous deadlocked convention. In the midst of a terrible heat wave, the delegates battled for seventeen days before they could agree on a platform and candidates. The year 1924 marked the point in the urbanization of America when an unfortunate equilibrium was struck between the urban Northeast and the rural South and West. Both the urban and rural elements made a bad showing at the convention. Democrats from the South and West emerged as racial bigots who championed the Ku Klux Klan (Texas delegates had to be dissuaded from burning a fiery cross); the New Yorkers appeared to no better advantage as they shouted down Bryan and behaved like Cockney rowdies. So closely was the convention divided that the vote not to mention the Klan by name in the platform was passed $543\frac{3}{20}$ to $542\frac{3}{20}$.

The convention divided in the same fashion on choosing a presidential nominee. For nine hot days the delegates deadlocked between New York's Governor Alfred E. Smith and McAdoo, the hero of the South and West. (Will Rogers wrote during the convention: "This thing has got to come to an end. New York invited you people here as guests, not to live.") Smith partisans in the galleries jeered at McAdoo, "Oil! Oil! Oil!" and boasted that there was "No Oil on Al." After 95 ballots, Smith and McAdoo withdrew by agreement; on the 103d ballot, the convention named John W. Davis for President and then chose Charles Bryan for Vice-President. Davis, Solicitor-General under Wilson and ambassador to Great Britain, was a man of ability and character ("the type," noted a political writer sardonically, "that street-railway conductors like to have for a superintendent—that is, 'a mighty fine man' "). As one of the leading corporation lawyers in the country, however, he was a red flag to the Progressive bulls. Moreover, naming William Jennings Bryan's younger brother as the vice-presidential candidate made the ticket look too obviously contrived, not the expression of a popular demand but the work of backroom politicians—Wall Street and Bryan on the same ticket. By the end of the convention, neither nomination was worth a lead nickel. Once again the Democratic party had revealed itself to be "merely an aggregation of local interests" resembling "the old Austrian Empire."

The Republican party pursued the shrewd strategy of ignoring the Democrats. Calvin Coolidge sat out the campaign in the White House, leaving the strenuous barnstorming to the Republican vice-presidential candidate Charles "Hell and Maria" Dawes. Dawes concentrated his fire on La Follette. Although the La Follette program was on the whole moderate, and although La Follette had flatly spurned Communist support (and was bitterly and unfairly maligned by the Communists), Dawes and the Republicans insinuated that the Senator was a Bolshevik agent. The issue in 1924, declared Coolidge, was "whether America will allow itself to be degraded into a communistic or socialistic state or whether it will remain American." Pointing to the Progressive pledge to reform the Supreme Court, and warning that a vote for La Follette might prevent any candidate from winning a majority and might thus throw the election into the House of Representatives, the Republicans argued that the only issue was, in George Harvey's phrase, "Coolidge or Chaos." In this curiously unreal campaign, the Democratic party made less impression on the popular mind than at any other time in its history. Davis could not get the Republicans to notice him, and La Follette could not for long distract the Republican press from the false issue of communism. The Republican campaign was a successful application of Philip Guedalla's dictum, "Any stigma would do to beat a dogma."

The Progressives, although they had a new interest in bread and butter issues, based their 1924 campaign on the old cry of the evil of monopoly. In the postwar years, noted one writer, an attack on the trusts seemed as outdated as the tandem bicycle and "trust-buster" was a term as much lost in the mists of the past as "free-soiler." In attempting to win public attention on the issue of monopoly, La Follette seemed, as Dos Passos later wrote, "an orator haranguing from the capitol of a lost republic." He appeared to be trying to turn back time to the pre-industrial society of the nineteenth century. The theme song of the 1924 campaign, a La Follette leader later observed, should have been "Tenting Tonight on the Old Camp Ground."

The Progressives waged the 1924 campaign under insurmountable handicaps. They had no state, county, or municipal tickets, for the unions and the farm organizations would not commit themselves to a third party; the Progressive movement of 1924 was not a third party but merely a presidential and vice-presidential ticket. The Progressives were crippled by lack of money; for every dollar Coolidge had in campaign funds, La Follette had four cents. Their appeal to the farmer was blunted by a sharp rise in farm prices. The AF of L, which indorsed La Follette in 1924 and thus broke its tradition of never making an outright indorsement of a Presidential candidate, gave little material aid to the Progressive campaign; some unions, like the Carpenters under Big Bill Hutcheson and the Mine Workers under John L. Lewis, even supported Coolidge.

Calvin Coolidge swept the country with 15 million votes, Davis was second with the unbelievably low total of 8 million, and La Follette trailed with somewhat less than 5 million votes. So great was the Republican margin that Coolidge got more votes than both his opponents put together in all but nine states. Eight years before, the Democrats had been the majority party. In 1924, they had sunk to such relative unimportance that not only were they engulfed by the Republican party but La Follette and the Progressives got four times as many votes as the Democratic ticket in California and twice as many votes as Davis in seventeen states west of the Mississippi. La Follette carried the city of Cleveland, a stronghold of the railway unions, and won 70,000 votes in San Francisco (Coolidge had 73,000), where Davis polled only 9,800. Yet the Progressives could draw little satisfaction from the election; they had not only helped produce the Coolidge landslide, by splitting the opposition and arousing the fear of "chaos," but La Follette was able to carry only the single state of Wisconsin in the Electoral College.

After the 1924 campaign the movement for a permanent farmer-labor party collapsed. The railway unions pulled out, and only a tiny fragment was left to struggle on for a few more years and then die. (The ideal of a farmer-labor party had always been something of a mirage. An Indiana farmer scolded Coolidge to "get the viewpoint of the broad prairie farmer. Don't be a narrow minded hill billy from Vermont dominated by selfish money and manufacturing and union labor interests all your life.") Before the war, progressivism had secured its greatest triumphs in an era of prosperity, but in the boom years of the Coolidge era, it got nowhere. When utilities announced high profits, people responded not with a wave of indignation but with a rush to buy utility stocks. In Congress the progressive bloc continued to score Pyrrhic victories, but even there the progressives were dispirited and discouraged.

Baffled progressives looked back nostalgically to their era

of influence, unable to puzzle out the reasons for their loss of prestige or to understand why so many of their former leaders had abandoned politics altogether. In a symposium in 1926, the economist Stuart Chase wrote of the prewar era:

Them was the days! When the muckrakers were best sellers, when trust busters were swinging their lariats over every state capitol, when "priviledge" shook in its shoes, when God was behind the initiative, the referendum and the recall—and the devil shrieked when he saw the short ballot, when the Masses was at the height of its glory, and Utopia was just around the corner. . . .

Now look at the damned thing. You could put the avowed Socialists into a roomy new house, Mr. Coolidge is compared favorably to Lincoln, the short ballot is as defunct as Mah Jong, Mr. Eastman writes triolets in France, Mr. Steffens has bought him a castle in Italy, and Mr. Howe digs turnips in Nantucket.

Shall we lay a wreath on the Uplift Movement in America? I suppose we might as well.

The 1920's marked a time of transition within progressivism from the old-style evangelical reformism, under leaders like La Follette and Bryan, to a new style urban progressivism, which would call itself liberalism. Liberalism would be less interested in the moral reformation of man and more in using the power of the federal government to provide specific economic and social benefits. Unlike progressivism, which drew its strength from the old-stock middle class of the small towns and the cities, with not a little support from rural areas, liberalism would be centered in the urban masses, often the "new" immigrant workers of the great cities.

Progressivism was frustrated in the 1920's because, even when it held the balance of power in Congress, it had no program to present; it was reduced to guerilla sniping at the conservatives, who knew what they wanted. Because the progressives had no program that required large-scale government spending, they eventually were forced, in the face of a bulging Treasury surplus, to agree to Mellon's tax cuts. Yet, although the progressives had few accomplishments in the 1920's, they were laying the basis for a change in attitude without which the New Deal would not have been possible. McNary-Haugenism committed the farmer to using the taxing power to subsidize agriculture; the Muscle Shoals fight paved the way for the public power projects of the 1930's; and the Railway Labor Act of 1926 was an important forerunner of the Wagner Act of 1935. At the same time, a corps of economists—men like Wesley Mitchell, Walton Hamilton, Paul Douglas, and Rexford Tugwell—were hammering out the theoretical foundations of the New Deal.

The new progressivism was already beginning to make its way in the 1920's, notably in the career of Fiorello La Guardia, who as congressman from New York City's East Harlem delighted in taunting the Old Guard leadership of the Republican party. La Guardia said to a reporter in 1922, "I stand for the Republicanism of Abraham Lincoln; and let me tell you that the average Republican leader east of the Mississippi doesn't know anything more about Abraham Lincoln than Henry Ford knows about the Talmud." La Guardia, who was a spokesman for the urban immigrant and thus was opposed to nativism and basically interested in cost-of-living issues, would link the older Progressives with the New Dealers; in the 1920's he was one of the few exceptions to the conservatism of the great cities. The new-style liberalism had not yet gained any considerable strength, while the old-style progressivism was dying out. Some men, of course, such as George Norris and even La Follette and Bryan to some extent, successfully combined elements of both. But in 1925 La Follette and Bryan died, and in 1926 Debs also passed away. ("It is hard," said Senator Borah after hearing of La Follette's death, "to say the right thing about Bob La Follette. You know he lived 150 years.") Until the urban progressives gained greater strength and until they found a national leader who could heal the breach between the two traditions, the progressives had little hope of winning national power.

VIII·

A Botched Civilization

A few years before World War I, the only literary tradition America had ever known came to an end. At the time it seemed less like a death than a beginning. "One's first strong impression," recalled Malcolm Cowley, "is of the bustle and hopefulness that filled the early years from 1911–1916. . . . Everywhere new institutions were being founded—magazines, clubs, little theatres, art or free-love or single-tax colonies, experimental schools, picture galleries. Everywhere was a sense of secret comradeship and immense potentialities for change." Intellectuals yearning for a "new republic" founded magazines; painters like John Marin and Marsden Hartley were creating new art forms; Isadora Duncan threw aside the rigid dance patterns of the past; Amy Lowell wrote free verse; and in an old stable in MacDougal Street the American theater got a fresh start with the founding of the Province-town Players. Woodrow Wilson caught the spirit of the age in the phrase, "the New Freedom." The poet Ezra Pound foresaw an inevitable "American Risorgimento" which would "make the Italian Renaissance look like a tempest in a teapot."

A Botched Civilization

Whenever numerous people speak of a renaissance, of the birth of a new culture, writes T. K. Whipple, "you may be sure that an era is dying. It is a law of literary history that these spectacular outbursts which look as if they were ushering in a new epoch are in truth ushering out an old one." The risorgimento of 1912 was an assault on the classical, rational assumptions of nineteenth-century America. Mabel Dodge, at whose salon on Fifth Avenue the rebels met, schemed to "upset America . . . with fatal disaster to the old order of things." The rebellious intellectuals of 1912, whether they turned to such philosophers of the irrational as Bergson or Nietzsche or continued the tradition of naturalism established by such writers as Zola and Ibsen, bristled at the Victorian standard of decorum. Holmes assailed formal jurisprudence, Dewey assaulted formal logic, and Veblen attacked classical economics. The same currents shook modern art; modern painting abandoned harmony, decorum, and the natural world.

The rise of the city disrupted class relationships and created, for the first time in America, a distinct body of intellectuals, large in numbers and pursuing their respective crafts on a full-time, professional basis. For the most part, the intellectuals came from a prosperous urbanized middle class, but because of the anonymity and mobility of city living they were indifferent to middle-class opinions and not bound by traditional ties to family or region or class. Joining this group were the sons of immigrants in the large cities, often with a background of learning such as European Marxism or the rabbinical tradition, who were educated in the burgeoning public high schools; cut off from their families by their intellectual tastes, they were even more rootless and had even fewer ties to American traditions than the intellectuals who sprang from the middle class. Out of such groups—it was inevitable even without World War I—arose a literature and an art that expressed a sharp cleavage with traditional American values and assumptions. Well before the war, the new intellectuals demonstrated that they were excited not by reason but by emotion, not by stability but by change. Politically, they were attracted not to the rational reforms of the progressives or of the "gas and water Socialists" but to the anarchists and the romantic violence of the IWW.

World War I completed the sense of disintegration. It destroyed faith in progress, but it did more than that—it made clear to perceptive thinkers that they had misread the Progressive era and the long Victorian reign of peace, that violence prowled underneath man's apparent harmony and rationality. "The plunge of civilization into this abyss of blood and horror," wrote Henry James in the first year of the European war, "so gives away the whole long age during which we have supposed the world to be, with whatever abatement, gradually bettering, that to have to take it all now for what the treacherous years were really making for and *meaning* is too tragic for any words." The war, wrote James, was an "unspeakable giveaway of the whole fool's paradise of our past"; he regretted that he had not died before it came. The war, with its pointless slaughter which decimated an entire generation in Europe, including some of its finest artists—the war which appeared to strip life and death of all human dignity— was taken as final evidence of the bankruptcy of a civilization. Men had died, wrote Ezra Pound,

> For an old bitch gone in the teeth,
> For a botched civilization.

A Botched Civilization

The war brought to an end four centuries of emphasis on human potentiality and returned men like Pound and his fellow poet T. S. Eliot to a medieval sense of man's wickedness. Eliot rebelled against nineteenth-century "cheerfulness, optimism, and hopefulness." "The Love Song of J. Alfred Prufrock," completed in 1911 but not published until 1917, is a hymn of weariness and impotence, of failure and loss of will. In 1922 Eliot's *The Waste Land* appeared. Throughout the long poem, in itself deliberately disconnected and fragmentary like the world and the emotions it evoked, are the repeated symbols of sterility and emptiness. *The Waste Land* not only excited the admiration and envy of other poets for its technique; it became the text of despair for a generation of intellectuals. It is, of course, a vulgarization of Eliot's work to view his poetry merely as expressing the despair of a generation. Apart from the fact that a work of art is not primarily an historical document but has a validity of its own, Eliot sought and achieved an expression of universality beyond any particular period of time. Nonetheless, his early work is studded with judgments on contemporary culture which clearly represent his sense of the doom of modern society and were so understood at the time. "The Hollow Men" (1925) carries the sense of despair and horror even deeper; men meet in a "valley of dying stars," in a world devoid of will or emotion—"shape without form, shade without color, paralyzed force, gesture without motion." Even death no longer has meaning: the world ends not with a bang but a whimper.

The disillusion of American writers centered in an attack on American "Puritanism." At least as early as Van Wyck Brooks's *The Wine of the Puritans* (1908), American writers argued that American culture had been soured by a Puritan tradition which had suppressed the pursuit of pleasure in favor of a pursuit of things and, ultimately, had diverted all American energy to technology and utilitarianism. Historically shaky at best, this argument quickly grew so banal that, as Charles Beard wrote, the term Puritan became an epithet for "anything that interfere[d] with the new freedom, free verse, psychoanalysis, or even the double entendre." Intellectuals seized on Sigmund Freud's concept of "repression" as proof that society blocked individual fulfillment and smothered emotion. In itself, this contention was not without substance, but American intellectuals believed it was something uniquely true of American society, as though sex taboos, for example, were known only to modern industrial civilization or to the land of the Puritans.

Hatred was directed less at historical seventeenth-century Puritanism than at nineteenth-century Victorianism, which the intellectuals saw as a blend of prudery, commercialism, and sanctimoniousness that added up to a denial of life. Well before the war, influenced by Oscar Wilde, Frank Harris, and George Bernard Shaw, American writers rebelled against the genteel tradition and in particular against Victorian reticence about sex. The postwar years brought to its climax what Edmund Wilson labeled the "liquidation of genteel culture." Intellectuals rejected the Victorian era—"the notorious Victorian era," Randolph Bourne called it—both because it was too vulgar and because it was too genteel; and they assaulted not only Victorian standards of morality and politics but also the nineteenth-century literary tradition. Above all, they loathed the Victorian trait of respectability, the "Cambridge ladies who live in furnished souls," that vast middle class which sought "culture" as it would shop for furniture, which measured everything in terms of money.

They despised capitalism as the foul offspring of Puritanism. They rebelled against what Waldo Frank called the "cold lethal simplicities of American business culture." The United States, they argued, was a gadgety, mechanistic culture, a place where people were bent only on getting a living, a country hostile to leisure and to art. America was, wrote one expatriate, "the enemy of the artist, of the man who cannot produce something tangible when the five o'clock whistle blows." The country was not without ideals, but its ideals were as immature and as vapid as the people who believed in them; American culture, Van Wyck Brooks argued in *America's Coming-of-Age* (1915), had been torn between an absurd Emersonian idealism and "catchpenny opportunism." The great photographer Alfred Stieglitz was even more blunt; on a picture of a horse's buttocks, he placed the title "Spiritual America."

The intellectuals found both evidence for their theory of the historical development of American culture and solace for their contemporary plight in the analogy between the United States in the 1920's and America in the years after the Civil War. Both eras were characterized by materialism, political corruption, and cultural vulgarity. Harding and the Ohio Gang had their counterparts in Grant and his cronies; Teapot Dome and the Veterans Bureau scandals had their forerunners in the Credit Mobilier, Black Friday, and the Whiskey Ring. In their interest in the Gilded Age, the intellectuals revived Herman Melville, awoke to Emily Dickinson, and were absorbed with Henry Adams. In *The Ordeal of Mark Twain* (1920), Van Wyck Brooks wrote of life in America in the

The Perils of Prosperity, 1914–32

Gilded Age as "a horde-life, a herd-life, an epoch without sun or stars, the twilight of a human spirit that had nothing upon which to feed but the living waters of Camden and the dried manna of Concord." Puritan, capitalist society, with its distorted system of values, its emphasis on the useful, its hostility to the artist, had succeeded both in crushing and in corrupting Twain, leaving him in his last days a bitter, frustrated man. Such too was the fate confronting the artist in the 1920's; he too was living in a "Tragic Era."

In 1916 Twain's *The Mysterious Stranger* had been published with its message that life was meaningless; in 1918 *The Education of Henry Adams* had appeared with its deeply pessimistic view of the American past and its prophecy of inevitable disaster. American writers, Van Wyck Brooks felt, were doomed to failure, however great their early promise. "There is no denying," wrote Brooks in 1921, "that for half a century the American writer as a type has gone down to defeat."

The intellectuals of these years did not just happen upon a sense of despair; they sought it out. Brooks became obsessed early in life with the great failures ("We were attracted to failure," he later conceded), while writers like Dos Passos could love only the defeated and scorned—the Wobblies, the Bournes, the La Follettes. The cult of bohemianism was half in love with easeful failure. "We had begun to develop an idea common to nineteenth century romantics and twentieth century bohemians, the idea that success was synonymous with philistinism," wrote Joseph Freeman. Quite "unable to distinguish between success and conventional standards of success, we made a cult of failure." The novelist Scott Fitzgerald, in particular, was fascinated by "the beautiful and damned."

A Botched Civilization

"All the stories that came into my head," he recalled, "had a touch of disaster in them."

The intellectuals felt cut off from the rest of the country. "What will you say to a man who believes in hell, or that the Pope of Rome wants to run this country, or that the Jews caused the war?" asked Ludwig Lewisohn. "How would you argue with a Methodist minister from an Arkansas village, with a Kleagle of the Klan, with a 'this-is-a-white-man's-country' politician from central Georgia?" Faced with such questions, some writers looked to themselves as leaders of a movement which would regenerate American society. Brooks, in particular, saw the artist as the guide to new directions for American culture; he accepted the Italian poet Leopardi's dictum that "in literature alone the regeneration of our country can have a substantial beginning." But most intellectuals had no such illusions; they felt superior to other men, had no desire to reform them or American society, and rejoiced in their separateness. They admired Flaubert not only for his sense of craft but for his contempt for the bourgeois philistines; indeed, the two seemed inseparable. In the poet E. E. Cummings' *The Enormous Room* (1922), there is a colloquy which states the conviction underlying the religion of art:

"What do you think happens to people who aren't artists? What do you think people who aren't artists become?"
"I feel they don't become: I feel nothing happens to them; I feel negation becomes of them."

Sherwood Anderson was the first writer canonized in the religion of art. No legend was more central to the idea that the artist could not survive in American business society, indeed that no meaningful life could be lived by any man in such a suffocating environment, than the story of Anderson's revolt. On November 27, 1912, Anderson walked out of his paint factory in Elyria, Ohio, in search of life. At the age of thirty-six, like Gauguin, he turned his back on the bourgeois world for the life of art, for a life with meaning. Such was the legend; in fact Anderson had suffered a nervous breakdown —the gap between the legend and reality was in itself as savage a commentary as the times could offer.

When so much of tradition seemed barren, when society seemed so bleak, art—craftsmanship and the concern for form —represented something true, something demanding yet clean and uncomplicated, a standard of integrity; and the writers were, if nothing else, devoted to mastering their art. "I want to be one of the greatest writers who have ever lived, on't you?" Scott Fitzgerald asked Edmund Wilson when they were Princeton undergraduates. The youthful, good-looking, blond, green-eyed Fitzgerald, whose *This Side of Paradise* (1920), as Glenway Wescott said, haunted the decade like a song, typified both the devotion to art and the romantic individualism of the period. "Fitzgerald," observes Lionel Trilling, "was perhaps the last notable writer to affirm the Romantic fantasy, descended from the Renaissance, of personal ambition and heroism, of life committed to, or thrown away for, some ideal of self."

The writers of the 1920's were concerned with the individual rather than with society, with private rather than public experience. They had faith only in the individual perception of experience; they were determined to write without regard for the pieties of American society. Yet it was difficult to tell the truth, for it was not easy to avoid using words which expressed what one ought to feel rather than what one did feel. Writers avoided adjectives, which were betraying, and pushed as far as they could with blunt nouns and verbs. In Ernest Hemingway's *A Farewell to Arms* (1929), when a character remarks that the Italians could not have fought the Austrians in vain, a friend observes:

> I was always embarrassed by the words sacred, glorious, and sacrifice and the expression in vain. We had heard them . . . and had read them, on proclamations that were slapped up by billposters over other proclamations, now for a long time, and I had seen nothing sacred, and the things that were glorious had no glory and the sacrifices were like the stockyards at Chicago if nothing was done with the meat except to bury it. There were many words that you could not stand to hear and finally only the names of places had dignity.

In rebelling against the standards of the day, the intellectuals were revolting against the ideas of progressive politics as well. A few years before the 1920's, men like Golden Rule Jones, the Toledo municipal reformer, and women like Jane Addams, the Chicago social worker, were exciting figures, rebels against the accepted ideas of their day. After World War I, they seemed to the new generation as dull as Henry Wadsworth Longfellow. H. G. Wells, whose reform writings had stirred the progressives, was dismissed as a "Fabian schoolmarm." Progressivism had become a kind of orthodoxy, and if you rebelled against orthodoxy, you rejected progressivism as well. Progressive education, recalled Malcolm Cowley, was "a topic that put us to sleep." All the new generation's efforts were bent on a rejection of middle-class values, and it did not matter whether those values appeared in the garb of conservatism or progressivism; nothing seemed worse than what Cowley called "an intolerable utopia of dull citizens."

Social reformers valued gains that could be measured—minimum wages and lower streetcar fares—and differed sharply from a tradition which centered on the individual soul and the individual imagination. Van Wyck Brooks described the reform movement as having been born middle-aged. There was none of the "tang and fire of youth in it, none of the fierce glitter of the intellect; there was no joyous burning of boats; there were no transfigurations, no ecstasies." Progressivism was indifferent to religion, other than social gospel religion, and to art. "In a world of electoral reform, plebiscites, sex reform and dress reform," wrote T. S. Eliot, "damnation itself is an immediate form of salvation." For years, bright young intellectuals had attempted to reform society, but what, they now asked, had they in common with society, or society with them. "Society," wrote Malcolm Cowley, recording the beliefs of his generation, "was terribly secure, unexciting, middle class, a vast reflection of the families from which we came. . . . Society was something alien, which our own lives and writings could never affect: it was a sort of parlor car in which we rode, over smooth tracks, toward a destination we should never have chosen for ourselves." Democracy implied the rule of middle-class values; the state was an instrument for suppressing dissent. Why should the intellectuals attempt to mobilize new majorities to suppress still more rights?

"The great problems of the world—social, political, economic and theological—do not concern me in the slightest," wrote the drama critic George Jean Nathan. "If all the Armenians were to be killed tomorrow and if half of Russia were to starve to death the day after, it would not matter to me in the least. What concerns me alone is myself, and the interests of a few close friends. For all I care the rest of the world may go to hell at today's sunset." Sending money for the relief of starving children abroad, remarked the novelist Joseph Her-gesheimer, "was one of the least engaging ways in which money could be spent." "If I am convinced of anything," observed the editor and writer H. L. Mencken, "it is that Doing Good is in bad taste."

In 1922 Harold Stearns edited his famous *Civilization in the United States,* a symposium of thirty different writers who concluded that American culture was in a desperate and perhaps hopeless state. In a notable article in *The Freeman,* Stearns asked, "What should a young man do?" His answer: There was nothing to do here, nothing at all. Get out of the country. After finishing the manuscript of *Civilization in the United States,* Stearns sailed for France. He was only one of a host of writers who gave up America entirely for some country where, they felt, the artist could breathe more freely; they left America, as Ezra Pound said, "in disgust." Sitting in sidewalk cafes in Paris, they wrote of Michigan and Wisconsin, especially of the small American town and of the wasted lives there. A few remembered America more fondly and wrote works like Stephen Vincent Benet's *John Brown's Body* (1928). Others simply lived the lives of Bohemian artists, following the pattern long since set by the French writer Henri Murger's *Scènes de la Vie de Bohême* (1848).

The exodus to Paris was a flight not merely from Puritan civilization but from modern industrialism, from the Machine Age itself. Although some artists attempted to come to terms with the machine and adapt themselves to an industrial society (ignoring Edmund Wilson's counsel, "Let the artist attend to his art and the age will attend to his adaptation"), most of the intellectuals of the 1920's saw the machine as a menace to be opposed, circumvented, or outwitted. Elmer Rice's play, *The*

The Perils of Prosperity, 1914–32

Adding Machine (1923), whose characters bear such names as Mr. Zero, and the Theater Guild production of the Czech playwright Karel Çapek's *R.U.R.*, which added the word "robot" to the language, were evidence of a pervasive concern with whether man himself was being transmogrified into a machine. Lewis Mumford warned that the assembly line was destroying the sense of pride and the sense of self of the craftsman. In fear and dislike of a machine age, many intellectuals turned toward more primitive societies, fleeing to Mexico or studying the art of the Congo or centering on the Negro as the symbol of pre-industrial man, uninhibited in his laughter and his sadness. In both the United States and Europe this took the form of a cult of jazz, for in a world of synthetic songs mechanically contrived on Tin Pan Alley, the rhythms of New Orleans and the delta country had the authentic ring of spontaneity.

Exile appealed most to younger men. The somewhat older generation of intellectuals typified by H.L. Mencken remained at home to become devastating critics of American society. Mencken did not merely attack democracy; he made the attack on the majority popular by his barbs at the "booboisie." Mencken's outspoken articles made each individual reader feel that he and the author (and possibly a few others in the "smart set") were laughing together at the stupid majority. No American institution was safe from Mencken's gibes. He declared that a clergyman was *ipso facto* a fraud and to be watched, especially when young girls or young boys were about. He told his readers that all Anglo-Saxons were cowards and that the Civil War was a third-rate war because only 200,000 men were killed in it. He advocated abolishing the public school system, defended prostitution, vivisection, and war, and denounced social workers as "settlement sharks." When he announced his candidacy for the presidency, it was on a platform of promising to take the Statue of Liberty beyond the three-mile limit and dump it in the ocean, to create vast stadia in which clergymen would be turned loose upon one another, and to give the Philippines to Japan.

He ridiculed all that "homo boobiens" cherished. In place of courting, he proposed that husbands and wives be matched by the common hangman. "Love," he remarked, "is the delusion that one woman differs from another." He drafted a bill legalizing the assassination of public officials. He derided the pet panacea of the civil service reformers by writing that to urge more gentlemen to go into politics was the same as arguing that the cure for prostitution was to send more virgins into brothels. For a decade he titillated his readers and enraged the objects of his scorn; no college fraternity house was complete without a copy of *The American Mercury*. At best, Mencken was a skeptic who cut through pretentiousness, barbarism, and the false affirmations of Rotarianism. As a critic, Mencken sponsored Theodore Dreiser and Frank Norris and, among Europeans, James Joyce, Gerhart Hauptmann, Havelock Ellis, and his favorite, Nietzsche. Some of these men he took up in the face of a vicious prudery; by his own courage or by his indifference to middle-class tastes he gained them an audience. Yet, as his fellow editor Charles Angoff has written, Mencken's "gift for literary criticism in the grand sense was very limited. He tended to like only those novelists who 'showed up' Americans. . . ." Mencken found everything absurd, the good as well as the bad; he was less a true satirist than a sophomoric nihilist.

Much the same might be said of Sinclair Lewis. Lewis's

novels, praised for their accurate portrayal of midwestern life, actually presented, as T. R. Fyvel has pointed out, a nightmare vision of American society; with monotonous consistency, Lewis revealed "on the one side a demonic American society from which there is no escape, on the other side a hero or heroine whose solitariness is complete." This grim caricature of American life, which might have produced despair, appears instead to have incited reform, of manners if not of character.

In September, 1928, in "Last Days of the Devastators," an article in the *Yale Review*, Henry S. Harrison commented on "the appetite of Americans for hearing themselves abused." Ever since the war, he noted, there had been a "strange orgy of flagellation," with the Boosters Clubs having their reverse counterpart in the "literature of self-depreciation." What these writers had essentially done, Harrison argued, was to come up with the not very original observation that "commonplace people act in a commonplace way," but they had nationalized this idea by giving the impression that it was something unique to America. In spite of themselves, their main impact was reformist; as the muckrakers had written of the "Shame of the Cities," they wrote of the "Shame of the Ohio Vulgarians." The result was that the work of the Lewises and Menckens guided the middle class in proper manners and aesthetic tastes. "The devastators are thus seen as the Emily Posts of our elementary aesthetics," Harrison concluded. "They teach the half-educated which cultural forks not to use."

Ironically, at the very time when intellectuals were complaining that art could not flourish in America, art burgeoned as it rarely, perhaps never, had before. When Amory Blaine, a character in *This Side of Paradise*, speaks for a generation "grown up to find all Gods dead, all wars fought, all faiths in man shaken," he is guilty of what Frederick Hoffman has called "the pathos of the adolescent." Many of the novels of the 1920's are peopled with characters who are neurasthenic, weak, unable to impose themselves on their world, fingering their grievances, nourishing a sentimental melancholia. Often the leading figures have no interest in themselves and are consequently at a handicap in invoking the interest of the reader. The Hemingway hero, as Wyndham Lewis remarked, is the man "things are done to." In the novels of the period, W. H. Auden has pointed out, man is "the absolute victim of circumstance and incapable of choice." Yet, Auden notes, American novelists "produced the only significant literature between the two great wars." There is an ironical disparity, Auden observes, between the vitality of the novelists and the "helpless victims" in their novels.

The writings of the period are often frankly nihilistic, most explicitly in Hemingway's "nada hail nada full of nada." Their view of social relations is often so distorted as to deny any kind of mature relationship or enduring tradition. Ezra Pound wrote of the adolescent "smothered in family."

> Oh how hideous it is
> To see three generations of one house gathered together!

Dos Passos' novel *1919* (1932) presents a shallow view of American culture, a crabbed, distorted image, which, as Maxwell Geismar has pointed out, breathes death, not life, revealing more about Dos Passos than it does about America. Nevertheless, the 1920's were years of wonderful creativity and, despite the negation of the themes of many of the novels and plays, of great gusto. Eugene O'Neill symbolized a revolutionary change in the quality of the theater; in Maxwell Anderson, Paul Green, Elmer Rice, Sidney Howard, and others, more talent was revealed in the 1920's than in all the previous history of the American theater. The novels of Ernest Hemingway, William Faulkner, Sherwood Anderson, F. Scott Fitzgerald, Willa Cather, and Sinclair Lewis, the short stories of Ring Lardner, the poetry of Hart Crane, E. E. Cummings, Conrad Aiken, Marianne Moore, and Wallace Stevens—these comprised just such a risorgimento as Pound had predicted.

No theme of the period was more hackneyed than the depiction of the Midwest as a cultural wasteland. The Midwest stood for all that was tedious, humdrum, and false about human existence; one could not change it, all one could do was flee. Yet Ford Madox Ford, who edited *transatlantic review* in Paris, wrote: "The Middle West was seething with literary impulse. It is no exaggeration to say that 80 per cent of the manuscripts in English that I received came from west of Altoona, and 40 per cent of them were of such a level of excellence that one might just as well close one's eyes and take one at random as try to choose between them."

It is not easy to explain the negativism of the artists of the 1920's in relation to their great creativity. The very rejection of tradition and of the earlier idealism, which might have resulted simply in a sterile Nay-saying, appears to have freed writers to experiment with new forms. There may well be a causal connection between intellectual productivity and the alienation of intellectuals. The writer of today, notes John Aldridge, is able to live "at least on terms of peaceable co-existence with society, and even though that has immensely improved his material circumstances, it has deprived him of that 'something' to push against which seems so necessary to the existence of his art." One thing is certain: the 1920's produced a literature that no era since has been able to match.

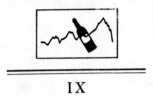

IX

The Revolution in Morals

The disintegration of traditional American values—so sharply recorded by novelists and artists—was reflected in a change in manners and morals that shook American society to its depths. The growing secularization of the country greatly weakened religious sanctions. People lost their fear of Hell and at the same time had less interest in Heaven; they made more demands for material fulfillment on Earth. The "status revolution" of the turn of the century undercut the authority of the men who had set America's moral standards: the professional classes, especially ministers, lawyers, and teachers; the rural gentry; the farmers; the urban patricians. The new urban minorities and *arriviste* businessmen were frequently not equipped—not even aware of the need either to support old standards or to create new ones. Most important, the authority of the family, gradually eroded over several centuries, had been sharply lessened by the rise of the city. "Never in recent generations," wrote Freda Kirchwey, "have human beings so floundered about outside the ropes of social and religious sanctions."

The Revolution in Morals

When Nora, the feminist heroine of *A Doll's House* (1879) by the Norwegian playwright Henrik Ibsen, walked out into the night, she launched against male-dominated society a rebellion that has not ended yet. The "new woman" revolted against masculine possessiveness, against "over-evaluation" of women "as love objects," against being treated, at worst, as a species of property. The new woman wanted the same freedom of movement that men had and the same economic and political rights. By the end of the 1920's she had come a long way. Before the war, a lady did not set foot in a saloon; after the war, she entered a speakeasy as thoughtlessly as she would go into a railroad station. In 1904, a woman was arrested for smoking on Fifth Avenue; in 1929, railroads dropped their regulation against women smoking in dining cars. In the business and political worlds, women competed with men; in marriage, they moved toward a contractual role. Once ignorant of financial matters, they moved rapidly toward the point where they would be the chief property-holders of the country. Sexual independence was merely the most sensational aspect of the generally altered status of women.

In 1870, there were only a few women secretaries in the entire country; by the time of World War I, two million women worked in business offices, typing the letters and keeping the records of corporations and countinghouses in every city in the nation. During the war, when mobilization created a shortage of labor, women moved into jobs they had never held before. They made grenades, ran elevators, polished locomotives, collected streetcar fares, and even drilled with rifles. In the years after the war, women flew airplanes, trapped beaver, drove taxis, ran telegraph lines, worked as deep-sea divers and steeplejacks, and hunted tigers in the jungle; women stevedores heaved cargoes on the waterfront, while other women conducted orchestras, ran baseball teams, and drilled oil wells. By 1930, more than ten million women held jobs. Nothing did more to emancipate them. Single women moved into their own apartments, and wives, who now frequently took jobs, gained the freedom of movement and choice that went along with leaving home.

After nearly a century of agitation, women won the suffrage in 1920 with the adoption of the Nineteenth Amendment. The American suffragettes modeled themselves on their British counterparts, who blew up bridges, hurled bombs, and burned churches, activities previously regarded as the exclusive privilege of Irish rebels. Using less violent methods, American women had greater success, and the adoption of the suffrage amendment climaxed a long debate in which suffragettes argued that the advent of the women's vote would initiate a new era of universal peace and benevolence, while their enemies forecast a disintegration of American society. (The chief result of women's suffrage, Mencken predicted, would be that adultery would replace boozing as the favorite pastime of politicians.)

As it turned out, women's suffrage had few consequences, good or evil. Millions of women voted (although never in the same proportion as men), women were elected to public office (several gained seats in Congress by the end of the 1920's), but the new electorate caused scarcely a ripple in American political life. Women like Jane Addams made great contributions, but it would be difficult to demonstrate that they accomplished any more after they had the vote than before. It was widely believed, although never proved, that women cast a "dry" vote for Hoover in 1928 and that women were likely to be more moved than men to cast a "moral-issue" vote. Otherwise, the earth spun around much as it had before.

The extreme feminists argued that women were equal to men, and even more so. "Call on God, my dear," Mrs. Belmont is alleged to have told a despondent young suffragette. "She will help you." Female chauvinists wanted not merely sexual equality but, insofar as possible, to dispense with sexuality altogether, because they conceived of sexual intercourse as essentially humiliating to women. "Man is the only animal using this function out of season," protested Charlotte Perkins Gilman. "Excessive indulgence in sex-waste has imperiled the life of the race." Chanting slogans like "Come out of the kitchen" and "Never darn a sock," feminist leaders rebelled against the age-old household roles of women; before long, even a woman contented with her familiar role felt called on to apologize that she was "just a housewife."

In Dorothy Canfield Fisher's *The Home-Maker* (1924), the process is taken to its logical conclusion: a woman who has been a failure as a mother succeeds in business while her husband, a failure in business, stays at home and makes a success of raising children. The literature of the time reflects the growing male sense of alarm, notably in D. H. Lawrence's morbid fear that he would be absorbed and devoured by woman but even more in a new American character represented by the destructive Nina Leeds of O'Neill's *Strange Interlude* (1928), the husband-exploiting title figure of George Kelly's *Craig's Wife* (1926), and the possessive "son-devouring tigress" of Sidney Howard's *The Silver Cord* (1927).

The new freedom for women greatly increased the instability of the family. By the turn of the century, women were demanding more of marriage than they ever had before and were increasingly unwilling to continue alliances in which they were miserable. For at least a century, the family had been losing many of its original social and economic functions; the state, the factory, the school, and even mass amusements robbed the family of functions it once had. The more that social usefulness was taken away from the family, the more marriage came to depend on the personalities of the individuals involved, and, since many Americans of both sexes entered marriage with unreasonable expectations, this proved a slender reed. In 1914, the number of divorces reached 100,-000 for the first time; in 1929, over 205,000 couples were divorced in a single year. The increase in divorce probably meant less an increase in marital unhappiness than a refusal to go on with marriages which would earlier have been tolerated.

As the family lost its other social functions, the chief test of a good family became how well it developed the personalities of the children, and parents, distrustful both of their own instincts and of tribal lore, eagerly sought out expert advice to avoid the opprobrium of having raised unhappy children. Dr. John B. Watson published the first edition of *Behaviorism* in 1914, but it was not until its third edition in 1925 that behaviorism—the idea that man was nothing but a machine responding to stimuli—took the country by storm. Since man was only a machine, environment alone was significant in determining both man's character and the nature of his society. "Give me a dozen healthy infants, well-formed, and my own specified world to bring them up in," declared Watson, "and I'll guarantee to take any one at random and train him to become any specialist I might select—doctor, lawyer, artist, merchant-chief, and yes, even beggarman and thief, regardless of his talents, tendencies, abilities, vocations and race of his ancestor." Watson's theories had the greatest impact on child-rearing; the Department of Labor incorporated behaviorist assumptions in its pamphlet *Infant and Child Care*, which, with emphasis on rigid scheduling of a baby's activities, became the government's leading best seller. Watson predicted that the time would come when it would be just as bad manners to show affection to one's mother or father as to come to the table with dirty hands. To inculcate the proper attitudes at an early age, Watson warned parents, "Never hug and kiss them, never let them sit in your lap."

Great as Watson's influence was, it could not hold a candle to that of Sigmund Freud. Before the war, Freud's name was known, outside of medical circles, only to a coterie of intellectuals. He had been referred to in the United States as early as 1895 by Dr. Robert Edes, but, a decade later, only a few well-informed medical men knew his name. By 1908, Dr. A. A. Brill, who had studied at Jung's Clinic of Psychiatry in Zurich, was won to Freudian theory and undertook the major task of translating Freud's work. In 1909, when Freud journeyed to the United States to give a series of lectures at Clark University, he was amazed that "even in prudish America" his work was so well known. The following year, Brill published the first of his translations of Freud, *Three Contributions to a Theory of Sex* (previously available only in the German *Drei Adhandlungen zur Sexual-Theorie*), and in 1913, Brill, at the invitation of the precocious Walter Lippmann, explained Freud to a group of American intellectuals gathered at Mabel Dodge's salon.

With startling speed Freudian doctrine was acknowledged

by a number of American intellectuals; in 1915 Lippmann and Max Eastman wrote perceptive articles on him, and his work, along with that of Nietzsche and Bergson, had strongly influenced Lippmann's *A Preface to Politics* (1914). Freud's sexual theories, particularly his contention that neurotic symptoms could be traced to sexual disturbances, were not popularly disseminated until after the war. But they were well enough known to New York social workers that, despite hostility and even revulsion at his blunt descriptions of infant sexuality, Brill was able to lecture on "Masturbation" to the ladies of the Child Study Association.

At the same time, Freudian theories made headway against vehement opposition in American medical circles. By 1916 there were some five hundred psychoanalysts, or people who called themselves that, in New York City. American participation in the war made the whole country psychology-conscious, if not Freud-conscious; more than one hundred psychologists served on the Surgeon-General's staff, and there was wide discussion of wartime medical phenomena like "shell shock." Even more important in popularizing psychology were the Army "intelligence" tests and the debates they aroused; during the war, hundreds of thousands of soldiers were asked to cross out the "g" in "tiger."

In the years after the war, psychology became a national mania. Books appeared on the *Psychology of Golf*, the *Psychology of the Poet Shelley*, and the *Psychology of Selling Life Insurance*. People talked knowingly of "libido," "defense mechanism," and "fixation," confused the subconscious with the unconscious, repression with suppression, and dealt with the tortuously difficult theories of Freud and of psychoanalysis as though they were simple ideas readily grasped after a few moments' explanation. One article explained solemnly that the immense popularity of the song "Yes, We Have No Bananas" was the result of a national inferiority complex. Psychiatrist Karl Menninger found himself badgered at parties to perform analyses of the personalities of guests as though he were a fortune teller. "When I refuse," he explained, "my questioners often show me how the thing is done." Neophytes were able to read books like *Psychoanalysis by Mail* and *Psychoanalysis Self-Applied*, while the Sears, Roebuck catalogue offered *Ten Thousand Dreams Interpreted* and *Sex Problems Solved*. Like the automobile, Freud was brought within the reach of everyone.

Freud's popularity had an inevitable effect on the "revolution in morals." It was assumed that he was arguing that unless you freely expressed your libido and gave outlet to your sex energy, you would damage your health; by the distortion of his work, a scientific imprimatur was given to self-indulgence. By a similar but more understandable misinterpretation, it was believed that Freud was denying the reality of love; his name was invoked in support of the dehumanization of sex. "I'm hipped on Freud and all that," observed a Scott Fitzgerald heroine, "but it's rotten that every bit of *real* love in the world is ninety-nine percent passion and one little soupçon of jealousy."

What only the initiate understood was that although Freud did emphasize the strong power of unconscious motivation, psychiatry was aimed not at stressing the irrational or at licensing indulgence but at making it possible for man to use his rational powers to control unconscious forces. Freud taught that the most "irrational" act had meaning. Psychiatrists used Freud's theories to enable men to control their emotions through a clearer understanding of their irrational impulses. The vast popularity of Freud in America, which was to move the center of psychiatry from Vienna to Park Avenue, alarmed many psychoanalysts. They realized that the popularity had been achieved less through an understanding of Freud than through a belief that he shared the American conviction that every man had the right not merely to pursue happiness but to possess it. This distortion had a number of unfortunate results, not least of which was the disappointment patients experienced when they came to realize that progress could be made only when self-indulgent fantasies were surrendered; but its ultimate effect was good. In Europe, psychiatry followed a course of near-fatalism in treating mental illness; in the more optimistic and more expectant American environment, psychiatry made greater gains and received far greater public support.

Freudian theories had a great impact on American writers, in part because they suggested new techniques for the exploration of human motivation, in part because they gave postwar intellectuals an invaluable weapon against the older standards. In some works the use of Freud was explicit; in others, as in the novels of Sherwood Anderson, where the influence of Freud seems obvious, there was apparently no conscious use of Freud at all. Eugene O'Neill turned to Freudian themes in his ambitious *Strange Interlude* (1928) as well as in his *Desire Under the Elms* (1924) and *Mourning Becomes Electra* (1931). Freud's greatest impact on the form of the novel was in the "stream-of-consciousness" technique, although its most important exponent, the Irish novelist James Joyce, was more directly influenced by Jung than by Freud. Stream of consciousness was employed in America most notably in William

The Revolution in Morals

Faulkner's *The Sound and the Fury* (1929) and in the works of the novelist and poet Conrad Aiken. "I decided very early," Aiken recalled, "that Freud, and his co-workers and rivals and followers, were making the most important contribution of the century to the understanding of man and his consciousness; accordingly I made it my business to learn as much from them as I could."

Freud's theories also opened up a new world to biographers anxious to understand the inner life of their subjects, but most of his effect on biography ran from the unfortunate to the disastrous. His own *Leonardo da Vinci* (1910), which should have served as a warning to biographers, became instead a model. In this essay Freud attempted with doubtful success to reconstruct Da Vinci's life and to interpret his works from a single fantasy that Da Vinci remembered. With similar fragmentary evidence, psychoanalytically oriented biographers tried to add a new dimension to their work; some of these ventures were serious, others were little more than vendettas on heroes of the past. Emerson and Thoreau, Ludwig Lewisohn wrote, were "chilled under-sexed valetudinarians." Even when new information or interpretations were established, it was not always clear what use could be made of them. "The superstition persisted," wrote Alfred Kazin, "that to have proved one's subject impotent was to have made a critical statement."

In the attempt to work out a new standard of relations between men and women, Americans in the 1920's became obsessed with the subject of sex. Some novelists wrote of little else, in particular James Branch Cabell, whose *Jurgen* (1919), actually a curiously unerotic novel despite its absorption with the subject, was praised for its "phallic candour."

The Perils of Prosperity, 1914–32

Radio singers crooned songs like "Hot Lips," "Baby Face," "I Need Lovin'," and "Burning Kisses." Magazines like *Paris Nights, Flapper Experiences,* and *Snappy Stories* covered newsstands. The newspaperman Frank Kent returned from a tour of the country in 1925 with the conviction that "between the magazines and the movies a lot of these little towns seem literally saturated with sex." Advertising, once pristine, began the transition which, as one writer remarked, was to transmute soap from a cleansing agent to an aphrodisiac and to suggest "that every woman buying a pair of stockings is aiming for an assignation, or at the very least for a rescue via a fire-ladder."

Absorption with sex was the life's blood of the newspaper tabloid. Developed by Lord Northcliffe in England, the tabloid first appeared in America with the founding of the New York *Daily News* in 1919. As a picture newspaper like the *Sketch* and the *Mirror* in England, the *News* caught on immediately; within five years it had the largest circulation of any newspaper in New York. Hearst followed with the *New York Daily Mirror,* a slavish imitation of the *News,* and in 1924 Bernarr MacFadden demonstrated how far salacious sensationalism could be carried with the *New York Evening Graphic.* The New York tabloids soon had their imitators in other cities. Although the tabloids won millions of readers, they did not cut into the circulation of the established newspapers; they found a new, semiliterate market.

Not even the tabloids exploited sex with the zeal of Hollywood; it was the movies which created the American love goddess. When the "vamp," Theda Bara, appeared in *The Blue Flame* in 1920, crowds mobbed theaters in eastern cities to get in. Movie producers found that films like *The Sheik* drew large audiences, while *Sentimental Tommy* or epics like *America* played to empty houses. When it was apparent that sex was infinitely more profitable than the prewar sentimental-patriotic fustian, the country got a steady diet of movies like *Up in Mabel's Room, Her Purchase Price,* and *A Shocking Night.* (Cecil B. De Mille changed the title of Sir James Barrie's *The Admirable Crichton* into *Male and Female.*) Clara Bow was featured as the "It" girl, and no one had to be told what "it" was. The only ones in Hollywood with "it," explained the novelist Elinor Glyn, were "Rex, the wild stallion, actor Tony Moreno, the Ambassador Hotel doorman and Clara Bow." Movie ads promised kisses "where heart, and soul, and sense in concert move, and the blood is lava, and the pulse a blaze."

Threatened by censorship bills in thirty-six states, the industry made a gesture toward reforming itself. Following the model of organized baseball, which had made Judge Kenesaw Mountain Landis its "czar" after the Chicago Black Sox scandal of 1919, the movie industry hired Harding's Postmaster-General, Will Hays, to be the "Judge Landis of the movies." All the Hays Office succeeded in doing in the 1920's was to add hypocrisy to sex by insisting on false moralizations and the "moral" ending. Movie ads continued to entice patrons with "brilliant men, beautiful jazz babies, champagne baths, midnight revels, petting parties in the purple dawn, all ending in one terrific smashing climax that makes you gasp."

Taboos about sex discussion were lifted; women talked freely about inhibitions and "sex starvation." Speech became bolder, and men and women told one another off-color stories that a short while before would have been reserved for the Pullman smoker. Novelists and playwrights spoke with a new bluntness; in Hemingway's *The Sun Also Rises* (1926), the word "bitch" recurs frequently. The woman who once was shocked by everything now prided herself, observed a writer in *Harper's*, on the fact that nothing at all shocked her; "immunity to the sensation of 'recoil with painful astonishment' is the mark of our civilization."

Parental control of sex was greatly lessened; the chaperone vanished at dances, and there was no room for a duenna in the rumble seat of an automobile. The bachelor girl had her own latchkey. Girls petted, and when they did not pet, they necked, and no one was certain of the exact difference; Lloyd Morris observed: "The word 'neck' ceased to be a noun; abruptly became a verb; immediately lost all anatomical precision." At one conference in the Midwest, eight hundred college girls met to discuss petting, to deal with searching questions like What do nice girls do? and How far should you go? "Whether or not they pet," said one writer, "they hesitate to have anyone believe that they do not." The consensus of the delegates was: "Learn temperance in petting, not abstinence."

Victorian dance forms like the waltz yielded to the fast-stepping Charleston, the Black Bottom, or slow fox trots in which, to the syncopated rhythms of the jazz band, there was a "maximum of motion in the minimum of space." Jazz made its way northward from the bordellos of New Orleans to the dance halls of Chicago during these years, crossed the ocean to Paris (where it was instantly taken up as a uniquely American contribution to music), and created its own folk heroes in the lyrical Bix Beiderbecke and the dynamic Louis Armstrong who, legend has it, once played two hundred different choruses of "Sweet Sue." The tango and the fox trot

The Revolution in Morals

hit the country before the war, but it was not until the 1920's that the more voluptuous and the more frenetic dance crazes swept the nation. Moralists like Bishop Cannon protested that the new dances brought "the bodies of men and women in unusual relations to each other"; but by the end of the period the fox trot was as popular and the saxophones wailed as loudly at the high-school dances of the Bishop's Methodist parishioners as in the dance halls of New York and Los Angeles.

What did it all add up to? Lord Birkenhead, the British Lord High Chancellor, observed in 1928: "The proportion of frail to virtuous women is probably constant throughout the ages in any civilization." Perhaps, but the meager evidence suggests otherwise. There appears to have been an increase in promiscuity, especially in sexual experience before marriage for middle-class women; there was probably an increase in extramarital experience as well. With effective contraceptive techniques widely used, the fear of pregnancy was greatly lessened. ("The veriest schoolgirl today knows as much as the midwife of 1885," wrote Mencken.) At the same time, quite possibly as a consequence, a great many brothels lost their customers and had to close their doors, while itinerant workers in the same field disappeared from the sidewalks. The degree of sexual experimentation in the 1920's has certainly been exaggerated, but there is a good deal to bear out Alexander Pope's aphorism that "every woman is at heart a rake."

Not only the American woman but the American girl was reputed to be freer with her sexual favors than she had ever been before, although serious periodicals published learned debates over whether this was fact or fiction. The flapper had as many defenders as accusers on this score, but no one doubted that every campus had its Jezebels. Smith College girls in New York, noted Malcolm Cowley, modeled themselves on Hemingway's Lady Brett. Certainly, girls were less reticent than they had been before the war. "One hears it said," lamented a Southern Baptist periodical, "that the girls are actually tempting the boys more than the boys do the girls, by their dress and conversation." They dressed more freely; they wore bathing suits which revealed more than had ever been revealed before. At dances, corsets were checked in cloakrooms; then even this pretense was abandoned. Above all, they were out for a good time. "None of the Victorian mothers," wrote F. Scott Fitzgerald in *This Side of Paradise*, "had any idea how casually their daughters were accustomed to be kissed."

Although Fitzgerald reported that the ideal flapper was "lovely and expensive and about nineteen," the flapper appeared bent on playing down her femininity and emphasizing her boyishness. She used the most ingenious devices to conceal the fact that she had breasts. Even the nudes at the Folies Bergères were flatchested and were picked for that reason, and in England, women wore the "Eton crop" and bound their chests with wide strips of ribbon to achieve a "boyish bust." The flapper wore dresses that suggested she had no hips at all; her waistline moved steadily southward. As one writer recalled, "Women not only lost their waists; they sat on them." She dieted recklessly in an effort to remove unwanted protuberances. Girls, noted Dr. Charles F. Pabst, were attempting to become "pathologically thin." "A strikingly sad example of improper dieting," he said, "was the case of a shapely motion-picture actress, who became a nervous wreck and blasted her career by restricting herself to tomatoes, spinach and orange juice." The flapper bobbed her hair and dyed it raven black. She concealed everything feminine but her matchstick legs. In 1919 her skirt was six inches above the ground; by 1927 it had edged about to her knees. The well-accoutered flapper wore a tight felt hat, two strings of beads, bangles on her wrists, flesh-colored stockings rolled below the knees, and unbuckled galoshes. Ironically, the more she adopted mannish styles, the more she painted her face, daubing her cheeks with two circles of rouge and her lips with "kissproof" lipstick; cosmetics became the chief way of distinguishing feminine members of the race.

The vogue of the flapper was only the most obvious instance of the new American cult of youth. "It is the glory of the present age that in it one can be young," Randolph Bourne wrote in 1913. In every age, youth has a sense of a separate destiny, of experiencing what no one has ever experienced before, but it may be doubted that there was ever a time in American history when youth had such a special sense of importance as in the years after World War I. There was a break between generations like a geological fault; young men who had fought in the trenches felt that they knew a reality their elders could not even imagine. Young girls no longer consciously modeled themselves on their mothers, whose experience seemed unusable in the 1920's.

Instead of youth modeling itself on age, age imitated youth. Scott Fitzgerald, looking back on the years of which he was the chief chronicler, recalled: "May one offer in exhibit the year 1922! That was the peak of the younger generation, for though the Jazz Age continued, it became less and less an affair of youth. The sequel was a children's party taken over by elders." "Oh, yes, we are collegiate" was the theme song of a generation yearning for the irresponsible, idealized days of youth. Everyone wanted to be young. Mrs. Gertrude Atherton's *Black Oxen* (1923) described how grandmothers might be rejuvenated through a glandular operation and once more stir up young men. It was the young girl who started the flapper ideal; it was her mother who kept it going.

Americans in the 1920's, at least on the surface, were less sinridden and more self-indulgent than they had ever been before. They broke the Sabbath apparently without compunction, missing the morning sermon to play golf, driving into the country in the afternoon instead of sitting stiffly in the parlor. The mood of the country was hedonistic; Omar Khayyam's quatrains took the colleges by storm. The ideal of hedonism was living for the moment, and if one can isolate a single spirit which permeated every segment of society in the postwar years, it was the obliteration of time.

Abandoning the notion of saving income or goods or capital over time, the country insisted on immediate consumption, a demand which became institutionalized in the installment plan. The President's Research Committee on Social Trends noted "the new attitude towards hardship as a thing to be avoided by living in the here and now, utilizing instalment credit and other devices to telescope the future into the present." Songs became obsolescent almost as soon as they appeared, and people prided themselves not on remembering the old songs but on knowing the latest. The imitation of youth by age was an effort to telescope the years, while youth itself tried to escape the inexorability of time. One of the younger generation, replying to its critics, observed: "The trouble with them is that they can't seem to realize that we are busy, that what pleasure we snatch must be incidental and feverishly hurried. We have to make the most of our time. . . . We must gather rose-buds while we may."

In the magazine *Secession*, a group of intellectuals, including Hart Crane, Kay Boyle, and Elliot Paul, signed a "Proclamation" declaring "Time is a tyranny to be abolished." Gertrude Stein's concept of a "continuous present" effaced not merely history and tradition but any sense of "time." "The future," she declared, "is not important any more." In Italy, the Futurists had cast out Petrarch and Dante and rejected harmony and sentiment; their present-mindedness had a direct impact on Ezra Pound, who found their chief spokesman, Marinetti, "thoroughly simpatico." The characters in the novels of the day, particularly those of Scott Fitzgerald, lived only for the moment, while Edna St. Vincent Millay penned the theme of the generation in "My candle burns at both ends." The spirit of hedonism of the decade, wrote Edmund Wilson, was "letting oneself be carried along by the mad hilarity and heartbreak of jazz, living only for the excitement of the evening."

The obliteration of time carried with it a conscious assault on the authority of history. The Dada movement, which developed in the war years in Zurich, adopted as its motto: "Je ne veux même pas savoir s'il y a eu des hommes avant moi" ("I do not wish even to know whether there have been men before me"). More remarkably, the very men who were the spokesmen for history and tradition led the onslaught; in this, Henry Ford and Charles Beard were one. Ford's interest in history was actually an anti-history. He took cottages in which Noah Webster and Patrick Henry had once lived and moved them to Dearborn, Michigan, where they had no meaning. He sentimentalized and pillaged the past, but he had no respect for it. "History is more or less the bunk," he said. "We want to live in the present, and the only history that is worth a tinker's dam is the history we make today." As early as 1907, the historians Charles Beard and James Harvey Robinson had deliberately attempted to subordinate the past to the present with the aim of enabling the reader "to catch up with his own times; . . . to know what was the attitude of Leo XIII toward the Social Democrats even if he has forgotten that of Innocent III toward the Albigenses." Beard's emphasis on current history had its counterpart in Veblen's dislike for dead languages, Holmes's skepticism about the value of learning as a guide in jurisprudence, and Dewey's emphasis on the functional in education.

The revolution in morals routed the worst of Victorian sentimentality and false modesty. It mitigated the harsh moral judgments of rural Protestantism, and it all but wiped out the awful combination of sanctimoniousness and lewdness which enabled Anthony Comstock to defame Bernard Shaw as "this Irish smut-dealer" and which allowed Teddy Roosevelt, with unconscious humor, to denounce the Mexican bandit Villa as a "murderer and a bigamist." It greatly extended the range of choice; "the conduct of life," wrote Joseph Wood Krutch, had been made "more thrillingly difficult." Yet, at the same time, it raised baffling problems of the relations between husband and wife, parent and child, and, in itself, provided no ready guides to conduct. The hedonism of the period was less a solution than a pathological symptom of what Walter Lippmann called a "vast dissolution of ancient habits," and it rarely proved as satisfying as people hoped. "Sons and daughters of the puritans, the artists and writers and utopians who flocked to Greenwich Village to find a frank and free life for the emotions and senses, felt at their backs the icy breath of the monster they were escaping," wrote Joseph Freeman. "Because they could not abandon themselves to pleasure without a sense of guilt, they exaggerated the importance of pleasure, idealized it and even sanctified it."

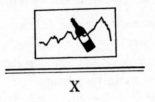

X

The Second Industrial Revolution

In the late eighteenth and early nineteenth centuries the industrialization of England accelerated at such a pace that historians have found no term adequate to describe it save one usually reserved for violent political change—revolution. In the late nineteenth century and early twentieth century the productive capacity of the American economy increased at a rate greater than that of the Industrial Revolution. After World War I, the United States, reaping the harvest of half a century of industrial progress, achieved the highest standard of living any people had ever known. National income soared from $480 per capita in 1900 to $681 in 1929. Workers were paid the highest wages of any time in the history of the country; essentially unchanged from 1890 to 1918, the real earnings of workers—what their income actually would buy at the store—shot up at an astonishing rate in the 1920's. At the same time, the number of hours of work was cut: in 1923 United States Steel abandoned the twelve-hour day and put its Gary plant on an eight-hour shift; in 1926 Henry Ford instituted the five-day week, while International Harvester announced the electrifying innovation of a two-week annual vacation with pay for its employees.

In 1922 the country, already enormously productive by comparison with other countries, started a recovery from the postwar depression—a recovery that maintained prosperity, with slight interruptions, until the fall of 1929. The key to the piping prosperity of the decade was the enormous increase in efficiency of production, in part the result of the application of Frederick W. Taylor's theory of scientific management, in part the outgrowth of technological innovations. In 1914 at his Highland Park plant Henry Ford had revolutionized industrial production by installing the first moving assembly line with an endless-chain conveyor; three months later his men assembled an automobile, down to its smallest parts, in 93 minutes. A year before it had taken 14 hours. During these same years, machine power replaced human labor at a startling rate: in 1914, 30 per cent of industry was electrified, in 1929, 70 per cent. The electric motor made the steam engine obsolete; between 1919 and 1927 more than 44 per cent of the steam engines in the United States went to the scrap heap. Since labor came out of the postwar depression with higher real wages—employers feared a new strike wave if they cut wages as sharply as prices fell—business was stimulated to lower production costs. With more efficient management, greater mechanization, intensive research, and ingenious sales methods, industrial production almost doubled during the decade, soaring from an index figure of 58 in the depression year of 1921 to 110 in 1929 (1933–39 = 100). This impressive increase in productivity was achieved without any expansion of the labor force. Manufacturing employed precisely the same number of men in 1929 as it had in 1919. The summit of technological achievement was reached on October 31, 1925, when Ford rolled a completed automobile off his assembly line every ten seconds.

The physical output of American industry increased tremendously. Between 1899 and 1929 the total output of manufacturing jumped 264 per cent. Petroleum products—new oil fields were discovered in Texas, Oklahoma, and California—multiplied more than sixteen times in this period, the basic iron and steel industry five times. The number of telephones installed grew from 1,355,000 in 1900 to 10,525,000 in 1915 to 20,200,000 in 1930. Most impressive was the growth of new industries, some of which did not even exist in 1914. Light metals like aluminum and magnesium experienced a meteoric rise; the output of aluminum more than doubled between 1914 and 1920. American factories turned out a host of new products—cigarette lighters, oil furnaces, wrist watches, antifreeze fluids, reinforced concrete, paint sprayers, book matches, dry ice, Pyrex glass for cooking utensils, and panchromatic motion-picture film.

Many of the new industries were geared to the American home. The American consumed a more varied diet than he ever had before. He thought it commonplace to have fresh fruit and vegetables in midwinter—Louisiana cherries and Arizona melons, Carolina peas and Alabama corn. In 1905, 41 million cases of food were shipped, in 1930, 200 million. Fresh green vegetables, many of them novelties, arrived in northern markets; shipments of lettuce grew from 13,800 carloads in 1920 to 51,500 in 1928, spinach from 2,900 in 1920 to 10,600 in 1927. As people moved into city apartments with kitchenettes, they gave a new spur to the canning industry. Canned fruits and vegetables more than doubled between 1914 and

The Second Industrial Revolution

1929; canned milk almost trebled. In many city homes the family sat down to a meal that started with canned soup, proceeded to canned meat and vegetables, and ended with canned peaches.

The chemicals industry, which started in the 1880's, was enormously stimulated by World War I. The war demonstrated how dependent the country was on foreign supplies of potash, nitrates, and dyes. Potash, essential for fertilizers, had come almost entirely from Germany before the war. When supplies were cut off, prices increased ten times, and this encouraged the creation of a domestic potash industry. When the United States could not import German indigo, the Dow Chemical Company's infant industry spurted. The government contributed more to the development of the chemicals industry than to any other industry. It confiscated German dye patents during the war and turned them over to American firms; it advanced nitrogen development by constructing a plant at Muscle Shoals in the Tennessee Valley and by operating a Fixed Nitrogen Research Laboratory in the War Department; and it gave high tariff protection to domestic chemicals and dyes.

The war also sparked the development of the new synthetics industry. Thousands of by-product ovens were built to produce coke needed in manufacturing explosives; after the war these ovens were used in the production of synthetic chemicals, especially of plastics. Synthetic plastics had been developed as early as 1869, with the creation of celluloid, but it was not until the postwar years that synthetic fibers and plastics became an important industry. The output of rayon, which transformed the textile business, multiplied sixty-nine times between 1914 and 1931. Bakelite, which was developed before the war, proved of enormous importance in the electrical and radio industries. In 1923, lacquers were introduced; easier to apply than paint, giving better protection and offering a wider range of colors, the quick-drying lacquers reduced the time needed to finish an automobile from twenty-six days to a matter of hours. In 1924, Du Pont established a "cellophane" plant in Buffalo; used to wrap everything from bacon to cigarettes, cellophane at least doubled its sales every year for the rest of the decade. In 1925, a Swiss chemist, who had been invited to America by the government during World War I to build a cellulose nitrate plant, placed "celanese" on the market; an artificial silk superior to rayon, celanese was an important step in the development of synthetic textiles. Scientific geniuses like George Washington Carver found new industrial uses for farm products, many of them surplus crops which were glutting the market. From peanuts, Carver extracted everything from shaving lotion to axle grease; from sweet potatoes, he got shoe-blacking, library paste, and synthetic tapioca.

The most important element in the prosperity of the 1920's was the increase in construction, in part because building had been halted during the war, in part to meet the drift from country to city and from city to suburbs. During the decade, New York got a brand new skyline. European travelers who in 1910 had been awed by 20-story skyscrapers returned in 1930 to find them dwarfed by new giants; some of the old structures had even been demolished to make way for 60-story buildings. The Grand Central section of Manhattan was almost entirely rebuilt; Fifth Avenue resounded with the staccato of riveters and the sharp clash of steel beams. High above the city streets, helmeted workers balanced themselves on girders; beneath them, men operated mammoth cranes or turned huge drums of concrete. Taller and taller the buildings soared; toward the end of the decade a race to erect the loftiest skyscraper became a fascinating new outdoor sport. On May 1, 1931, the race ended when the Empire State Building climbed past the Bank of Manhattan's 71 stories and the Chrysler Building's 77 stories. Built in less than a year, the 86-story Empire State Building, topped by a graceful mast, was the tallest building in the world.

What New York had, every interior city had to have too, and those on the prairies erected their own towers. Cities the size of Beaumont, Memphis, and Syracuse boasted buildings of at least 21 stories. Tulsa and Oklahoma City, which did not even exist when the first skyscraper was built, had skylines by the end of the decade. Cleveland pointed proudly to its 52-story Terminal Tower, Houston to its Petroleum Building, Chicago to its Tribune Tower. The skyscraper was as certain an expression of the ebullient American spirit as the Gothic cathedral was of medieval Europe. Denounced by many American critics as a vulgar evidence of commercialism and an indiscriminate passion for bigness, the skyline was recognized by European observers for what it was—a radiant, defiant display of American energy and optimism. Too often banal in conception, the skyscraper was at its best—as in Raymond Hood's News Building in New York—a symmetrical rectangle of stark beauty.

Outside the great cities, construction went on at an even faster rate, as people fanned out into the suburbs. The borough of Queens, across the East River from Manhattan, doubled its population in the 1920's. Grosse Point Park near Detroit grew 700 per cent, Shaker Heights outside Cleveland

1,000 per cent, and the movie colony of Beverly Hills 2,500 per cent. Save for California, the greatest real estate boom in the country took place in Florida. Flivvers with northern license plates clogged Miami's Flagler Avenue in the 1920's; not only the man of wealth, who headed for Palm Beach or Boca Raton, but the man of moderate income decided to winter in Florida. "Realtors" converted swamps into Venetian lagoons, and much of the population of Florida was engaged in selling lots. In Coral Gables a real estate man hired William Jennings Bryan to sit on a raft under a beach umbrella and lecture on the beauties of Florida climate; Bryan was followed with dancing by Gilda Gray. The land-speculation mania in Florida reached its high point one day in the summer of 1925 when the Miami *Daily News*, crowded with real estate advertisements, printed an issue of 504 pages, the largest in newspaper history. In 1926, after a hurricane had driven the waters of Biscayne Bay over the cottages of Miami, the land boom collapsed. But still the resorts were strung from Jacksonville to Key West. Miami, once a mangrove swamp, grew 400 per cent in the decade.

The construction of roads and highways poured fresh public funds into the economy. While Secretary Mellon endeavored to cut back federal spending, state and local governments stepped up spending at a rate which more than offset the Mellon program of deflation. Construction programs for highways and buildings employed more men and spent more money than any single private industry. In 1914, there were almost no good roads outside of the East, and crossing the continent was an adventure. Automobiles sank to their hubs in gumbo muds; travelers crossing Iowa were often forced to wait several days until the roads dried before moving onto the next town. Perhaps because cars were viewed as pleasure vehicles, parsimonious state legislatures were reluctant to vote public funds to improve roads.

The Federal Aid Road Act of 1916 offered federal funds to states which would organize highway departments and match federal grants. Spurred by federal initiative, every section of the country launched ambitious road-building programs in the postwar years. In 1906, local governments appropriated 96 per cent of all highway funds; by 1927, they were providing only 53 per cent, while the states spent 37 per cent, and the federal government 10 per cent. Florida built the Tamiami Trail through the swamps of the Everglades; Arizona constructed a road across the desert west of Phoenix; Utah laid a highway over a sea of mud, a relic of ancient Lake Bonneville, near the Nevada line; and in Massachusetts the magnificent Mohawk Trail climbed the Hoosac Range. New York pioneered with the construction of the beautiful Bronx River Parkway which curved its way out of New York City northward through the Westchester countryside. By 1928, the tourist could drive from New York as far west as St. Mary's, Kansas, on paved highways, but it was still not advisable to drive down the Santa Fé Trail southwest of St. Louis in the rainy season, and mountain passes west of Salt Lake City were seldom passable during the winter or early spring.

Without the new automobile industry, the prosperity of the Roaring Twenties would scarcely have been possible; the development of the industry in a single generation was the greatest achievement of modern technology. As recently as 1900, Vermont had enforced a law requiring every motorist to employ "a person of mature age" to walk one-eighth of a mile ahead of him bearing a red flag. That year there was not a single filling station in all the country. In 1902, San Francisco, Cincinnati, and Savannah still maintained speed limits of eight miles an hour. While lawmakers were attempting to keep pace with technology, an enormous change took place within the industry. Ransom Olds started mass production in automobiles; Henry Leland demonstrated that cars could be made with interchangeable parts; and Henry Ford quickly took over both principles and carried them to lengths that left his competitors far behind.

The production of automobiles soared almost at a geometric rate, and the auto industry gave a shot in the arm to the whole economy. In 1900, there had been an annual output of 4,000 cars; by 1929, 4,800,000 automobiles were being produced in a single year, and Americans were driving more than 26 million autos and trucks. In the United States, there was one automobile to each five persons—almost one car per family—as compared to one car to 43 persons in Britain, one to 325 in Italy, one to 7,000 in Russia. In America, the possession of an automobile was not, as in Europe, a class privilege. The auto industry was the most important purchaser of rubber, plate glass, nickel and lead; it bought 15 per cent of the steel output of the nation and spurred the petroleum industry to a tremendous expansion. There was scarcely a corner of the American economy which the automobile industry did not touch; it stimulated public spending for good roads, extended the housing boom into the suburbs, and created dozens of new small enterprises from hotdog stands to billboards.

Detroit became the Mecca of the modern world and Ford its prophet. Russian and German scholars talked reverently of "Fordismus," and industrial missions came from all over

The Second Industrial Revolution

the world to study American techniques. "Just as in Rome one goes to the Vatican and endeavours to get audience of the Pope," wrote one British traveler, "so in Detroit one goes to the Ford Works and endeavours to see Henry Ford." "As I caught my first glimpse of Detroit," recorded another Briton, "I felt as I imagine a Seventeenth Century traveller must have felt when he approached Versailles." Ford was worshiped as a miracle-maker: a group of college students voted the Flivver King the third greatest figure of all time, surpassed only by Napoleon and Christ. When Ford announced the Model A early in 1928, 500,000 people made down payments without having seen the car and without knowing the price.

Ford personified the farmboy-mechanic who in a single lifetime reached the top. He fulfilled the dream of an acquisitive society committed to a belief in individual advancement. He brought the automobile to the masses of the world; he was the magical tinkerer who revolutionized human life. He was the high priest of mass production, which people the world over saw as more important than any ideological doctrine as a solution to the curse of poverty. His firm was family-owned; he was hostile to Wall Street; he founded, so it was believed, the doctrine of high wages and low prices, of sharing the benefits of his genius with the world—he was, in short, the Good Businessman. He resolved the moral dilemma of a Puritan-capitalist society. He achieved material success without losing his primal innocence.

"Machinery," declared Ford solemnly, "is the new Messiah." Dazzled by the prosperity of the time and by the endless stream of new gadgets, the American people raised business in the 1920's into a national religion and paid respectful homage to the businessman as the prophet of heaven on earth. As government looked only to the single interest of business, so society gave to the businessman social pre-eminence. There was no social class in America to challenge the business class. To call a scientist or a preacher or a professor or a doctor a good businessman was to pay him the most fulsome of compliments, for the chief index of a man's worth was his income. "Brains," declared Coolidge, "are wealth and wealth is the chief end of man." The opinions of a man like Ford, who believed in reincarnation, hated Jews, doctors, Catholics, and bankers, and abominated tobacco (it was "bad for the bowels"), were listened to with reverent respect, not only when he spoke on business matters but also when he made pronouncements on culture and public morals. "The man who builds a factory builds a temple," observed Coolidge, "the man who works there worships there."

Americans had less interest in a hereafter than in salvation on earth. Material comfort became not a means to an end but the final end of life itself. People continued to go to church, but church rituals were accepted less with reverence than with politeness. The functions of the church were gradually replaced by institutions committed to the ideal of service, to "organized altruism." Forced to accommodate themselves, the churches stressed not the divinity but the humanity of Christ. Churches installed swimming pools, game rooms, and gymnasiums with, as one foreign visitor noticed, "the oxygen of good fellowship" permeating everything. When a British journalist visited one American church, its young preacher invited him to "come and inspect his plant."

The classic statement of the secularization of religion and the religiosity of business was Bruce Barton's *The Man No-*

The Second Industrial Revolution

body Knows, a best seller in 1925 and 1926. Barton praised Jesus handsomely as a topnotch businessman. "He picked up twelve men from the bottom ranks of business and forged them into an organization that conquered the world." Jesus was an A-1 salesman, and the parables were "the most powerful advertisements of all time." No one need doubt that business was the main focus of His concern. Why, Jesus Himself had said: "Wist ye not that I must be about my father's business?"

Religion was valued not as a path to personal salvation or a key to the riddles of the universe but because it paid off in dollars and cents. The dean of the University of Chicago Divinity School told a reporter that a man could make more money if he prayed about his business. Reading the Bible, explained another writer, meant money in your pocket. Insurance men were advised that Exodus offered good tips on risk and liability, while a Chicago bond salesman confided that he had boosted his income by drawing arguments from Ezekiel. "Of all the Plenipotentiaries of Publicity, Ambassadors of Advertising and Bosses of Press Bureaus, none equals Moses," said Elbert Hubbard, for it was Moses who "appointed himself ad-writer for Deity." Taught to write advertising copy for their churches, pastors billed their sermons under captions like "Solomon, a Six-Cylinder Sport." Sermons were entitled after a popular cigarette slogan, "They Satisfy," or after a flour advertisement, "Eventually, Why Not Now?" (an appeal for conversion), or "Three-in-One Oil" (the Trinity).

Encouraged by the friendly disposition of the federal government, the concentration of industry stepped up sharply in the postwar years. Although the merger movement had reached its apex before the war, it found new areas like the utilities in the 1920's. Most mergers brought together not competitive firms but companies engaged in the same business in different cities. Between 1919 and 1930, 8,000 businesses disappeared. "So long as I am Attorney General," explained Harry Daugherty, "I am not going unnecessarily to harass men who have unwittingly run counter with the statutes." Despite Daugherty's intentions, the Federal Trade Commission occasionally proved obstreperous and interceded to block consolidations and discourage trade associations. When in 1925 Coolidge appointed the lumber attorney William E. Humphrey to the chairmanship of the commission, large-business interests moved into control of the FTC. Humphrey himself denounced the FTC as "an instrument of oppression and disturbance and injury instead of help to business" and a "publicity bureau to spread socialistic propaganda." After Humphrey's accession, the commission approved trade associations and smiled on business agreements to lessen "cutthroat" competition.

Few businesses grew as rapidly as the electric light and power industry—the chief field for mergers in the 1920's. Between 1902 and 1929, the output of electric power multiplied more than 19 times—from 6 billion kilowatt-hours to 117 billion. Almost as much new hydroelectric power was developed between 1920 and 1930 as in all the years before 1920. As local electric light and power companies, which once served a single town, were interconnected in vast regional grids, financiers used the holding-company device to merge small firms into great utility empires. Between 1919 and 1927 over 3,700 utility companies vanished. Promoters organized a group of utility giants starting with the United Light and Power Company and the American Superpower Corporation in 1923 and ending with the Niagara Hudson Company and the Commonwealth and Southern Corporation in 1929. By 1930 ten holding-company groups controlled 72 per cent of the country's electric power.

The most spectacular of the new utility titans was Samuel Insull. Starting as an office boy in London at five shillings a week, Insull rose to the top of a holding-company empire which controlled gas and electric companies in twenty-three states. Operating out of Chicago, he extended his domain over businesses as remote as the Androscoggin Electric Company in Maine and the Tidewater Power Company in North Carolina. Chairman of the board of sixty-five different firms, Insull was involved in business operations in almost every conceivable field, from Mexican irrigation projects to the pathetic attempt to make Port Isabel, Texas, "the Venus of the South." His dairy herd, bathed in ultra-violet rays, was surrounded by electric screens that electrocuted flies. Respected as a philanthropist and a patron of the arts, he built the Chicago Civic Opera an ornate skyscraper opera house. An intimate of mayors and senators, he was accused of buying political influence and suborning public officials.

The merger movement accelerated rapidly in American banking. The large banks swallowed the little banks or established branch banks which took away their business. In 1920, there were 1,280 branch banks; in 1930, 3,516. The greatest of the branch bankers was a newcomer, Amadeo Peter Giannini, who developed a chain of 500 banks throughout the state of California under a single holding company. His Bank of America National Trust and Savings Association in San Francisco became the fourth largest bank in the country, larger than any bank outside New York. In Manhattan, the National City Bank took over the Farmers Loan & Trust Company; the Guaranty Trust amalgamated with the Bank of Commerce; and the Chase National absorbed the Equitable Trust Company. By 1929, 1 per cent of the banks in the country controlled over 46 per cent of the banking resources of the nation.

Chain stores grew enormously in the postwar years. Chain-store units rose from 29,000 in 1918 to 160,000 in 1929; between 1919 and 1927 their sales jumped 124 per cent in drugstores, 287 per cent in groceries, and 425 per cent in the clothing business. The Great Atlantic and Pacific Tea Company's chain of red-fronted grocery stores grew from 400 in 1912 to 15,500 in 1932. By the end of the period, the A & P was selling a greater volume of goods than Ford at his peak; its billion dollar a year grocery business accounted for one-tenth of all food sold at retail in the United States. In these same years, the Woolworth "five and tens" crowded out many old neighborhood notion stores; for a dime or less, the customer could buy everything from Venetian Night Incense to Mammoth Tulip Sundaes, Hebrew New Year cards to poker chips, gumdrops to French Guiana stamps. A mammoth holding company, Drug, Incorporated, owned 10,000 Rexall drugstores and 706 Liggett stores, as well as the Owl chain on the Pacific Coast, and owned huge drug companies like Vick Chemical, Bayer Aspirin, and Bristol-Myers. By 1932, chain stores accounted for 22 per cent of the retail trade in Baltimore, 31 per cent in Atlanta, 37 per cent in Chicago. In some places the independent grocery store of 1914 had almost disappeared; Philadelphia bought two-thirds of its food in chain stores.

By the end of the decade the consolidation movement in

The Second Industrial Revolution

American business reached boom proportions. In 1919, there were 80 bank mergers, in 1927, 259. In 1928, the Chrysler Corporation took over Dodge Brothers, Postum Company amalgamated with Maxwell House Coffee, and Colgate merged with Palmolive-Peet. Two advertising agencies combined to form the wonderfully sonorous firm of Batten, Barton, Durstine & Osborn. By 1929, the 200 largest non-financial corporations in America owned nearly half the corporate wealth of the nation, and they were growing much faster than smaller businesses. From 1924 to 1928, their assets expanded three times as fast as those of smaller corporations. Four meat packers controlled 70 per cent of the production in their industry; four tobacco companies accounted for 94 per cent of the output of cigarettes.

Many industries—textiles, clothing, and bituminous coal, in particular—remained boisterously competitive, however. The growth of oligopoly—domination of an industry by a few firms—often meant more rather than less competition. Although consolidation accelerated in the 1920's, there was not as much actual monopoly—that is, domination of an industry by only one company. No longer did a single firm lord it over the steel or the oil industries. Although the chain-store movement spelled national consolidation, it also destroyed the monopoly of the merchant in the small American town.

The benefits of technological innovation were by no means evenly distributed. While workers' income went up 11 per cent from 1923 to 1929, corporate profits rocketed 62 per cent and dividends 65 per cent. Despite the high productivity of the period, there was a disturbing amount of unemployment. Factory workers in "sick" industries like coal, leather, and textiles saw little of the boom prosperity. The Loray Mill in Gastonia, North Carolina, site of a bloody strike in 1928, paid its workers that year a weekly wage of $18 to men and $9 to women for working a 70-hour week. At the height of Coolidge prosperity, the secretary of the Gastonia Chamber of Commerce boasted that children of fourteen were permitted to work only 11 hours a day. Perhaps as many as two million boys and girls under fifteen continued to work in textile mills, cranberry bogs, and beet fields. In 1929, 71 per cent of American families had incomes under $2,500, generally thought to be the minimum standard for a decent living. The 36,000 wealthiest families in the United States received as much income as the 12,000,000 American families —42 per cent of all those in America—who received under $1,500 a year.

Yet, if one focuses exclusively on farm poverty or on depressed West Virginia coal towns, it is easy to get a distorted picture of life in the 1920's. As Henry May writes, "Sometimes even prosperity—an important fact despite its exceptions—is belittled almost out of existence." If prosperity was by no means as pervasive as Chamber of Commerce publicists claimed, it was still widespread enough to change markedly the life of millions of Americans. The change resulted less from a considerable increase in income for the average American—by later standards the increase does not seem so impressive—than from the fact that Americans could buy things with their paychecks that they had never been able to get before.

People could get into their automobile—almost everyone owned a car—and drive into the country or visit neighbors in the next town. For the first time, they saw America, taking trips to distant campsites or historic shrines and most of all discovering the glories of California and Florida. Electricity —all but farm homes had it by the end of the decade—meant not only electric lights but also a wide range of electric appliances. Women could buy vacuum cleaners and washing machines, toasters and electric sewing machines; in 1921, the production of refrigerators was only 0.6 per cent of what it was to be in 1929. Women of all classes wore clothing luxuries. They discarded cotton stockings and underwear for silk and rayon (in 1900, 12,000 pairs of silk stockings were sold, in 1930, 300 million), and the American woman became known as "America's greatest fur-bearing animal."

On week ends Americans went to the ballpark. Organized sport in America had captivated the country for decades, but it was not until the 1920's that spectator sports took on a central role in American life. In the Cathedral of St. John the Divine in New York, a bay was built with windows depicting various sports. On July 2, 1921, 91,000 fans at Boyles' Thirty Acres in Jersey City paid more than a million dollars to watch Jack Dempsey fight "gorgeous" Georges Carpentier. Dempsey knocked him out in the fourth round, but more important, the country had seen the first "million dollar gate." It was the Golden Age of Sports—of Babe Ruth, Bobby Jones, and Bill Tilden. It was the era of the Dempsey-Tunney fight, the decade when Ruth hit sixty home runs in a season. The biggest change took place in college football. People who had never been near a college crowded the vast new college stadiums to cheer the Four Horsemen of Notre Dame or the Galloping Ghost of Illinois. On one memorable fall afternoon in Urbana, Harold "Red" Grange scored four touchdowns against Michigan in the first twelve minutes of the game. By the end of the 1920's college football had become a major industry, with gate receipts each year of over $21 million.

People could walk down to the neighborhood theater and see the latest movie. Already flourishing before the war, motion pictures after the war became one of the ten great industries of the country, with an invested capital of a billion and a half dollars. In 1922, movie theaters sold 40 million tickets every week; by 1930, the average weekly attendance was 100 million. The faces of Charlie Chaplin and Harold Lloyd were known in every corner of the globe, and "youngsters playing in the back streets of Hull or Newcastle," noted one British writer, "threatened one another with *the works*." Every respectable American town had its own movie palace. The movie houses became the temples of a secular society. In New York, Roxy's called itself "The Cathedral of the Motion Picture," the Capitol described itself as "The Theater with a Soul," and the Fifty-Fifth Street Theater advertised itself as "The Sanctuary of the Cinema."

Even more intriguing was the new invention of radio. There are many claimants to the honor of being the first station, but radio really arrived on the night of November 2, 1920, when KDKA at East Pittsburgh broadcast the presidential election returns. By 1922 there were radios in three million homes; that year the sale of sets was already a $60 million a year industry. Seven years later $852 million worth of radio sets were sold. Men bought cone-speakers and amplifiers and talked endlessly about how to eliminate static. They introduced a whole new vocabulary and within a few months used the terms—"tune in," "network," "airwaves"—so casually that the words lost their gloss of technological novelty. People clamped on earphones to hear Roxy and His Gang, the

The Second Industrial Revolution

Clicquot Club Eskimos, the Ipana Troubadours or the A & P Gypsies. Grantland Rice broadcast the World Series, Floyd Gibbons narrated the news with a machine-gun staccato, and Rudy Vallee warbled the latest songs. From speakers in homes all over America came the sound of the ubiquitous ukelele.

Within a decade the radio and the movie nationalized American popular culture, projecting the same performers and the same stereotypes in every section of the country. In movie theaters everywhere, when olive-skinned Rudolph Valentino carried an impeccably blonde heroine across the burning Sahara and flung her into his tent, women swooned. Men scoffed at the Valentino craze, but barbers reported that men who once had called for bay rum now demanded pomades to make their hair sleek. There was even something of a vogue of sideburns, while dance schools offering the tango did a flourishing business. Endless interviews with Valentino appeared in national periodicals, including one with the inevitable title, "I'm Tired of Being a Sheik."

In the fall of 1929 two former vaudevillians, Freeman Gosden and Charles Correll, began a radio comic strip called "Amos 'n Andy." Within a few months the two blackface comedians, broadcasting over the N.B.C. network, had taken the country by storm. Many people refused to answer their telephone while the program was on the air. Movie theaters in smaller cities were forced to interrupt their show and turn on the broadcast; if they did not, they knew they would lose most of their patrons until the program was over. Millions of Americans followed avidly the affairs of the Fresh Air Taxicab Company, and Madame Queen and the Kingfish became household words. One man inserted an advertisement in a newspaper to ask his friends not to disturb him while the program was being broadcast. Senator Borah referred to Amos and Andy in a debate on the Philippines.

As the country solved the problems of production, greater emphasis was placed on distribution; the old-style manufacturer and tycoon became less important than the salesman and the promoter. In the 1920's the advertising man and the public relations expert came into their own. To staff the agencies of distribution and the "service" industries, a new white-collar class developed in the cities. Together with the civil servant, the salesman, and the salaried manager, these white-collar clerks constituted a "new middle class."

This shift in emphasis produced important changes in the national character. In place of the idea that saving was a virtue, an article of faith as old as the first colonial settlements and the chief conviction of Benjamin Franklin's Poor Richard, a new conviction developed that thrift could be socially harmful and spending a virtue. "We're too poor to economize," wrote Scott Fitzgerald jauntily. "Economy is a luxury." The nineteenth-century man, with a set of personal characteristics adapted to an economy of scarcity, began to give way to the twentieth-century man with the idiosyncrasies of an economy of abundance.

Aggressively optimistic, he was friendlier but had less depth, was more demanding of approval, less certain of himself. He did not knock, he boosted. He had lots of pep, hustle, and zip. He joined the Rotary or Kiwanis, and he believed in "service," a word that was repeated *ad nauseum* during the decade. Sinclair Lewis painted his portrait as George Babbitt, and Babbitt acknowledged that it was a reasonable likeness. "Dare to Be a Babbitt!" urged *Nation's Business*. What the world needed was more Babbitts, "good Rotarians who live orderly lives, and save money, and go to church, and play golf, and send their children to school."

The problem for the twentieth-century man was not the material environment but other people. "Our future," wrote Walter Weyl in 1919, "may depend less on the hours that we work today than on the words or the smile we exchange with some anonymous fellow-passenger in the office-building elevator." Men aimed less at improving their character and more at improving their personality. Neither health nor education nor even one's own "personality" was valued for itself alone, but for what it would do toward making one a "success," success meaning not merely greater income but the social acceptance necessary to stifle self-doubt. The main social knowledge a man had to acquire was how to "sell himself."

The nineteenth-century man coveted individual success; the twentieth-century man sought a place for himself in the bureaucracy. Probably the most important development within corporations during these years was the divorce of ownership from control. In 1900, there were four million owners of stocks; by 1930, twenty million. Control of business policy passed from the hands of owners, many of whom had not the remotest curiosity about or knowledge of the firm in which they held stock, and into the hands of a salaried bureaucracy. By the end of the decade a "managerial revolution" had occurred: plant managers and corporation executives, rather than owners, made the chief decisions. Young men no longer aimed to found their own businesses, to be Carnegies or Vanderbilts; they wanted to rise to a high position as a hired manager or a salaried executive. The businessman was less interested in risk and more in stabilizing his business. Unlike the nineteenth-century tycoon with the attitude of the "the public be damned," the postwar businessman was extremely self-conscious about how he appeared to others.

Business developed ingenious methods to transform anxiety about scarcity into a desire for "luxury consumption of leisure and the surplus product." The advertising man and the salesman assaulted the older virtues of thrift and prudence. Behaviorist psychology, with its manipulative view of man, was perfectly adapted to mass advertising; Watson himself left the Johns Hopkins University under fire to become vice-president of an advertising agency. Advertisers sold not products but qualities like social prestige, which the possession of the products would allegedly secure. With debt no longer regarded as shameful, people bought on installment. Three out of every four radios were purchased on the installment plan, 60 per cent of all automobiles and furniture. "You furnish the girl; we furnish the home," advertised one furniture factory. Ten years after the war, conspicuous consumption had become a national mania. When a French perfume would not sell at ordinary rates, the manufacturer raised its price and made a fortune.

Henry Ford had built the Model-T flivver, a sturdy, simply constructed car without grace or beauty, and he had sold millions of them. When he started to lose sales in the 1920's to the more modern General Motors car, he refused to admit that the Model T was no longer marketable. "The customer," he snapped, "can have a Ford any color he wants—so long as it's black." But by the mid-1920's the country had less interest in price than in style and comfort. The purchase of an automobile had been a male prerogative—only men knew what lay under the hood—and men mostly bought cars that offered the soundest mechanical features. As women increasingly decided which car the family would buy, carburetors and gaskets became less important than the color of an automobile and the texture of its upholstery. In May, 1927, Ford surrendered; he halted production on the Model T, and when the Model A came out, it had modern design and construction and could be bought in a choice of colors from Dawn Gray to Arabian Sand.

The Coolidge era is usually viewed as a period of extreme conservatism, but it was thought of at the time as representing a great stride forward in social policy, a New Era in American life. During these years employers embarked on a program of welfare capitalism. They built clean, trim, well-lighted factories, with safety devices to forestall injury. They installed cafeterias, complete with trained dieticians, and formed glee clubs and baseball teams. The Hammermill Paper Company sold its employees cut-rate gasoline; L. Bamberger and Company provided free legal service; and Bausch and Lomb set up eye and dental clinics for its workers. In part to avert unionization, employers replaced tyrannical foremen with trained personnel men and organized company unions. They instituted group insurance plans and introduced profit-sharing; probably more than a million workers owned stock by 1929, an innovation which proved of dubious value by the end of the year. "If every family owned even a $100 bond of the United States or a legitimate corporation," declared Franklin D. Roosevelt, "there would be no talk of bolshevism, and we would incidentally solve all national problems in a more democratic way."

Although the new prosperity favored an exceptionally materialistic view of life, it resulted in more than just increased sales of cigarette lighters and kitchen gadgets. The country spent more than twice as much as it had before the war on libraries, almost three times as much for hospitals. The United States in 1928 paid out as much for education as all the rest of the world. In 1900 a child had only one chance in ten of going to high school; by 1931 he had one chance in two. In 1900 he had only one chance in thirty-three of going to college; by 1931 he had better than one in seven. In part the result of increased wealth—which financed research, improved sanitation, and made possible better nutrition—science in the first third of the twentieth century increased American life expectancy from 49 to 59 years, cut infant mortality two-thirds, and slashed the death rate of typhoid from 36 to 2 per 100,000, of diphtheria from 43 to 2, of measles from 12 to 1.

In December, 1928, President Coolidge declared: "No Congress of the United States ever assembled, on surveying the state of the Union, has met with a more pleasing prospect than that which appears at the present time." By 1928, Coolidge had the assent of many of the New Era's former critics. "The more or less unconscious and unplanned activities of business men," noted Walter Lippmann, "are for once more novel, more daring, and in general more revolutionary than the theories of the progressives." "Big business in America," wrote Lincoln Steffens, who had long been a fierce critic of American capitalism, "is producing what the Socialists held up as their goal; food, shelter and clothing for all. You will see it during the Hoover administration."

New Era publicists argued that a new kind of "economic democracy" had been established. The businessman, enjoying high profits, shared them in "high wages" with his worker. The worker himself, by investing in the stock market, open to all, could own a share of industry. "We are reaching and maintaining the position," declared Coolidge as early as 1919, "where the property class and the employed class are not separate, but identical." The consumer, spending his dollars, it was said, cast votes to determine what should be produced. Soundly based on technological innovations, its gains dispersed through high wages, administered by enlightened businessmen, a new civilization appeared to be emerging. Without the class hatred or bureaucratic despotism of communism, the United States, it seemed, was on its way toward the final abolition of poverty.

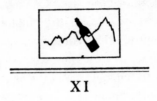

XI

Political Fundamentalism

Despite prosperity, the United States in the postwar years felt deeply threatened from within. The American people suddenly felt thrust upon them the responsibilities of war and the making of peace, and their contact with Europe and power politics was bitterly disillusioning. In a world of Bolshevik revolutions and Bela Kuns, of general strikes and Mussolini's march on Rome, there was a danger that America too might be infected by the social diseases of the Old World. Yet the threat of foreign contagion was not as terrifying as the fear of change from within. In part the danger seemed to come from enclaves of the foreign-born, not yet adapted to American ways, in part from the rise of the metropolis, with values different from those of nineteenth-century America, in part from the new intellectual currents of moral relativism and cosmopolitanism. Not a little of the anxiety arose from the disturbing knowledge that Americans themselves no longer had their former confidence in democracy or religion. "They have," observed André Siegfried, "a vague uneasy fear of being overwhelmed from within, and of suddenly finding one day that they are no longer themselves."

Political fundamentalism was an attempt to deny real divisions in American society by imposing a patriotic cult and coercing a sense of oneness. Admiration for the Constitution became a tribal rite; in the 1920's, Americans, as one English writer noted, were "a people who, of all the world, craved most for new things, yet were all but Chinese in their worship of their Constitution and their ancestors who devised it." Constitution-worship was a kind of magical nativism, a form of activity in which, as the anthropologist Ralph Linton writes, "the society's members feel that by behaving as the ancestors did they will, in some usually undefined way, help to recreate the total situation in which the ancestors lived."

Every effort toward social change was condemned as un-American. "Individualism?" cried an American Legion commander in California. "Down with all Isms!" This resistance to change and this insistence on conformity intertwined with the desire of rural churchmen to turn back modernism in religion and compel morality by statute. In 1924, Protestant fundamentalists wove together both movements in a "Bible-Christ-and-Constitution Campaign," while the Ku Klux Klan's warcry was "Back to the Constitution."

The country was hostile to everything foreign; isolation in foreign affairs had its counterpart in a determination to curb immigration, to avoid foreign contamination, and to preserve the old America ethnically before it was too late. In the late nineteenth century and the early years of the twentieth century, the drive for immigration restriction foundered on presidential vetoes. Restrictionism could not overcome the industrialists' demand for cheap labor or, more important, America's confidence in its ability to absorb large numbers of foreign-born. World War I badly shook American self-confidence. The war revealed that the sympathies of millions of Americans were determined by their countries of origin, and the fight over the League of Nations reflected the animosities of Irish-Americans, German-Americans, and other "hyphenated Americans." In his defense of the Versailles Treaty, Wilson charged: "Hyphens are the knives that are being stuck into this document." By the end of the war years many Americans agreed with Walter Hines Page: "We Americans have got to . . . hang our Irish agitators and shoot our hyphenates and bring up our children with reverence for English history and in the awe of English literature."

The drive for immigration restriction after the war was based, to a far greater degree than before, on a pseudo-scientific racism. Men with little knowledge of either science or public affairs were accepted as experts on "race," although their writings revealed neither insight nor good judgment. In *The Passing of the Great Race* (1916), Madison Grant contended that race was the determinant of civilization and that only Aryans had built great cultures. "The man of the old stock," alleged Grant, "is being crowded out of many country districts by these foreigners, just as he is to-day being literally driven off the streets of New York City by the swarms of Polish Jews. These immigrants adopt the language of the native American, they wear his clothes, they steal his name and they are beginning to take his women, but they seldom adopt his religion or understand his ideals. . . ." Lothrop Stoddard in *The Rising Tide of Color* (1920) and Professor Edwin East of Harvard warned that white races were being engulfed by the more fertile colored races. Most influential of all were the widely read articles by Kenneth Roberts in the *Saturday Evening Post*. Roberts urged that the immigration laws be revised to admit fewer Polish Jews, who were "human parasites"; cautioned against Social-Democrats, since "social democracy gives off a distinctly sour, bolshevistic odor"; and opposed unrestricted immigration, for it would inevitably produce "a hybrid race of people as worthless and futile as the good-for-nothing mongrels of Central America and Southeastern Europe."

In the first fifteen years of the century an average of one million immigrants a year had entered the United States. Slowed to a trickle by the war, the stream of immigration became a swollen torrent after the armistice. From June, 1920, to June, 1921, more than 800,000 persons poured into the country, 65 per cent of them from southern and eastern Europe, and consuls in Europe reported that millions more were planning to leave. By February, 1921, Ellis Island was so jammed that immigration authorities had to divert ships to Boston. Alarmed almost to the point of panic, Congress rushed through an emergency act to restrict immigration; it passed the House in a few hours without a record vote and was adopted by the Senate soon after by 78–1.

For a time, industrialists continued to set themselves against restriction. T. Coleman du Pont protested that critics of the immigrant were suffering from "sheer Red hysteria, nothing more," while Judge Gary denounced the 1921 law as "one of the worst things that this country has ever done for itself economically." With the new prosperity of 1923 and increased mechanical efficiency, which reduced the need for mass labor, the chief obstacle to permanent immigration restriction was removed at the same time that industrialists, agitated by the Red Scare, grew increasingly nativist. In 1924 Congress passed, over scant opposition, the National Origins Act, which fixed a total annual immigration quota and stipulated that national quotas be calculated on the basis of the proportion of descendants of each nationality resident in the country in 1920. In addition, it forbade all Oriental immigration—a gratuitous insult which was marked in Japan with a day of national mourning. "It is a sorry business," wrote Hughes, "and I am greatly depressed. It has undone the work of the Washington Conference and implanted the seeds of an antagonism which are sure to bear fruit in the future."

The law, reflecting racist warnings about a threat to the "Anglo-Saxon" stock, aimed at freezing the country ethnically by sharply restricting the "new" immigration from southern and eastern Europe. In the debate on the bill, Congressmen reviled the foreign-born of the great cities, particularly of New York, to whom were attributed every evil of the day. "On the one side," asserted Representative Tincher of Kansas, "is beer, bolshevism, unassimilating settlements and perhaps many flags—on the other side is constitutional government; one flag, stars and stripes. . . ." For three hundred years English squires and cutthroats, French Huguenots, Spanish adventurers, pious subjects of German duchies, and, above all in recent years, peasants from Calabria to the Ukraine had come to America in search of gold, or land, or freedom, or something to which they could not put a name. Now it was over. One of the great folk movements in the history of man had come to an end.

The immigration restriction movement drew on the fear that America might be transformed ethnically by an invasion of alien elements from without. The Ku Klux Klan preyed on the fear that the country was already in peril from elements within. Both saw their chief enemy in the rise to dominance of the great city. The Klan was organized on Stone Mountain in Georgia on Thanksgiving night, 1915, in the light of a blazing cross, by William J. Simmons, a former Methodist circuit rider and organizer of fraternal organizations. Modeled on the hooded order of Reconstruction days, the Klan admitted "native born, white, gentile Americans" who believed in white supremacy; by implication, they could not be Catholics. Although it took the name of an old southern society, the Klan was more a part of the nativist tradition of Know-Nothingism, having its greatest appeal not to the deep South but to the Southwest, Midwest, and Far West, where people were worried less by the Negro than by the encroachment of "foreigners."

The Klan centered in the small towns and recruited the poorer and less educated. It drew its chief support from the sense of desperation experienced by Protestant townsmen of native stock in these years, when they felt themselves eclipsed by the rise of the city, engaged in a battle which their failing birth rates doomed them to lose. Many Klansmen feared that they had organized too late; in part, this explains why otherwise decent Americans shut their eyes to Klan terrorism. In its elaborate ritual, its stark pageantry, its white-hooded sheets, its titles of "Exalted Cyclops," "Klaliff," "Klokard," "Kligrapp," and "Klabee," it appealed to the lodge vogue of middle-class America, and it gave a sense of oneness to men who felt themselves being overwhelmed. When the Klansman sang "klodes" with his neighbor and klasped his hand in a secret grip, he felt reassured.

The Perils of Prosperity, 1914–32

For several years the Klan made little headway; in 1920 it had less than 5,000 members. World War I bequeathed a great well of unexpressed violence; millions of Americans were whipped up to hate the Kaiser, armed with modern weapons, and left with no enemy to fight, so quickly did the war end. The Klan provided an outlet for pent-up hatred. In 1920 two professional fund-raisers who saw the financial possibilities in the Klan, Edward Y. Clarke and Mrs. Elizabeth Tyler, raised initiation fees and introduced the methods of modern salesmanship. The Klan added 100,000 members. In 1922, Hiram W. Evans, a Texas dentist with his eye on the main chance, brushed aside Simmons, took over as Imperial Wizard, and pushed the Klan into Southwest politics.

In Texas, Charles Culberson, a senator for twenty-four years, opposed the Klan and went down to defeat in a senatorial primary in 1922 at the hands of a Klan-backed candidate. In Oklahoma, Governor J. C. Walton called all the citizens of the state into military service and declared martial law in an effort to put down the organization; the Klan-controlled legislature retaliated by impeaching him and removing him from office in November, 1923. In staunchly Republican Oregon, a state settled by eastern and midwestern Protestants, the Klan elected a Democratic governor, Walter Pierce, by the largest majority in state history and adopted by initiative a law that wiped out parochial schools by requiring parents to send all children between eight and sixteen to public schools. (In 1925, the Supreme Court [*Pierce* v. *Society of Sisters*] declared the law unconstitutional.) Strongest in the Far West, Southwest, and Midwest, the Klan reached its greatest power in Indiana, where David Stephenson took over the Republican party and put in one of his henchmen, Ed Jackson, as Governor. At its height, the Klan may have enrolled as many as five million members.

Wherever the Klan entered, in its wake came floggings, kidnappings, branding with acid, mutilations, church burnings, and even murders. In the South the Klan was an attempt to use terror to preserve a social system that was swiftly changing. Half a million Negroes had been drafted, and another half-million had migrated north, creating a new independence on the part of Negro labor. Yet even in the South, terror, although it was used against the Negro (a bellhop in Texas was branded on the forehead with the initials "KKK," and Negro homes were burned in Florida to discourage voting), was employed more often against Catholics or political enemies or bootleggers or, most important, against individuals deemed immoral. In Birmingham, a Klansman murdered a Catholic priest in cold blood and was acquitted; in Naperville, Illinois, two hours after a monster Klan ceremony, a Roman Catholic church was burned. When the mayor of Columbus, Georgia, ignored demands of the Klan that he remove the city manager, his home was dynamited. After the triumph of the Klan ticket in Alabama in 1927, a Negro woman was flogged and left to die; a white divorcee was punched into unconsciousness; a naturalized citizen was lashed for marrying a native-born woman; a Negro was beaten until he sold his land to a white man for less than it was worth.

The Klan reached the heights in Indiana, and in Indiana it toppled to its death. Some 350,000 white-sheeted Klansmen took over the state. Many of them sauntered brazenly through town with their hoods flung back, not even bothering to conceal their identity. On parade nights in Kokomo, the police force vanished and white-sheeted figures, bearing a curious resemblance to the absent patrolmen, directed the traffic of the town. A gross, corrupt man with a taste for sadism, David Stephenson under the title "Dragon" not only ran Indiana but commanded the Klan throughout the Midwest. He made himself a political power and a multimillionaire overnight through his Klan activities. Finally, he overreached himself: he forced Madge Oberholtzer, a twenty-eight-year-old State House secretary, onto a Chicago-bound train and brutally assaulted her. When she took poison, his henchmen spirited her to a hotel and held her for several days without medical aid; a month later she died. In November, 1925, Stephenson was convicted of second-degree murder and sentenced to life in prison. When his crony, Governor Jackson, refused to pardon him, Stephenson opened a "little black box" which sent a congressman, the mayor of Indianapolis, and other officials to jail; Jackson was indicted for bribery but escaped because of the statute of limitations.

As early as 1924 the Klan had been put on the run in Oklahoma, Louisiana, and Texas. The conviction of Stephenson, who had attacked petting parties and warred on vice, sealed its doom. Although the Klan played a part in stirring up anti-Catholic feelings against Al Smith, the Democratic presidential nominee in the 1928 campaign, it quickly petered out after that. (If the Klan spirit was evident in 1928, it is no less true that it was powerless to prevent the nomination of a Catholic on a major party ticket.) Throughout the history of the Klan runs a sordid thread of corruption. Many of the Klan leaders joined the organization primarily for personal profit; many who preached righteousness were morally corrupt. Feeding on a millennial lust for rule by a league of the pure, the

Klan, once in power, licensed the very evils it said it would exterminate. Its ugly side lay in the fact that it appealed to many who were frustrated by the rigid moral code of the small town. Klansmen often felt tempted by that which they were condemning—the city, sexual freedom, modern life—and their frustration often took a sadistic turn, as when they stripped "fallen" women naked and whipped them. The Stephenson episode revealed everything that was seamy about the Klan—the disloyalty of its leaders, the financial corruption, the political subversion, the moral hypocrisy, the sadism. The Klan never recovered.

It is not surprising that the Klan had some of its fiercest encounters with the liquor interests, for both the Klan and the prohibition movement centered in the rural areas of the country, especially in the villages where the Baptist or Methodist preacher could speak with authority on matters of politics and morals. The prohibitionists viewed the immensely complex problem with which they were dealing only in moral terms, and their picture of the world of drink was a nightmare vision. The Anti-Saloon League, for example, reported that "nearly 3,000 infants are smothered yearly in bed by drunken parents." Drink was said to be the potion of the immigrant masses of the city and of the rich. It was associated with the saloonkeepers who ran the city machines and who used the votes of the whiskey-loving immigrant. It was associated with the German brewers and their "disloyal" compatriots who drank beer and ale. It was associated with the rich men who operated their "whiskey rings" and served wine at Belshazzar's Feast. The cities, which resisted the idea that "thou shalt not" was the fundamental precept of living, were always hostile to prohibition. The prohibitionists, in turn, regarded the city as their chief enemy, and prohibitionism and a pervasive anti-urbanism went hand in hand.

In December, 1917, Congress adopted and sent to the states the Eighteenth Amendment, prohibiting the manufacture, sale, or transportation of alcoholic beverages; in January, 1919, the thirty-sixth state ratified the amendment. In October, 1919, Congress, over Wilson's veto, passed the Volstead Act to extend wartime prohibition and define "alcoholic" rigidly as one-half of 1 per cent alcohol by volume. The Prohibition Commissioner promised that no liquor would be manufactured "nor sold, nor given away, nor hauled in anything on the surface of the earth or under the earth or in the air." In rural Protestant areas, despite moonshine and hard cider, prohibition brought a decline in drinking, and this may have been true for the country as a whole; there were fewer deaths from alcoholism and fewer arrests for drunkenness. Yet from the first, prohibition was unpopular with a sizable minority of the country, particularly in the great cities. Prohibition enforcement agencies never had enough officers, and the agents they had were often venal political hacks, quick to resort to violence. Public fury was aroused at the prohibition agents, who on occasion sprayed bullets over waterfront streets or invaded private premises of minor offenders; they appeared to be as lawless and reckless as the men they were pursuing.

Before long, millions of Americans sided with the lawbreakers. On one occasion, thousands of bathers at Coney Island watched an encounter between Coast Guard cutters and rumrunners: they cheered the rumrunner as it opened a lead on the pursuing government boats. In areas hostile to prohibition, agents were almost helpless. In wet cities like

Political Fundamentalism

New York and San Francisco, a stranger could most easily locate a "speakeasy"—a saloon operating on the sly—by asking an obliging policeman, who could usually point out one just a few doors away. In 1929 Mrs. Mabel Walker Willebrandt, who had been Assistant Attorney-General of the United States in charge of prohibition prosecutions, conceded that liquor could be bought "at almost any hour of the day or night, either in rural districts, the smaller towns, or the cities."

Ingenious means were devised to get illegally what the law denied. Redistilling industrial alcohol was one source, prescriptions from compliant druggists another. Liquor schooners plied Rum Row off the New Jersey coast, and ice sleds ran liquor across Canadian rivers in winter. Saloons disguised themselves as private associations like "The Bombay Bicycle Club." E. B. White slyly proposed that the government nationalize speakeasies. "In that manner," he wrote, "the citizenry would be assured liquor of a uniformly high quality, and the enormous cost of dry enforcement could be met by the profits from the sale of drinks."

Many people made their own home brew; in large cities, hardware stores openly displayed copper stills along with yeast, hops, and other ingredients. Other people bought their whiskey from bootleggers who claimed they were selling the best imported brands from Canada or Scotland, and sometimes did. More often, they passed off inferior products—at worst substances like Jamaica ginger, better known as "jake," which paralyzed thousands of people, Jackass Brandy, which caused internal bleeding, Soda Pop Moon from Philadelphia, containing poisonous isopropyl alcohol, Panther Whiskey, based on esters and fusel oil, or Yack Yack Bourbon from Chicago, which blended iodine and burnt sugar.

The Perils of Prosperity, 1914–32

Bootlegging produced the chief income for gangs which infested the large cities and frequently bought or coerced their way into city governments. In 1920 "Scarface" Al Capone, a New York hoodlum from the Five Points Gang, moved to Chicago and set up an empire in alcohol, gambling, prostitution, and drugs. By 1927 he was operating a $60 million business and had a private army of close to one thousand hoodlums who "rubbed out" rival bootleggers attempting to cut into Capone's "territory." In 1926 and 1927 there were 130 gang murders in Cook County, and not a single murderer was apprehended. Capone drove the streets of Chicago in a $30,000 armor-plated automobile, convoyed by scout cars, and went to the theater with a score of bodyguards. On one occasion when the police brought Capone in for questioning, the Detective Bureau was besieged by nearly one hundred gangsters.

The gangsters in many of the great cities either took over the government or were permitted to create their own private governments. In Chicago, the Terrible Gennas had five police captains and four hundred policemen on their payroll. In New York, speakeasies paid "protection" money to gangsters like Dutch Schultz, who were allied with Tammany Hall powers like Jimmy Hines. By consolidating independent units, observed Lloyd Morris, tongue in cheek, Schultz "eliminated waste, promoted efficiency, and replaced the disorder of obsolete individualism with rigorous discipline." In Philadelphia, bootleggers established an inner government with a judge before whom attorneys practiced and whose decisions were enforced by gunmen.

By the close of the decade there was a swelling movement for repeal of the Eighteenth Amendment. This demand centered in urban industrial states and was led by Governor

Political Fundamentalism

Alfred E. Smith of New York and Governor Albert Ritchie of Maryland. New York had repealed its "Baby Volstead Act" as early as 1923, while feeling was so strong in Maryland, which never passed a state enforcement law at all, that in June, 1922, a mob of wets stormed the jail at Ocean City and freed two men arrested for drunkenness. Repeal sentiment was strong among parched voters in the cities, who had always hated prohibition, and among men like Representative George Tinkham of Massachusetts, who argued, "The more advanced a country is, the higher its alcoholic content." More consequential was the growing antagonism of people who were worried by the contempt for law which prohibition bred, and by the great gap between profession and practice, which applied even to many of the prohibitionists themselves. In Virginia, prohibition had been enacted when a state senator, ill with a hangover from carousing the night before, cast the decisive vote in its favor. By the end of the decade prohibition still appeared to have the support of the majority of the nation, but its days were numbered.

The campaign to preserve America as it was, to resist the forces of change, came to a head in the movement of Protestant fundamentalism climaxed by the Scopes trial. Although the publication of Darwin's *Origin of Species* in 1859 had touched off a controversy between science and theology which rocked the Western world for the next two decades, men like Asa Gray in the United States and Charles Kingsley in England succeeded in reconciling evolution and Christianity; by the time of World War I, an attack on Darwin seemed as unlikely as an attack on Copernicus. When in 1922 the Kentucky legislature came within a single vote of banning the teaching of evolution in the schools, the country suddenly

217

awoke to a deep-seated hostility to science in rural America which it thought had been scotched a half-century before.

In rural areas and small towns, particularly in the mountain country of the South, many Protestant ministers had never subscribed to Darwinism; they continued to believe that the only true account of the origin of the world could be obtained by a literal reading of the first two chapters of Genesis. The attempts of modernists to accommodate religion to scholarly criticism of the Bible had, the fundamentalists argued, shattered the chief tenets of Christianity. One fundamentalist wrote: "The Modernist juggles the Scripture statements of His deity and denies His virgin birth, making Him a Jewish bastard, born out of wedlock, and stained forever with the shame of His Mother's immorality." To attempt to preserve religion while denying the truth of Christ's resurrection, wrote the editor of a Baptist periodical, "is like saying that the title to the house which you prepared as a habitation for your old age is a fraud. . . . If Jesus Christ did not rise from the dead, we cannot depend upon a word of what he said."

Strengthened by popular anger against Germany (the home of modernist religion) and by the Red Scare (which linked atheism with communism), fundamentalism made modest gains during and after the war, but it amounted to little until William Jennings Bryan joined the anti-evolution movement. Bryan was a man to reckon with; for three decades he had been the folk hero of the Mississippi Valley heartland. A man of transparent sincerity, courageous in the face of repeated defeats, a man whose belief in democracy was instinctive, Bryan was the authentic representative of the tradition of Jacksonian democracy (with a leaven of nineteenth-century evangelical Christianity) in his suspicion of the expert and the university-educated as members of a privileged class. "It is better," wrote Bryan, "to trust in the Rock of Ages than to know the age of rocks; it is better for one to know that he is close to the Heavenly Father than to know how far the stars in the heavens are apart."

Always a factionalist, Bryan threw himself into the anti-evolution campaign with the same zeal he had marshaled against the "goldbugs" in 1896. Bryan, wrote Heywood Broun, "has never lived in a land of men and women. To him this country has been from the beginning peopled by believers and heretics." Under Bryan's leadership, the campaign to coerce the teaching of a biology which conformed to the account of the origin of man in Genesis quickly caught the attention of the nation. It was a war of country and small town against the city, a war largely centered in the South. In the Northeast, the anti-evolutionists got nowhere. When a bill was introduced in the Delaware legislature to forbid teaching that man evolved from lower animals, it was referred facetiously to the Committee on Fish, Game, and Oysters. In many southern states anti-evolution efforts were turned back by counterattacks from university presidents and urban newspapers, but in Oklahoma, Florida, and North Carolina the anti-evolutionists won partial victories. When the Texas legislature turned down a bill to censor textbooks, Governor "Ma" Ferguson took matters in her own hands and blacklisted or bowdlerized the books to remove any mention of Darwinism. "I am a Christian mother," the Governor declared, "and I am not going to let that kind of rot go into Texas textbooks."

The first smashing victory for the anti-evolutionists came in Tennessee, where a farmer named George Washington Butler, who was a part-time school teacher and clerk of the

Round Lick Association of Primitive Baptists, was elected to the legislature on the single plank of advocating an anti-evolution law. Bryan and a powerful fundamentalist lobby moved in on Nashville to support Butler; in March, 1925, the legislature made it illegal "for any teacher in any of the universities, normal, and all other public schools of the state, to teach any theory that denies the story of the divine creation of man as taught in the Bible and to teach instead that man has descended from a lower order of animals."

That spring, in the mountain town of Dayton, Tennessee, John T. Scopes, a slim bespectacled young biology teacher at Central High School, a man with an engaging modesty and wit, was sipping lemon phosphates at Robinson's Drug Store with several of his friends, and in particular with George Rappelyea, manager of the local mine, and druggist Robinson, who was chairman of the county schoolbook committee. They talked about the Butler law, which they disapproved, and about the fact that the American Civil Liberties Union had offered counsel to any Tennessee teacher who challenged the act. More in the spirit of fun than of social protest, the mine manager and the teacher hatched a scheme. The next day Scopes lectured from Hunter's *Civic Biology* and Rappelyea filed a complaint with the local officials; the police hailed Scopes before the justices of the peace, and he was bound over to a grand jury.

To Scopes's defense came Clarence Darrow, the most famous defense lawyer in the country and an admitted agnostic, Arthur Garfield Hays, a civil liberties attorney, and Dudley Field Malone, who in other years had campaigned with Bryan for the Democratic cause. Retained by the World's Christian Fundamentals Association to assist the prosecution was Wil-

Political Fundamentalism

liam Jennings Bryan. Bryan announced that the trial would be a "duel to the death" between Christianity and evolution. "He gave the impression," observed *Le Matin*, "of one returned to the earth from the wars of religion."

The Scopes trial is usually seen simply as a struggle for academic freedom against Tennessee Hottentots. Certainly this was the most important substantive issue in the case, and there is little to be said for the bizarre attempt to force teachers to give their students a wholly inaccurate account of the evolution of man. Yet the case was not simply a morality play between the good forces of intellectual freedom and the evil spirits of obscurantism. In the Scopes trial, the provincialism of the city was arrayed against the provincialism of the country, the shallowness of Mencken against the shallowness of Bryan, the arrogance of the scientists against the arrogance of the fundamentalists.

The very faith in science, as C. E. Ayres pointed out, had reached the point where it had become "superstition, in another guise." In the 1920's the nation was captivated by scientific developments in electricity, by the new world of radioactivity, even by more mundane matters like calories and vitamins; science, many people believed, was a universal balm that would answer every human need. High priests of the science cult dismissed traditional concerns as remnants of an irrational age. "No one," declared Watson, the behaviorist psychologist, "has ever touched a soul, or has seen one in a test tube." Churchgoers were rightly concerned about a cult of science which stripped away myths, provided no adequate system of ethics, offered little sustenance in times of grief, and provided a partial, limited glimpse of man and the universe.

The Perils of Prosperity, 1914–32

Fundamentalism made sense to men in isolated rural areas still directly dependent on nature for their livelihood; they distrusted human capacity and relied on divine intervention, because it had been their own experience that men had to rely on the rains for the crops and were all but helpless when disease struck. Their adversaries in the city found fundamentalism incomprehensible because the rational methods of production in the factory and life in the metropolis suggested that man, through science and education, could solve the major problems of living and might even be able someday to solve the ultimate questions of human existence.

At the Dayton trial the court contended that the only issue properly before it was whether Scopes had violated the law, which he clearly had. The defense attempted to shift the emphasis to the law itself. Scopes's attorneys, who argued that a belief in evolution was consistent with Christian faith and that Genesis was allegorical, were frustrated in their efforts to demonstrate that the law was either wicked or foolish, until Hays hit upon the idea of calling Bryan to the stand as an expert on the Bible.

Bryan declared that the whale had swallowed Jonah (although he thought it was a fish rather than a whale), that Eve had been made from Adam's rib, that all languages derived from the collapse of the tower of Babel, and that Joshua had literally made the sun stand still. Professing himself an authority on religion and science, Bryan was revealed by Darrow's devastating probing to be a man of dense ignorance. Bryan made a fatal admission: he conceded that when the Bible said the world had been created in six days, it did not necessarily mean that a "day" was twenty-four hours long; it might be a million years. Thus Bryan, whose position was grounded on the conviction that the Bible must be read literally, had himself "interpreted" the Bible, thereby destroying the basis for opposition to both modernism and evolution.

Scopes was found guilty, as had been anticipated from the first, and fined $100. The Tennessee supreme court later threw out Scopes's fine on a technicality, thereby blocking his attorneys from testing the constitutionality of the law. Scopes himself received a scholarship to attend the University of Chicago, where he was trained as a geologist. Scopes had lost, but, in another sense, Scopes had won. In the last minutes of Darrow's cross-examination, there was raucous laughter at Bryan, derision from his own followers. A terrible sense of pathos filled Bryan's last days; soon after the trial he died, after having written an autobiographical statement to prove that he was neither an ignorant nor an uneducated man. The anti-evolutionists won victories in three more southern states, but with Bryan's death the heart went out of the movement, and it quickly subsided.

The aftermath of the Scopes trial is symbolic of the fate of political fundamentalism in the 1920's. Immigration restriction, the Klan, prohibition, and Protestant fundamentalism all had in common a hostility to the city and a desire to arrest change through coercion by statute. The anti-evolutionists won the Scopes trial; yet, in a more important sense, they were defeated, overwhelmed by the tide of cosmopolitanism. Such was the fate of each of the other movements. By the end of 1933 the Eighteenth Amendment had been repealed and the Klan was a dim memory. Immigration restriction, which apparently scored a complete triumph and certainly did win a major one, was frustrated when (since the law did not apply to the Western Hemisphere) Mexicans, French Canadians, and Puerto Ricans, most of them "swarthy" Catholics, streamed in. Ostensibly successful on every front, the political fundamentalists in the 1920's were making a last stand in a lost cause against the legions of the city.

XII

The Sidewalks of New York

The United States in the 1920's neared the end of a painful transition from a country reared in the rural village to a nation dominated by the great metropolis. In 1910, 54.2 per cent of the country lived in villages of fewer than 2,500 inhabitants; by 1920, only 48.6 per cent—for the first time in our history, less than half the people dwelt in small villages and on farms. During the decade, some six million people abandoned the farm for the city. The city of Los Angeles jumped from 319,000 in 1910 to more than 1,238,000 in 1930. By 1930, the United States was only 44 per cent rural.

Not only were the cities outstripping the villages and small towns in population, but there was during these years a conscious rejection of rural values. In *Spoon River Anthology* (1915), Edgar Lee Masters pictured American small-town life as mean and narrow; in *Winesburg, Ohio* (1919), Sherwood Anderson painted a series of haunting portraits of the human spirit stifled by an Ohio town; in *Main Street* (1920), Sinclair Lewis held up to public inspection the faults of a typical American prairie community; in *Look Homeward, Angel*

(1929), Thomas Wolfe gave a far more savage view of a southern town. Scattered across the continent, wrote Van Wyck Brooks, were thousands of villages, "frostbitten, palsied, full of a morbid, bloodless, death-in-life." No theme of American literature of the period was more pervasive than what Carl Van Doren called "the revolt from the village." In the last chapter of the representative novel of the day, the hero went to the railroad depot of the midwestern town to buy a one-way ticket to Chicago or New York, the bright metropolises shiny with promise.

The city was self-conscious in its superiority to rural mores, and it made no effort to conceal its contempt for small-town America. Mencken contended that the farmer was not a member of the human race. The *New Yorker*, founded in 1925 and in itself the perfect symbol of urban humor light-years removed from rural wit, boasted that it was "not for the old lady in Dubuque." In Dorothy Parker's epigrams at the Hotel Algonquin, in the joyously raucous nasality of Al Jolson, and in the New York City provincialism of Jimmy Walker and Texas Guinan, the city created a world in which the traditions of small-town America were almost unrecognizable.

Rural leaders in turn attacked the city as the modern Gomorrah, raising the ancient cry of the debauchery of the metropolis. The Broadway theater, expostulated the Methodist Board of Temperance, Prohibition and Public Morals, was "naked, profane, blasphemous and salacious." The city, rural traditionalists expounded, was the home of the alien and the uprooted Negro, of a people lost to fundamental American values. "New York," wrote the *Denver Post* in 1930, "has been a cesspool into which immigrant trash has been dumped for so long that it can scarcely be considered American any more." New York was the seat of the Union Theological Seminary and modernism, the home of the nightclub and the gangster, of Wall Street and Tammany Hall; it was, as Bryan had long ago said of the East, "the enemy's country." It was a city cruel and impersonal, the abode of the rootless, a place where, as one writer noted, "nobody seemed to have parents."

Critics viewed the city as a great incubus sucking the life's blood of the countryside. Sociologists raised the nightmare of a barren urban society which could not reproduce itself, dooming America to depopulation and decay. The German philosopher Oswald Spengler, who enjoyed a vogue in the 1920's, warned that urbanization spelled the degeneration of Western culture. In 1915 the nation's birth rate was 25.0; by 1932 it had skidded to 17.4. During the first four decades of the twentieth century, citydwellers did not bear enough children to maintain a stable population in the next generation. Yet the population of urban America increased 27 per cent between 1920 and 1930 while rural America grew only 4 per cent. The cities outdistanced the rural areas chiefly by depopulating the countryside.

The war between the country and the city had been fought for decades. What was new about the situation in the 1920's was the tension within each camp as well. On the one hand, people on farms and in the small towns could not help but know, even if they would not always admit, how deeply their own lives had been affected by the appeal of the city. They knew that not merely was America changing but they themselves were changing. On the other hand, the very men who symbolized the triumph of the city were themselves among the most reluctant to see the death of the old order.

Mencken's celebration of the virtues of New York was so boisterous because deep down he felt uneasy whenever he was in the big city; he was always happiest when he was headed home to the quieter confines of Baltimore. Beneath Sinclair Lewis's satire of Gopher Prairie lay a deep love of the place. "If I seem to have criticized prairie villages," Lewis wrote in 1931, "I have certainly criticized them no more than I have New York, or Paris, or the great universities. I am quite certain that I could have been born and reared in no place in the world where I would have had more friendliness."

In no writer is this ambivalence more apparent than in Sherwood Anderson. The main character of *Winesburg, Ohio* turns his back on the small town, true enough. But no one can read Anderson without being aware of his abiding affection for the small town and its skilled craftsmen and his loathing of the "filth and disorder of modern civilization." The character of the harness maker Joe Wainsworth, who in his hatred of machinery kills his assistant, is the symbol of the earlier order venting its wrath on the modern age. The same Anderson who wrote of the thwarted lives in "the little frame houses, on often mean enough streets in American towns" could also recall fondly "men and lads together on chairs and upturned boxes before livery-stable doors or before country-town hotels at evening, breeding lines being discussed and fought over, great names mentioned, the master reinsmen, Murphy, Budd Doble, Walter Cox, and the great master of them all, Pop Geers." With not a little sadness, Anderson protested: "We never did get a fair break from our writers on some of the sweeter sides of our American life."

Some men sought not merely to retain the rural character

of American society, but to turn back the clock and restore the pristine America of yesteryear. At the head of this movement was Henry Ford, who collected a great variety of Americana at "Greenfield Village" and constructed a replica of a nineteenth-century rural community. Censuring modern dancing as immoral because it occurred "mostly above the feet," Ford revived old-fashioned folk dancing, importing dozens of fiddlers to Dearborn and turning up old folk tunes like "Arkansas Traveler" and "Paddy on the Turnpike." He not only supported a back-to-the-soil movement; he subsidized a printing of selections from the *McGuffey Readers* and distributed them to libraries around the country. Yet at the same time, Ford in his massive automobile factories was doing more than any man to destroy rural America beyond recall. His celebration of rural values had about it something of the synthetic-reactionary character of a Balkan peasant party. Ironically, Ford himself had turned toward tinkering with machines because he loathed farm work.

Until the 1920's the tension between city and rural values had not entered the national political arena. For more than a century American politics had been dominated by the country; no political appeal was more certain of success than birth in a log cabin. Even when, in the years after the Civil War, the United States moved rapidly from an agrarian to an industrial nation, its chief political figures were cut from the familiar mold. They were farmboys, or men from the small town, or, if they came from the city, they had not cut their ties with rural America and were as acceptable to the crossroads town as to the metropolis. In the 1920's, for the first time, a man who was unmistakably of the city made a bid for national power; in the career of Alfred E. Smith and the dramatic campaign of 1928 all the tensions between rural and urban America came to a head.

Born in 1873 in a tenement on New York's Lower East Side, in the shadow of Brooklyn Bridge, Smith lived the life of a boy in a great city. Instead of currying his pony or shooting squirrels on a smoky October afternoon, Al climbed among packing crates and boxes along the waterfront. Instead of playing one o'cat in the old apple orchard, he cuffed handballs against a warehouse wall. Instead of splashing in a swimming hole of a rural brook, Al leaped from dirty wharves into the East River. From the age of seven until he was fourteen, he served seven o'clock Mass as altar boy in the neighborhood Catholic church. At the age of fifteen, he was forced to quit school to go to work; four years later, he was hired as salesman and assistant bookkeeper in the Fulton Fish Market at $12 a week and all the fish he wanted.

He joined the Tammany Hall organization, as inevitable an institution as one could find in the Fourth Ward, and, leaving the fish markets behind him, worked for eight years in the commonplace political job of subpoena server. In 1903, at the age of thirty, as a reward for faithful service, Smith was sent to the New York state legislature as assemblyman. He made a brilliant record in the legislature. He handled the bills resulting from the insurance probe conducted by Charles Evans Hughes, and investigated the terrible Triangle Fire, which took the lives of 145 girls in a shirtwaist factory and awakened the country to the need for social legislation. Ultimately he became, as Elihu Root said, the best-informed man on legislative matters in the entire state. In 1918 he was elected governor; save for 1920, when he was submerged in the Harding landslide, Smith remained in Albany until 1928.

The Sidewalks of New York

As governor, Smith was viewed as the spokesman for the new urban masses, and under his leadership a number of important social reforms were achieved. In the 1930's, when Smith joined the forces opposing the New Deal, he was lampooned in political cartoons for betraying his old friends, casting away his brown derby for a top hat. This was unfair; Smith, like many of the new urban leaders, was from the first fundamentally conservative. He was a young man on the make, and politics was one of the few avenues of social mobility open to a young Irish Catholic boy from the East Side. He was attempting to win success, like the young farmboys described in his schoolbooks, who rose to power at the heads of corporations. Smith never questioned the assumptions of capitalist society, certainly not the profit motive or the virtue of success, and the notion of a planned society was as repugnant to him as to Hoover. It was this combination of humanitarianism with economic orthodoxy, which emphasized administrative reform and greater economy, that accounted for much of his appeal. "Governor Smith," wrote Nathan Straus, "has been a champion of the people without being a demagogue."

Smith personified the desire of the sons of urban immigrants to make a place for themselves in the world, and politics was one of the most obvious ways they could do so. Smith was not the first man to discover this. He was part of a tradition at least as old as the election of the German immigrant John Peter Altgeld to the governorship of Illinois in 1892, a tradition which embraced in the early years of the century Irish boys like David I. Walsh in Massachusetts and Joe Tumulty in New Jersey. But he was the first to ask acceptance by the people for the highest office in the land. It was for this reason that Smith was so taken to heart by the Irish of the Northeast; he was a test case of how far an Irish Catholic boy could go, and how soon. "Al Smith," wrote William Allen White, "must rise or fall in our national life, if ever he should enter it, as our first urbanite."

One of the ablest state officers in American history, a man with an amazing record of electoral success, four times elected governor of the most populous state in the country, Smith was, save possibly for McAdoo, the first man of national stature the Democratic party had produced since Wilson. He was the logical candidate for the presidential nomination in 1928. Despite lingering bitterness over the Madison Square Garden convention, even many of the old McAdoo supporters recognized that if Smith could not win in 1928, no Democrat could. "In my present state of mind," wrote a West Virginia Democrat, "I am for 'Rum, Romanism and Rebellion.' " Although he was opposed by a variety of southern rivals at the Houston convention, Smith won the Democratic nomination handily.

When Coolidge announced laconically, "I do not choose to run," the Republicans turned to Herbert Hoover, born in Iowa, as their presidential candidate and named Senator Charles Curtis of Kansas as his running mate. For the first time in history, both candidates of a major party hailed from west of the Mississippi. After a long career as mining engineer and promoter in every corner of the earth, Hoover had first caught national attention in the war years as Food Administrator and administrator of Belgian relief. John Maynard Keynes observed that he was "the only man who emerged from the ordeal of Paris with an enhanced reputation," while Justice Louis D. Brandeis remarked that he was "the biggest figure injected into Washington life by the war." Hoover was the epitome of the new capitalism, with its emphasis on efficiency, distribution, co-operation, and "service." Smith could make the appeal of a great humanitarian and a friend of business interests at the same time; it was his misfortune to run against a man in 1928 who could make precisely the same claims and did not have Smith's political liabilities.

The Democratic party in the 1920's faced a problem similar to that of the Republican party under the New Deal. If it attempted to compete with the Republican party by showing it was just as conservative, if it adopted a "me too" position, it had little chance of success, because the Republican party had established itself too firmly as the party of prosperity. On the other hand, if it attempted to adopt a widely differing policy and take a more radical line, it ran smack against the conservative temper of the decade. Either way, it was licked, just as was the Republican party under the New Deal. It could hope for success only as the Republicans of the 1930's could hope for success—first, by a change in the national temper and the creation of new issues, second, by the emergence of a strong national leader in their own ranks.

For the most part, the Democratic party in 1928 chose to take a "me too" position. After their resounding defeat in the 1924 election, the Democrats grew even more cautious than they had been before. In 1925 John W. Davis wrote to a follower: "When will we get done with the fool idea that the way to make a party grow is to scare away everybody who has an extra dollar in his pocket? God forbid that the Democratic party should become a mere gathering of the unsuccessful!" To head his campaign in 1928, Smith named John Raskob, a Republican who had voted for Coolidge in 1924, who had run the Finance Committee of General Motors, and who listed himself in *Who's Who* as "capitalist." Raskob made a deliberate attempt to identify the Democratic party with business interests and to assure the country there was no real difference on this score with the Republicans. He proudly announced that Harkness of Standard Oil, Spreckels the sugar titan, and James the New York financier were supporting Smith; not one of them "considers that his interests are in the slightest degree imperilled," Raskob told the nation. On every important issue, the Democratic platform of 1928 paralleled that of the Republicans. As Newton Baker ruefully observed, "McKinley could have run on the tariff plank and Lodge on the one on international relations."

Smith's inability or unwillingness to establish a progressive position sharply different from Hoover's permitted the campaign to focus on religion, prohibition, and personalities. Well before the battle began, foes of Smith warned that his election would mean the control of the White House by a foreign pope, and his nomination unleashed a vicious whispering campaign against him. Scurrilous pamphlets were distributed with titles like "Traffic in Nuns" or "Alcohol Smith," and as the Democratic campaign train moved across Oklahoma, the candidate could see fiery crosses burning in the fields.

"No Governor can kiss the papal ring and get within gunshot of the White House," announced Methodist Bishop Adna Leonard of Buffalo, while Methodist Bishop Cannon of Virginia referred contemptuously to Raskob as "this wet Roman Catholic Knight of Columbus and chamberlain of the Pope of Rome." It was not merely extremists like Leonard and Cannon who injected the religious issue into the campaign; the liberal Protestant publication, *Christian Century*, observed that Protestants could not "look with unconcern upon the seating of a representative of an alien culture, of a mediaeval Latin mentality, of an undemocratic hierarchy and of a foreign potentate in the great office of President of the United States."

Anti-Catholicism was not all a handicap, for it appears to have solidified the Catholic vote for Smith and, indeed, to have brought out numbers of Catholics to vote for the first time. One of the outstanding features of the 1928 election was the exceptionally high popular vote, 67.5 per cent of those eligible, a decided increase over the 51.1 per cent turnout in 1924. There is considerable impressionistic evidence that one of the reasons for the high vote was an outpouring of Catholic women voters for the first time. The Catholic vote was formidable enough to move Rhode Island and Massachusetts into the Democratic column. In Boston the vote was a staggering 44 per cent heavier than in 1924. Yet the divisive religious issue certainly damaged Smith far more than it helped him, for it cut into his support in his own party, particularly in the Protestant South.

Probably more important than religion in alienating the South was the prohibition issue. Herbert Hoover called prohibition a "great social and economic experiment, noble in motive and far reaching in purpose," while Smith's skepticism about prohibition was raised to a basic issue of the campaign by his nomination of Raskob, the leading wet in the country, as his campaign manager. In the 1920's prohibition was the most avidly discussed question of the day, a subject of far more popular concern than any issue of foreign policy, and the forces in favor of prohibition were well organized and politically powerful, centered in the Methodist Church under the fanatical leadership of Bishop Cannon. As Will Rogers observed: "A Preacher just can't save anybody nowadays. He is too busy saving the Nation. . . . Every Crossroad Minister is trying to be a Colonel House." For Bishop Cannon and his followers, the campaign resolved itself into one overwhelming question: "Shall Dry America elect a 'cocktail President'?"

Hoover won the election with 21 million votes to Smith's 15 million, taking the Electoral College by the decisive margin of 444 to 87. Smith won fewer electoral votes than any Democratic candidate since Horace Greeley in 1872 and a smaller proportion of electoral votes than any Democrat since General McClellan in 1864. For the first time since Reconstruction, the Republicans split the Solid South, taking Virginia, Texas, Tennessee, North Carolina, Florida, Kentucky, and Maryland and almost capturing Alabama as well. The election, explained Bishop Cannon, was a repudiation "of the wet sidewalks of our cities, aided and abetted by a selfish, so-called liberal element of high society life."

Buried in the election returns was one significant development that was overlooked at the time. In 1924, the Republicans had carried the dozen largest cities in the country by a 1.3 million margin; in 1928, the Democrats gained a slight edge in the same cities. Smith swung 122 Republican counties into the Democratic column, 77 of them predominantly Catholic. For the first time, the Democrats cracked the industrial east, hitherto the most Republican section of the country, the stronghold of protectionism. Until 1928, the Democrats had not been particularly an urban party. In 1928, the Democrats won the battle for the allegiance of the city and laid the foundation for the urban-based party of the 1930's.

The urban-rural division between Hoover and Smith was much more complex in the South. The anti-urban sentiments aroused there by Smith were probably stronger than in any other section of the country; yet it was the rural South that was the chief Smith stronghold and the urban South that swung to Hoover. In the rural black belts where Negro concentration was heaviest, the whites would not risk breaking Democratic solidarity; of the 191 counties more than 50 per cent Negro, only 7 voted for Hoover. On the other hand, the southern city, with lower Negro concentrations, felt freer to break party ranks; largely populated by old stock, southern cities were repelled by Smith's new immigrant associations and attracted to Hoover as spokesman for a chromium-shiny new capitalism. Hoover captured Dallas, Fort Worth, Birmingham, Nashville, Chattanooga, Winston-Salem and other southern cities.

Given the temper of the 1920's and the success of the Republican party in identifying itself with prosperity, given the aura of legitimacy about the Republican party since the days of the Civil War, Smith's setback in 1928 was only to be expected. If Smith had been Protestant, dry, and born in a log cabin of good yeoman stock, he still would have been defeated on the Democratic ticket. In the atmosphere of the 1920's, the Republican party was almost unbeatable.

Historians have been more perplexed by why Smith lost so much of the normally Democratic areas of the country. Was prohibition or Catholicism the more important cause? The whole question may well be a fruitless one; the campaign reflected a deep antagonism between rural and urban America which went beyond any single issue. The rural voter or the city voter loyal to traditional values and mores did not stop to ask himself whether he was dismayed by Smith's religion or by his views on alcohol; he responded to Smith as a symbol of a great many attitudes and beliefs which were alien to his own. Once this tension developed, every episode in the campaign tended to exacerbate the sense of alienation which non-urban and non-eastern voters felt toward Smith. The way he said "raddio," his brown derby, even the way he smoked his cigar, marked Smith as an outlander.

Hoover, on the other hand, established the image of himself as an Iowa farmboy steeped in the traditions of rural America. He spoke of the swimming hole under the willows, of trapping rabbits in cracker boxes in the woods down by the Burlington track, and of bellywhopping down Cook's Hill on winter nights. He recalled being taught by a neighboring Indian boy how to bring down pigeons and prairie chickens with a bow and arrow. Fishing, wrote Hoover, was "good for the soul of man," for all men were equal before fishes. He sung the praises of "the willow pole with a butcher's-string line, fixed with hooks ten for a dime, whose compelling lure is one segment of an angleworm and whose incantation is spitting on bait." When he wrote his letter accepting the Republican nomination in 1928, Hoover referred to himself as "a boy from a country village, without inheritance or influential friends. . . ."

Smith was seen as the spokesman for the foreigner, a man who, if elected, would flood the nation with a new tide of European immigrants, a man who had gained the nomination only because he held the suffrage of the big-city aliens who were threatening to take over the country. "I'll tell you, brother, that the big issue we've got to face ain't the liquor question," the Reverend Bob Jones told a Birmingham meeting. "I'd rather see a saloon on every corner in the South than see the foreigners elect Al Smith President!"

George Fort Milton, the Tennessee editor and historian,

wrote that Smith's appeal was "to the aliens, who feel that the older America, the America of the Anglo-Saxon stock, is a hateful thing which must be overturned and humiliated; to the northern negroes, who lust for social equality and racial dominance; to the Catholics who have been made to believe that they are entitled to the White House, and to the Jews who likewise are to be instilled with the feeling that this is the time for God's chosen people to chastise America yesteryear. . . . As great as have been my doubts about Hoover, he is sprung from American soil and stock."

In the rabidly nationalistic years of the twenties, America insisted that the country be represented by a symbol of the old values; Smith could not fulfil this function as the United States viewed itself in 1928. "It is not that Governor Smith is a Catholic and a wet which makes him an offense to the villagers and town dwellers," wrote William Allen White in 1928. "The whole Puritan civilization which has built a sturdy, orderly nation is threatened by Smith." One of Smith's supporters of 1928 was later to report: "Recently I spent a pleasant weekend in Virginia. I visited the tombs of Thomas Jefferson, Robert E. Lee and 'Stonewall' Jackson to renew my faith. I feel that it did so, and I have reached the conclusion that neither Jefferson, Lee or Jackson could have been born on the East side in New York."

Smith, with his East Side mannerisms, when placed alongside the marble figures of Jefferson or Lee frightened rather than reassured a nation trying to come to terms with the city. As Walter Lippmann observed: "Quite apart even from the severe opposition of the prohibitionists, the objection to Tammany, the sectional objection to New York, there is an opposition to Smith which is as authentic, and, it seems to me, as poignant as his support. It is inspired by the feeling that the clamorous life of the city should not be acknowledged as the American ideal." A man of great ability, Al Smith arrived too early on the political scene to be accepted as a national symbol. His rejection, particularly the manner in which he was denied, not only embittered Smith but left a wound in his ardent admirers that has not yet wholly healed.

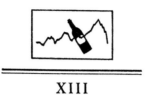

XIII

Smashup

The prosperity of the 1920's produced the contagious feeling that everyone was meant to get rich. The decade witnessed a series of speculative orgies, from "get-rich-quick" schemes to the Florida real estate boom, climaxed in 1928 and 1929 by the Great Bull Market. Before the war, stock market investment had been almost wholly a preserve of the wealthy; in the 1920's clerks and bootblacks talked knowingly of American Can or Cities Service and bought five shares "on margin." In later years it was frequently said that by the end of the twenties "everyone was in the market," but there were actually fewer, probably far fewer, than a million people involved. What is closer to the truth is that millions of Americans followed the market with avid interest; it became, remarks Professor Galbraith, "central to the culture."

No one can explain what caused the speculative wave of 1928. It is true that credit was easy, but credit had been easy before without producing a speculative mania. Moreover, much of the speculation was carried on at rates of interest which by any reasonable standard were tight. More important were the sense of optimism which permeated the decade and the conviction that, especially in the economic world, anything was possible. "We grew up founding our dreams on the infinite promises of American advertising," Scott Fitzgerald's wife Zelda once remarked. "I still believe that one can learn to play the piano by mail and that mud will give you a perfect complexion." The faith people had that they too could be rich was deliberately cultivated by responsible bankers and heads of investment trusts, who gave every indication of believing what they were saying. In an article called "Everybody Ought to Be Rich," John Raskob argued in the *Ladies' Home Journal* that anyone who saved fifteen dollars a month and bought sound common stocks would in twenty years be worth $80,-000. Since commodity prices were remarkably stable throughout the boom, economists were reassured that, despite the speculative fever, the economy was basically sound.

The volume of sales on the New York Stock Exchange leaped from 236 million shares in 1923 to 1,125 million in 1928. That was a year when everything one touched seemed to turn to gold: industrial stocks went up the astonishing total of 86.5 points. Customers crowded into brokers' offices in midmorning and stood staring at the blackboard or inspecting the tape until closing time. They borrowed money, bought more stock, watched the stock go up, and borrowed still more money to buy still more stock. By 1928 the stock market was carrying the whole economy. If it had not been for the wave of speculation, the prosperity of the twenties might have ended much earlier than it did. Coolidge's deflationary policies had withdrawn government funds from the economy, consumers had cut spending for durable goods in 1927, and the market for housing had been glutted as early as 1926. But with the economy sparked by fresh funds poured into speculation, a depression was avoided and the boom continued.

The stock market frenzy began in March, 1928. On Saturday, March 3, Radio sold at 94½. By the next Friday it had surged to 108. On the next day it bounded to 120½. It seemed impossible, but when the market closed on Monday morning, Radio had gained another 18 points and was selling at 138½. The next morning, Radio opened at 160, a gain of 21½ points overnight. And it did not stop. After a few days of relative quiet, Radio jumped 18 points on March 20. The Big Bull Market was under way. Not long before he left office, President Coolidge announced that stocks were "cheap at current prices." The summer of 1929 not only bore out his dictum but made the gains of 1928 look modest in comparison. In three months—from June to August—industrials climbed 110 points; in a single summer the value of industrial stocks increased by almost a quarter.

Even by the summer of 1928 the market had drawn people who never dreamed they would be caught in the speculative frenzy. How much longer could you hold out when your neighbor who bought General Motors at 99 in 1925 sold it at 212 in 1928? There were stories of a plunger who entered the market with a million dollars and ran it up to thirty millions in eight months, of a peddler who parlayed $4,000 into $250,000. The Bull Market was not simply a phenomenon of New York and Chicago; there were brokerage offices in towns like Steubenville, Ohio, and Storm Lake, Iowa. Even non-investors followed the market news; like batting averages, it touched the statistical heart of the country.

Men in Saginaw and Amarillo opened their newspapers and turned first to the stock market reports. They shared the same worries, often heard the same tips, that moved men to buy and sell in the canyons of Wall Street. In an era of prohibition, as Charles Merz points out, the broker's office took the place of the barroom; it had "the same swinging doors, the same half-darkened windows." In midmorning men would slump into the mahogany chairs of the smoke-filled room to search the blackboard or the hieroglyphics of the chattering ticker tape for news of the fate of Anaconda or Tel. and Tel.

In early September, 1929, the stock market broke, rallied, then broke again. By early October, Radio had tumbled 32 points, General Electric over 50 points, Steel almost 60 points. Still there was no panic. "Stock prices," announced Professor Irving Fisher of Yale, in what was to become a classic statement, "have reached what looks like a permanently high plateau." In the last week in October the situation turned suddenly worse. On October 23, rails and industrials fell 18 points. On Thursday, October 24, prices broke violently, and a stampede set in. The gains of many months were wiped out in a few hours. Radio opened at 68¾, closed at 44½. For a few days a determined effort by bankers led by the House of Morgan held the market steady, but the next week the downward plunge resumed with reckless fury. On Monday U.S. Steel lost 17½, Westinghouse 34½, General Electric 47½. The next day, Tuesday, October 29, was a day of sickening disaster. The ticker closed two and a half hours behind; when the last sales had been listed, industrial stocks had zoomed down 43 points.

On November 13 the decline came to a temporary halt, as the market reached the lowest point it was to hit that year. On that day industrial stocks were 228 points lower than they had been in early September; their value had been cut in half.

Smashup

This was only the beginning of the end. In September industrials had stood at 452; in November, 1929, they were 224. On July 8, 1932, at the bottom of the depression, they would sink to 58. In three years General Motors plummeted from 73 to 8, U.S. Steel from 262 to 22, Montgomery Ward from 138 to 4.

The prosperity of the 1920's had been founded on construction and the automobile industry. Residential construction, which had stood at five billion dollars in 1925, was down to three billion by 1929. The automobile industry continued to grow, but after 1925 it grew at a much slower rate, cutting back purchases of steel and other material; the cycle of events, whereby an increase in car production produced rapid increases in steel, rubber, glass, and other industries, now operated in a reverse manner to speed the country toward a major depression. By 1929 the automobile industry—and satellites like the rubber-tire business—were badly overbuilt. Since there was no new industry to take the place of automobiles and no policy of federal spending to provide new investment (Mellon, in fact, was working in the opposite direction), it was inevitable that as investment fell off and the rate of production slackened in the key industries, a serious recession would result.

There was no single cause of the crash and the ensuing depression, but much of the responsibility for both falls on the foolhardy assumption that the special interests of business and the national interest were identical. Management had siphoned off gains in productivity in high profits, while the farmer got far less, and the worker, though better off, received wage increases disproportionately small when compared to profits. As a result the purchasing power of workers and farmers was not great enough to sustain prosperity. For a time this was partly obscured by the fact that consumers bought goods on installment at a rate faster than their income was expanding, but it was inevitable that a time would come when they would have to reduce purchases, and the cutback in buying would sap the whole economy.

With no counteraction from labor unions, which were weak, or from government, which had no independent policy, business increased profits at twice the rate of the growth in productivity. So great were profits that many corporations no longer needed to borrow, and as a result Federal Reserve banks had only minimal control over speculation. With no other outlet, profits were plunged into the stock market, producing a runaway speculation.

The policies of the federal government in the 1920's were disastrous. Its tax policies made the maldistribution of income and oversaving by the rich still more serious. Its monopoly policies added to the rigidity of the market and left business corporations too insensitive to changes of price. Its farm policies sanctioned a dangerous imbalance in the economy. Its tariff policies made a difficult foreign-trade situation still worse. Its monetary policies were irresponsible; at critical junctures, the fiscal policy of the Coolidge administration moved in precisely the wrong direction. The administration took the narrow interests of business groups to be the national interest, and the result was catastrophe.

The market crash played a major role in precipitating the Great Depression. It shattered business confidence, ruined many investors, and wiped out holding company and investment trust structures. It destroyed an important source of long-term capital and sharply cut back consumer demand. Yet business would have been able to weather even the shock of the crash, if business had been fundamentally sound. The crash exposed the weaknesses that underlay the prosperous economy of the twenties—the overexpansion of major industries, the maldistribution of income, the weak banking structure, and the overdependence of the economy on consumer durable goods.

During the 1920's almost seven thousand banks failed; no industrial nation in the world had as unstable and as irresponsible a banking system as the United States. "The banks," noted one writer, "provided everything for their customers but a roulette wheel." In the 1920's wrote Professor Schumpeter, "a new type of bank executive emerged who had little of the banker and looked much like a bond salesman"; the new type of banker-promoter financed speculation and loaded the banks with dubious assets. Nothing did more to turn the stock market crash of 1929 into a prolonged depression than the destruction of business and public morale by the failure of the banks.

A year after the crash, six million men walked the streets looking for work. By 1932, there were 660,000 jobless in Chicago, a million in New York City. In heavily industrialized cities the toll of the depression read, as one observer noted, like British casualty lists at the Somme—so awesome as to become in the end meaningless, for the sheer statistics numbed the mind. In Cleveland 50 per cent were jobless, in Akron 60 per cent, in Toledo 80 per cent. In Donora, Pennsylvania, only 277 of 13,900 workers held regular jobs. In the three years after the crash, 100,000 workers were fired on the average every week.

By 1932, the physical output of manufacturing had fallen

to 54 per cent of what it had been in 1929; it was a shade less than production in 1913. All the gains of the golden twenties were wiped out in a few months. By the last year of the Hoover administration, the automobile industry was operating at only one-fifth of its 1929 capacity. As the great auto plants in Detroit lay idle, fires were banked in the steel furnaces on the Allegheny and the Mahoning. By the summer of 1932, steel plants operated at 12 per cent of capacity, and the output of pig iron was the lowest since 1896. Between 1929 and 1932, freight shipments were cut in half, and major railroad systems like the Missouri Pacific, the Chicago and North Western, and the Wabash passed into receivership.

The farmer, who had seen little of the prosperity of the 1920's, was devastated by the depression. The crash—and the ensuing financial debacle—destroyed much of what remained of his foreign markets. American foreign trade declined from $10 billion in 1929 to $3 billion in 1932. Foreign capital issues fell from $1500 million in 1928 to the abysmally low figure of $88 million in 1932. As foreign nations erected new barriers to American products and unemployment cut heavily into the domestic market, crop prices skidded to new lows. Wheat fell from $1.05 a bushel in 1929 to 39 cents in 1932, corn from 81 cents to 33 cents a bushel, cotton from 17 cents to 6 cents a pound, tobacco from 19 cents to 10 cents a pound. The result was catastrophic. Gross farm income fell from nearly $12 billion to the pitiful sum of $5 billion.

Like a cold bay fog, fear of the bread line drifted up into the middle class. Detroit counted 30 former bank tellers on its relief rolls. The universities graduated thousands of engineers, architects, and lawyers who had not the slightest prospect of a job. With no hope of employment, young people postponed marriage or, if they were married, did not have children. In 1932, there were 250,000 fewer marriages than in 1929, and the birth rate slipped from 18.8 to 17.4 per thousand. Hundreds of thousands of working women returned to their homes. Economy-minded school boards halted building projects and slashed teachers' salaries. Chicago teachers, unpaid for months, lost their savings, had to surrender their insurance policies, and were forced to borrow from loan sharks at 42 per cent annual interest. By the middle of 1932, over 750 had lost their homes.

The depression touched every area of American life. Bergdorf Goodman slashed sables 40 per cent, Marcus and Company offered a $50,000 emerald ring for $37,500, and the Pullman Company cut rates on upper berths 20 per cent. The Yankees mailed Babe Ruth a contract for the 1932 season with a $10,000 salary cut, and the Giants offered their star first baseman, Bill Terry, 40 per cent less. The United Hospital Fund reported that donors not only reneged on pledges but even asked that the previous year's contributions be returned to them. Off Broadway, theater lights were darkened; on Fifth Avenue, strollers no longer heard the sound of riveters. The managers of the Empire State Building ended all pretext that its offices were rented; elevators stopped running from the 42d to the 67th floors.

The nation's first response to the depression was fatalistic. Business cycles were inevitable, the fatalists argued, and there was nothing to do but wait out this latest disaster. Any attempt to interrupt the process would only make matters worse. The *New York Times* contended that "the fundamental prescriptions for recovery [were] such homely things as savings, retrenchment, prudence and hopeful waiting for the turn." Businessmen, especially bankers, demanded a ruthless deflation. "To advise people to spend," declared one banker, "would be seditious." Above all, governments must reduce expenditures, and relief budgets must be cut to the bone. The depression revived an emphasis on Puritan virtues which the 1920's had rejected, and bankers linked their insistence on deflation to Calvinist morality. President John E. Edgerton told the National Association of Manufacturers in the autumn of 1930 that it was important to make people understand that the suffering of the unemployed was not the product of an economic breakdown but was the direct result of their moral infirmity.

The financial community purported to see the depression as a blessed occurrence which would improve the national character by chastening the spirit. The crash, announced the leading banking periodical, "should be highly beneficial." Nevertheless, as Gilbert Seldes dryly remarked, "No one ever proposed to continue the depression in order to continue its benefits." Even hard-shelled British Tories were shocked by the tenacious resistance of American businessmen to unemployment insurance. "I do not sympathize," wrote Winston Churchill, "with those who think that this process of compulsory mass saving will sap the virility and self-reliance of our race. There will be quite enough grind-stone in human life to keep us keen."

The country hoped to lick the depression through magical incantation and by showing the same kind of booster spirit that had made Zenith hum. "Just grin," urged Charles M. Schwab, "keep on working." Thousands of people in Cincinnati wore buttons reading: "I'm sold on America. I won't talk depression." The vice-president of one Wall Street firm took a bunch of white carnations to his office every morning for each of his department heads, so that they would exude confidence and cheer. New York's Mayor Jimmy Walker asked movie theaters to show only cheerful films. Businessmen and government officials issued periodic bulletins declaring that the depression would be over in 30 or 60 or 90 days. Julius Rosenwald even announced that he was afraid there might soon be a serious labor shortage. The prayer offerings met with indifferent success. "Some leading Republicans are beginning to believe there is some concerted effort on foot to use the Stock Market as a method of discrediting the Administration," complained Republican National Chairman Simeon Fess. "Every time an Administration official gives out an optimistic statement about business conditions, the market immediately drops."

President Hoover has been flayed by his critics as a tool of Wall Street and as a "do-nothing" President. He was neither. He strongly disapproved of the bankers' insistence on deflation, and he used governmental power to check the depression in an unprecedented manner. Hoover had little patience with men like Secretary Mellon, who urged him to "liquidate labor, liquidate stocks, liquidate the farmers, liquidate real estate." The President stepped up federal construction, urged state and local governments to accelerate spending, and gained promises of increased capital investment from the railroads and utilities. He summoned the leading businessmen of the country to a White House conference and obtained a pledge from them to maintain wage rates. Earlier in 1929, Congress had passed the Agricultural Marketing Act, which aimed to stabilize agriculture through federal encouragement of farm co-operatives. By 1930, a Grain Stabilization Corporation and a Cotton Stabilization Corporation were invading the open market to bolster crop prices.

Hoover's approach to unemployment relief was more orthodox. To provide relief for the jobless, Hoover relied on local government initiative and private charity. He created national committees of volunteers to solicit funds, but he set himself firmly against all proposals for federal relief. A federal dole would involve huge appropriations which would unbalance the budget and thus jeopardize the national credit, he thought. It would invite reckless spending on "pork-barrel" projects. Most important, federal relief projects, Hoover argued, would destroy the character of the recipients and create a class of public wards.

Within a few months, the assumptions on which Hoover based his relief policies were shot to bits. Private charity proved wholly inadequate, and local governments soon exhausted their treasuries. Relief payments, which at most reached $5 a week for an entire family, were $2.39 a week in New York and still less elsewhere. Dallas and Houston gave no relief at all to Mexican or colored families. When cities were forced to borrow, they found they could secure funds from bankers only by agreeing to cut families from relief and reduce the pittance the jobless received. Detroit's relief rolls were swelled by thousands of discharged auto workers, but Detroit could tax neither Ford nor Chrysler, because their plants were beyond the city line. When Detroit's Mayor Frank Murphy tried to borrow, he could obtain funds from the auto companies only by agreeing to slash welfare funds drastically. Detroit dropped more than one-third of the families on relief.

The worse the depression got, the less the cities did. New

Smashup

Orleans refused all new applicants, and St. Louis cut half the relief families from its rolls. Save for New York—and to a lesser extent Illinois, Pennsylvania, New Jersey, and Wisconsin—the state governments did almost nothing. As the situation in the automobile plants grew desperate, Michigan cut its relief funds from over $2 million in 1931 to $860,000 in 1932. More than 100 cities had no relief appropriations at all for 1932.

Unable to pay rent or meet mortgage payments, many families were dispossessed from their homes. In empty lots on the edge of industrial cities, homeless men, sometimes with families, built crude shelters of packing crates and old pieces of metal. In the larger cities, whole colonies of these "Hoovervilles" were established. When municipal lodging houses became overcrowded, men huddled in empty freight cars or in shutdown factories. In New York's Central Park, a group of squatters nested in "Hoover Valley," the bed of a drained reservoir. In Arkansas, men were found living in caves. By the Salt River in Arizona, miners camped under bridges. In the great cities, girls slept on subways. Thousands of Americans wandered the country aimlessly, in quest of a job, or relief, or just a sense of motion. In 1929, the Missouri Pacific counted 13,745 migrants; in 1931, 186,028. By 1932, there were from 1 to 2 million men, including a few hundred thousand young boys, roaming the country.

In the cities, long queues of hungry men, their shoulders hunched against December winds, edged along sidewalks to get a bowl of broth from charity "soup kitchens." While most families were able to make out on shorter rations, the plight of the utterly destitute—and by 1932 they numbered millions—was appalling. In the St. Louis dumps, small groups of men, women, and children dug for rotten food. In Chicago, they stood outside the back doors of restaurants for leavings or scoured the market districts for spoiled fruit and vegetables. In the coal hills of Pennsylvania, families were fed on weeds and roots. While there were few deaths from starvation, 238 persons suffering from malnutrition or starvation were admitted to New York hospitals in 1931. Forty-five of them died.

In the three years after the crash, factory wages shrank from $12 billion to $7 billion. Although wages fell, the wage *rate*, which employers had promised Hoover they would maintain, held up remarkably well in the first two years of the depression. From the first, bankers declared a relentless war on the high-wage philosophy. *The Commercial and Financial Chronicle* conducted a persistent campaign for wage-slashing as "an intelligent step in the return of prosperity." "The man who relies upon the wage he receives for his daily toil," declared the *Chronicle*, "must realize that employers have suffered even as has the employee; and much beyond the same." On September 22, 1931, U.S. Steel announced a 10 per cent wage cut; General Motors, Bethlehem Steel, and other corporations immediately followed. The wage front was broken. Within a year, sweatshops had mushroomed all through the East. In one factory, 13-year-old packing girls were paid 50 cents a day; in another plant, apron girls received a daily wage of 20 cents.

To alleviate the misery of the depression and to use public funds to revive investment, a group of Senate progressives demanded federal action. Senator Robert Wagner of New York introduced bills for advance planning of public works and to create a federal employment service and an agency to gather unemployment statistics. Together with Wagner, Senators Robert M. La Follette, Jr., of Wisconsin, Edward P. Costigan of Colorado, and Bronson Cutting of New Mexico advocated federal spending for public works and direct relief. Hoover peremptorily opposed all these bills. While the relief situation was rapidly nearing the point of total breakdown, Hoover issued sanguine statements minimizing the number of unemployed and the degree of suffering.

Hoover was quite right in issuing reassuring statements; it would have been far worse if he had been panicky. It is also understandable that he would attempt, at first, to rely on local initiative. Hoover's failure lay in his refusal to admit the collapse of his program and in his rigid rejection of the need for a new course. When the President's own relief experts reported that unemployment was mounting to incredible levels, he would not believe them. When they urged him to launch a huge public works program, he disregarded them. Because of "an aroused sense of public responsibility," Hoover claimed, "those in destitution and their children are actually receiving more regular and more adequate care than even in normal times."

In the spring of 1931, a slow upturn in production and employment led some economists to believe that the United States was pulling out of the depression. Then disaster struck from abroad. The withdrawal of American dollars from Europe after the 1929 crash had created serious financial stringency in Europe. In March, 1931, French bankers called in short-term German and Austrian notes, a move made partly for political reasons. Unable to meet the demands, the Kreditanstalt in Vienna buckled. The collapse of the greatest bank in Austria in turn set off a chain reaction. Heavy withdrawals of gold from Germany forced the Weimar Republic to default on its reparations payments. Fearing Germany would go Communist, President von Hindenburg appealed to Hoover for help.

In June, 1931, President Hoover proposed a one-year moratorium on reparations payments and intergovernmental debts. It was a superb move, but Hoover received so little cooperation from the French that much of its value was dissipated. In August, the British, who had gone to the aid of both Austria and Germany, were caught short themselves. In September, Great Britain abandoned the gold standard. The British decision marked the virtual end of the system of international exchange of nineteenth-century capitalism.

The American banking system was exceptionally vulnerable to these financial upheavals. In 1929, 659 banks failed; in 1930, 1,352; in 1931, 2,294. In November, 1930, a panic, starting in Nashville, swept through the Middle South and closed 129 banks. The following month, a little before Christmas, the Bank of the United States in New York City, an institution with 400,000 depositors, collapsed. The ruin of the Bank of the United States, which held the life savings of thousands of recent immigrants, affected a third of the people of New York City and was the worst bank failure in the history of the Republic. Millions of Americans who in 1929 had regarded banks as the epitome of security withdrew their money and hid it under flagstones. By the fall of 1931, a billion dollars had been taken from banks and put in safe deposit boxes or stuffed in old mattresses.

The European financial debacle created a fresh crisis in the United States. As Europeans demanded gold, American banks in turn had to call in their loans to American businesses, and a new wave of liquidations followed. When in October, 1931, Philadelphia's banks were threatened, President Hoover got the more substantial bankers of the country to set up a National Credit Corporation so that strong banks could bolster the weak ones. The strong banks, animated by a sense of *sauve qui peut*, refused to co-operate.

By the autumn of 1931, bankers had carried out the policy of deflation so relentlessly that they were caught in their own web. The endless downward spirals of liquidation had reached the point where they threatened the existence of the banks themselves. By October, 1931, bankers were complaining that people were "economizing extravagantly." Once the deflation threatened the financial structure, bankers were curiously unwilling to experience the spiritual benefits of chastening. Although they continued to advocate deflation for every other segment of the economy, the bankers demanded government protection from the consequences of deflation to themselves. Fearing that if the policy of deflation was not arrested, bankers would pull their own houses down, Hoover, in December, 1931, proposed the creation of a Reconstruction Finance Corporation. Based on the War Finance Corporation of World War I, the RFC was chartered by Congress in January, 1932, to lend funds to banks, railroads, building and loan associations, and similar institutions.

Hoover followed up the RFC with a series of other antideflationary measures. In January, 1932, new capital was provided for the Federal Land Banks. The Glass-Steagall Act released gold to meet foreign withdrawals and, by liberalizing Federal Reserve requirements, expanded credit. The Federal Home Loan Bank Act, aimed at saving the mortgage market, bolstered building and loan associations. In July, 1932, after

Hoover vetoed the Garner-Wagner relief bill, which provided direct relief aid and vast public works, Congress passed a new law authorizing the RFC to lend money to states and municipalities for self-liquidating public works and to lend a smaller sum for relief to states whose resources were exhausted.

Although the RFC helped shore up railroads on the verge of bankruptcy and cut down, at least for a time, bank closings, it did nothing to get the economy rolling again. Bankers viewed the RFC not as a way to expand the volume of credit but as a means of preserving their own and other institutions from bankruptcy. The RFC virtually ignored its role as a public works agency; it moved with exasperating slowness in spending the public works and relief appropriations Congress granted it in 1932. The rest of Hoover's program met with even less success. The railroads and utilities, which had promised to expand construction, contracted their operations instead. New capital issues—investment in stocks and bonds—fell from $10 billion in 1929 to $1 billion in 1932. This was not enough new capital even to maintain the country's industrial plant. Although Hoover increased federal spending on public works, state and local governments cut back so sharply that total public construction declined. The grain and cotton corporations accumulated huge warehouses of surpluses they could not sell. Despite their efforts, the prices of grain and cotton plummeted, and the Federal Farm Board wound up with losses of $184 million. Disgusted with Hoover's insistence on voluntarism, the Board advocated federal compulsion to reduce farm production.

In the months after the crash, people continued to look to the business leaders they had revered in the 1920's to lift them out of the depression. As the months went by, and the outlook blackened, it became clear that the business titans were not miracle workers but as fallible as other mortals. Businessmen, who had claimed credit for the prosperity of the 1920's, were now blamed for producing the depression of the 1930's. As federal deficits mounted, Andrew Mellon, who had been all but canonized in the 1920's, was mocked as "the greatest Secretary of the Treasury since Carter Glass." In April, 1932, Hoover, who was convinced that a malicious conspiracy of bears was driving down the market, instigated a Senate investigation of Wall Street. The Senate probe revealed that J. P. Morgan and his nineteen partners paid no federal income taxes for 1931 and 1932 and that Morgan kept a list of insiders who were allowed to buy at less than the market price.

In March, 1932, Ivar Kreuger, one of the most respected international financiers, committed suicide in his Paris apartment. When his affairs were disentangled, it was found that the Swedish Match King had fleeced American investors of a quarter of a billion dollars by duping Lee, Higginson and other presumably astute American investment firms. American financiers had permitted Kreuger to take $50 million in securities from the vaults of the International Match Company without anyone knowing it, and Lee, Higginson had sold Kreuger's issues to the American public without insisting on the elementary step of an independent audit. That same month, Samuel Insull's utility empire collapsed, with a total loss to investors of nearly $700 million. The stock of Insull Utility Investments fell from 107½ in 1929 to 1⅛ in March, 1932. Soon it was completely worthless. The scapegoat for other businessmen, Insull fled to Paris and crossed the Mediterranean in a dirty Greek steamer to avoid extradition to face a Cook County jury.

The Perils of Prosperity, 1914–32

Nothing struck a harder blow at the prestige of American business than the phenomenon of want in the midst of plenty. While people went hungry, granaries bulged with wheat no one could sell. While people froze for lack of fuel in winter, snow drifted over the mouths of idle coal pits. With billions of dollars locked up in the banks, Iowa towns issued scrip and stores in the state of Washington issued and accepted wooden money. Knoxville, Atlanta, and Richmond printed their own currency.

Abundance stalked the canefields and the grain belts. "From Ocala south and east to Orlando and the fertile Indian River region," reported one writer after a tour of Florida, "oranges and grapefruit hang heavy on the trees and cover the ground beneath." When a terrible drought struck the country in 1930, many farmers rejoiced, and stock prices soared on Wall Street. The Federal Farm Board urged southern planters to plow under every third row of cotton, and even the boll weevil was viewed with a friendlier eye. Brazil burned thousands of bags of coffee and shoveled scowloads of coffee into the Atlantic. Rubber planters were jubilant when they discovered a new pest was attacking their trees.

Technology was the god of the 1920's. When the depression struck, technology was denounced for bringing the curse of plenty. Men relentlessly sabotaged the production on which they had preened themselves in the Coolidge years. In 1932, Representative Hatton Sumners of Texas urged that the Patent Office cease giving patents on labor-saving devices. In the winter of 1930, Newark abandoned machines for hand excavation, and Minneapolis used picks and shovels. Boston stored away its snow-loading machines to give men work with snow shovels that winter. When Henry Ford, who had done as much as any man to mechanize agriculture, hired men to harvest crops on his farms, he equipped them only with old-fashioned hoes. Kansas, the most highly mechanized agricultural state in the country, restored hitching racks in front of courthouses.

Many Americans who had never had a "radical" thought before in their lives began to question the virtues of American capitalism. Scott Fitzgerald, who by the summer of 1932 was reading Karl Marx, wrote: "To bring on the revolution, it may be necessary to work inside the communist party." How, critics asked, could one justify a system that wilfully destroyed its crops and cast aside its machines? "When I think of what has been happening since unemployment began, and when I see the futility of the leaders," declared Father John A. Ryan, "I wish we might double the number of Communists in this country, to put the fear, if not of God, then the fear of something else, into the hearts of our leaders. . . ."

As the bread lines lengthened, the mood of the country became uglier. In July, 1931, 300 unemployed men stormed the food shops of Henryetta, Oklahoma. An army of 15,000 pickets marched on Taylorville, Illinois, and stopped operations at the Christian County Mines in 1932. In Washington, D.C., 3,000 Communist "hunger marchers" paraded. None of these demonstrations matched in importance the rebellion of American farmers. From Bucks County, Pennsylvania, to Antelope County, Nebraska, farmers banded together to prevent banks and insurance companies from foreclosing mortgages. When sheriffs attempted to carry out foreclosures, mobs of farmers, brandishing pitchforks and dangling hangman's nooses, persuaded the sheriffs to retreat. In Iowa—the center of stable Republican farm life—once prosperous farmers, leaving their neat white houses and rich lands behind, barricaded highways to prevent milk from getting to market in a vain effort to force up prices. In a national radio broadcast, John A. Simpson, president of the National Farmers' Union, denounced the wealthy as "cannibals that eat each other and who live on the labor of the workers."

Nothing seemed more unreasonable to farmers than to deprive a man of a farm when, through no fault of his own, he could no longer meet his obligations, and, on this one question, the farmer was almost beside himself. A. N. Young, president of the Farmers' Union of Wisconsin, told a Senate committee: "They are just ready to do anything to get even with the situation. I almost hate to express it, but I honestly believe that if some of them could buy airplanes they would come down here to Washington to blow you fellows all up. . . . The farmer is naturally a conservative individual, but you cannot find a conservative farmer today. . . . I am as conservative as any man could be, but any economic system that has in its power to set me and my wife in the streets, at my age—what can I see but red?" For the first time in history, Lloyd's of London sold large sums of "riot and civil commotion insurance" to Americans.

Demanding immediate and full payment of bonuses for their service in World War I, an army of 15,000 to 20,000 unemployed veterans moved on Washington in the spring of 1932. The House passed the bonus bill, but when the Senate voted the bill down by an overwhelming margin, half the men left the city. The rest stayed on; they had no jobs, no homes, no place else to go. Most of them lived in mean shanties on the muddy Anacostia flats, some camped in unused government buildings. General Glassford, the head of the District police, treated the men with decency and with discretion, but, as the men stayed on day after day, Hoover and his officials panicked. On July 28, 1932, the Government decided precipitately to evict a group of bonus marchers from vacant government buildings on Pennsylvania Avenue. Two veterans were killed and several District police were injured in a scuffle that followed. President Hoover summoned the U.S. Army to take over.

With machine guns, tanks, and tear gas, brandishing sabers and drawn bayonets, the Army, in full battle regalia, advanced on the ragged group of bonus marchers. Led by the Army Chief of Staff, Douglas MacArthur (Dwight Eisenhower and George Patton were two of his junior officers) the Army dispersed the marchers and burned their billets. Hoover, whose attack on the veterans had aligned much of the country against him, made matters worse by releasing a report of the Attorney-General accusing the bonus army of being composed of Communists and criminals. General MacArthur, who called the veterans "a mob . . . animated by the essence of revolution" added to the sense that the government had lost its sense of proportion. If Hoover had "let it go on another week," MacArthur declared, "I believe that the institutions of our Government would have been very severely threatened."

By the summer of 1932, Hoover was subject to open contempt. None of his efforts seemed to do much good, and a great deal that he had said was less than honest. The country was convinced that Hoover, who more than any American of his generation had won the reputation of Great Humanitarian, was a cold-hearted man, indifferent to suffering. Scurrilous biographies were circulated accusing Hoover of having indulged in slave-trading, profited from Belgian relief, and even having caused the execution of Nurse Edith Cavell. His name became a trademark for every artifact of the depression. Men who slept on park benches dubbed the newspapers with which they covered themselves "Hoover blankets." A pocket turned inside out was a "Hoover flag." In the Southwest, harvest hands sang "Hoover made a souphound outa me."

Hoover was victimized by the excessive expectations which public relations men had built up in 1928. A man of great administrative ability, he possessed almost no political gifts. He had an aversion to the tortuous practices of democracy. Lacking skill at political maneuver, he met every situation with the directness of a rhinoceros. No one could question his devotion to his office. Hoover, observes Allan Nevins, worked "as hard as any resident of the White House since James K. Polk worked himself to death there." But, apart from his political failings and his questionable economic policies, he did not have the personality to inspire the people. In his early years he had traversed the globe from the Transvaal to the Malay Peninsula, from western Australia to Mandalay, living the life of a Richard Harding Davis hero. Yet Hoover, as Arthur Schlesinger, Jr., observes, "transmuted all adventure into business as a Davis hero would transmute all business into adventure." When asked to stir the people, President Hoover would tell his friends glumly: "I have no Wilsonian qualities."

Since it seemed almost certain that the Democrats would win in November, a keen contest developed for the Democratic presidential nomination. When New York's Governor Franklin D. Roosevelt won re-election by a landslide in 1930, he immediately established himself as the leading contender. A distant cousin of Theodore Roosevelt, he had much of

Teddy's gusto. Although he took some time to grasp the seriousness of the depression—he dismissed it at first as a "little Flurry down town"—he soon was meeting it with Rooseveltian vigor. His economics was Victorian; at the Governor's Conference in Salt Lake City in June, 1930, Roosevelt attacked Hoover for attempting to violate the natural laws of economics and the principle of laissez faire. Yet Roosevelt established the first state relief agency in the country and by 1932 had won almost every progressive in the party to his cause. In his humanitarian approach to politics, in his love of experimentation, and in his impatience with economic fatalism, Roosevelt suggested that beneath his cautious platitudes lay the promise of an audacious program.

The fight for the Democratic nomination quickly settled down to a stop-Roosevelt campaign. Al Smith, piqued by Roosevelt's rise to eminence while Smith's fortunes were declining and riled at Roosevelt's refusal to retain Smith's advisers in Albany, led the opposition. Although the conflict was essentially a clash of personalities, Smith injected an ideological note in the campaign as well, for he was aligned with the most conservative elements in the Democratic party. When Roosevelt in April, 1932, pleaded for "the forgotten man at the bottom of the economic pyramid," Smith, his face red with anger, retorted, "This is no time for demagogues." Although it seemed unlikely that Smith could win the Democratic nomination himself, it was quite conceivable that Smith could muster enough votes to block Roosevelt's nomination and throw the honor to someone else. Of the myriad of other candidates, John Garner, the Democratic Speaker in the House, had the strongest support, but astute observers believed that, if the convention deadlocked, the nomination might well go to Wilson's Secretary of War, Newton Baker, an internationalist who was conservative on economic issues.

At the Democratic convention in Chicago in June, Roosevelt took a sizable lead over his nearest rivals, Smith and Garner, but when, after three ballots, Roosevelt was unable to obtain the two-thirds vote necessary for victory, it appeared that he might be denied the nomination. At this critical juncture, California decided to throw its Garner votes to Roosevelt. The reasons for the California decision are not certain, but there is a persistent belief that it was based on the determination of William Randolph Hearst to prevent the convention from turning to the internationalist Baker. Even more important was Garner's refusal to permit the Democratic party to deadlock and destroy itself as it had in 1924. On the fourth ballot, Senator William McAdoo, whose presidential hopes had been frustrated by Smith in 1924, announced California's switch. As he stalked to the platform, he allegedly whispered: "Here's where I even up scores." The California vote turned the tide for Roosevelt; Garner, possibly as the result of an informal deal, gained the vice-presidential nomination.

Neither convention seemed as concerned about the depression as it did about the prohibition issue. "Here we are in the midst of the greatest crisis since the Civil War," wrote John Dewey, "and the only thing the two national parties seem to want to debate is booze." Save for prohibition—the Democrats were wringing wet, while the Republicans hedged—there were few important differences between the parties. The one major distinction established during the campaign was that Roosevelt, who, for an old Wilsonian, had become strongly nationalist, traced the depression to domestic causes, while Hoover emphasized its European origins.

At times, Roosevelt's campaign speeches anticipated the New Deal; he talked of the need for experimentation, indorsed social welfare legislation, outlined the idea of the Civilian Conservation Corps, and urged public power development and government regulation of utilities. But a great deal of what he said was double talk. While he promised expensive national reforms, he pledged at the same time a 25 per cent cut in the budget and censured Hoover's administration as "the greatest spending administration in peace times in all our history"—one which had "piled bureau on bureau, commission on commission. . . ." His tariff policy was contradictory; his farm speech at Topeka was designed to mean all things to all men. Running safely ahead, Roosevelt saw no point in unnecessary militancy. On Election Day, the country gave Roosevelt 22,800,000 votes to Hoover's 15,750,000. Roosevelt captured all but six states; he swung every state south and west of Pennsylvania.

The vote was less a triumph for Roosevelt than a rejection of Hoover. In the weeks after the election, as another depression winter approached, the country was deep in gloom. "For after a three years' deflation of the smart man, who is there in whom we can put our confidence?" asked Elmer Davis. "The leaders of industry and finance? They are about as thoroughly discredited as any set of false prophets in history and most of them know it. . . . Confidence in the politicians? The mere suggestion is enough to make anybody laugh. . . ." America no longer seemed a land saturated with hope and promise of the future. In 1932, 36,000 immigrants entered the country; 103,000 emigrants left. By the end of the 1930's, it would be clear that the self-confidence of the United States had not been shattered but only badly jarred. At the time, men felt that they had come to the end of an era. "Has the prophecy of Henry Adams, that we are all on a machine which cannot go forward without disaster and cannot be stopped without ruin, come true?" asked William Dodd. Of all the losses wrought by the depression, the ebullient optimism of 1914 was the chief casualty.

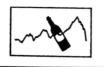

Epilogue

Never was a decade snuffed out so quickly as the 1920's. The stock market crash was taken as a judgment pronounced on the whole era, and, in the grim days of the depression, the 1920's were condemned as a time of irresponsibility and immaturity. "It was an easy, quick, adventurous age, good to be young in," wrote Malcolm Cowley, "and yet on coming out of it one felt a sense of relief, as on coming out of a room too full of talk and people into the sunlight of the winter streets."

Time was ruthless to the heroes of the decade. In 1929, with horrible appropriateness, Zelda Fitzgerald suffered a mental breakdown. Scott Fitzgerald aged like Dorian Gray; he wrote excellent work which, in the serious-minded thirties, was dismissed as trivia. Fitzgerald himself entered that "dark night of the soul" where it was "always three o'clock in the morning." The insouciant Jimmy Walker continued to make the rounds of New York nightclubs, but in the depression days his antics no longer amused, and he was driven from office. Mencken, who had been the savant of the college generation of the twenties, was brushed aside by the college generation of the thirties, if they read him at all, as an antiquated reactionary.

In 1933 the nation repealed the prohibition amendment, and with it went the world of the speakeasy; that same year, Texas Guinan died. Sound movies ended the careers of many of the silent stars. Clara Bow, who recalled halcyon days—"I'd whiz down Sunset Boulevard in my open Kissel (flaming red, of course) with seven red dogs to match my hair"—entered a sanitarium. When the sound track revealed that the screen's greatest lover, John Gilbert, had a high-pitched voice, his contract was not renewed. At 38 he was dead, the sound era's most conspicuous victim. In 1931 the Ziegfeld Follies opened for the last time. In 1932, bankrupted by the depression, Florenz Ziegfeld died. In the spring of 1932 vaudeville went to the grave when the Palace gave its last all-vaudeville bill. The law caught up with Al Capone in 1931, and he was sentenced to eleven years in prison for federal income tax evasion. The underworld caught up with Dutch Schultz and riddled him with bullets in a Newark barroom; dying, he uttered the baffling metrical sentence: "A boy has never wept, nor dashed a thousand kim." Dempsey's defeat, Gene Tunney's retirement, and the death of Tex Rickard brought the golden age of boxing to an end in 1929. In 1934 Babe Ruth, a pathetic waddling figure, tightly corseted, a cruel lampoon of his former greatness, took off his Yankee uniform for the last time.

The depression years killed off the symbols of simplicity the 1920's had cherished. In January, 1933—eight weeks before Franklin Roosevelt took office—Calvin Coolidge died. Henry Ford, the folk hero of the Coolidge era, was damned in the 1930's as a tyrannical employer. When he instituted the five-dollar day, he had been honored as the laboring man's warmest friend. In the depression days, Ford was hard put to defend the actions of his private police headed by a former prize fighter, Harry Bennett, a mean-tempered man with close friends in the Detroit underworld. Charles A. Lindbergh, the tousled blond airman whose flight to Paris in 1927 made him

Epilogue

America's golden boy, suffered the trials of Job in the 1930's. On the night of March 1, 1932, his twenty-month-old son was kidnapped from his home. Seventy-two days later, the child's body was found in a patch of woods. Cruelly badgered by the press and exploited by publicity-seekers, Lindbergh and his family abandoned America for Europe in December, 1935. The magnificent Lone Eagle of the 1920's, Lindbergh, by 1940, was detested as an associate of Nazis and an avowed racist.

Throughout the 1920's, demure Mary Pickford had remained the curly-locked Pollyanna of prewar American innocence. She refused to play "bad girl" roles. Rebelling against the fashions of the time, she refused to cut her hair. In 1927, she wrote: "Sometimes it is a dreadful nightmare, when I feel the cold shears at the back of my neck, and see my curls fall one by one at my feet, useless, lifeless things to be packed away in tissue paper with other outworn treasures." In the first year of the depression, her curls were shorn, and she appeared on the screen portraying bad women.

In the 1920's the events of half a century finally caught up with America. Ever since the Civil War the United States had been industrializing at an astonishing rate—erecting great factories, filling up the empty spaces of the West, expanding its cities to gargantuan size. In the years after World War I the productive capacity of the American economy suddenly exploded at the very same time that, in large part because of the growth in productivity, the United States became the greatest of the world powers, and the city overtook the country in the race for dominance. All the institutions of American society buckled under the strain.

It was a time of paradoxes: an age of conformity and of

271

liberation, of the persistence of rural values and the triumph of the city, of isolationism and new internationalist ventures, of laissez faire but also of government intervention, of competition and of merger, of despair and of joyous abandon. Many of the apparent paradoxes can be explained by the reluctance of the American people to accept the changes that were occurring and by their attempt to hold on to older ways of thought and action at the same time that they were, often against their will, committed to new ones. The very men who were taken as symbols of the old order were the ones who undermined it—the Victorian statesman Woodrow Wilson, who presided over the transition to a strong state and the breakdown of isolation; the antiquarian Henry Ford, who disrupted the nineteenth-century world with revolutionary industrial technology; even Herbert Hoover, whose triumph in 1928 over Smith appeared to be a rejection of urban mores, but who himself was the unwitting architect of a new era.

The 1920's, despite rhetoric to the contrary, marked the end of nineteenth-century liberalism. In the same week in October, 1922, Lloyd George paid his last official visit as Prime Minister to the King and Mussolini marched on Rome. Although Republican ideologues like Hoover sounded the praises of laissez faire and business-minded administrators like Andrew Mellon attempted to diminish the role of government, the state continued relentlessly to augment its power. Both the civil and military functions of the federal government doubled between 1915 and 1930.

The 1920's have been dismissed as a time of immaturity, the years when America was hell-bent on the "gaudiest spree in history." But there was a great deal more to the era than raccoon coats and bathtub gin. "The world broke in two in 1922

Epilogue

or thereabouts," wrote Willa Cather. The year may not be accurate, but the observation is. The United States had to come to terms with a strong state, the dominance of the metropolis, secularization and the breakdown of religious sanctions, the loss of authority of the family, industrial concentration, international power politics, and mass culture. The country dodged some of these problems, resorted to violence to eliminate others, and, for still others, found partial answers. The United States in the period from 1914 to 1932 fell far short of working out viable solutions to the problems created by the painful transition from nineteenth-century to modern America. But it is, at the very least, charitable to remember that the country has not solved these problems yet.

Important Dates

1914   Outbreak of World War I
First moving assembly line with endless-chain conveyor
Strand Theatre in New York begins exclusive showing of
    motion pictures
T. S. Eliot abandons Boston for London

1915   Sinking of the "Lusitania"
Ku Klux Klan organized
Nonpartisan League formed

1916   Preparedness movement
House-Grey memorandum
Gore-McLemore resolutions
"Sussex" affair

1917   Wilson's "peace without victory" speech
Zimmermann telegram
American declaration of war
Creation of war economy
First United States troops land in France
Bolshevik Revolution in Russia

1918   *Hammer* v. *Dagenhart*
Wilson announces Fourteen Points
War Industries Board
Sedition law

Important Dates

Battle of the Argonne
Victorious end of World War I

1919 Peace conference and Versailles pact
Eighteenth Amendment (prohibition)
Senate rejects United States membership in League of Nations
Red Scare
Founding of American Communist parties
First ads showing woman holding a cigarette

1920 Nationwide Palmer raid
Senate rejects United States membership in League of Nations for second and final time
Nineteenth Amendment (women's suffrage)
Main Street
This Side of Paradise
Start of postwar depression
KDKA broadcasts news of Harding's victory
Studebaker stops making horse-drawn wagons

1921 Emergency immigration restriction law
Organization of the farm bloc
Washington conference on disarmament and Far East

1922 Fordney-McCumber tariff
Bailey v. *Drexel Furniture Co.*
The Waste Land
Recovery from postwar depression

1923 United States Steel abandons twelve-hour day
Death of President Harding
Adkins v. *Children's Hospital*
Revelation of scandals of Harding administration

1924 National Origins Act (immigration restriction)
Dawes Plan on reparations
Progressive ticket headed by Robert La Follette

1925 Scopes trial
Third edition, Watson's *Behaviorism*
The New Yorker founded

The Perils of Prosperity, 1914–32

Bryn Mawr rescinds rule against smoking by students in college buildings

1926   *The Sun Also Rises*

1927   Lindbergh flies the Atlantic to Paris
Execution of Sacco and Vanzetti
The Jazz Singer—first feature sound film
Start of "Good Neighbor Policy" in Latin America

1928   The Big Bull Market
Kellogg-Briand Pact

1929   *Look Homeward, Angel*
Agricultural Marketing Act
Wall Street Crash

1930   Hawley-Smoot Tariff Act

1931   Empire State Building
Hoover moratorium on intergovernmental debts
Japan invades Manchuria

1932   Reconstruction Finance Corporation
Bonus Army episode
Election of Franklin D. Roosevelt

Suggested Reading

Every account of this period begins with Frederick Lewis Allen, *Only Yesterday* (1931), a social history written in such a lively style that academicians often underrate its soundness. Allen's *The Big Change* (1952), which covers the first half of the twentieth century, is less perceptive. Lloyd Morris, *Postscript to Yesterday* (1947), offers a secondhand account of the social history of the twentieth century, sometimes penetrating, often superficial. Morris's *Not So Long Ago* (1949) concentrates on the cultural changes wrought by the automobile, movies, and the radio. Isabel Leighton (ed.), *The Aspirin Age* (1949), collects ten essays on America between Versailles and the crash, including a hilarious article on prohibition by Herbert Asbury, a study of Coolidge by Irving Stone, the fantastic life story of Aimee Semple McPherson by Carey Mc-Williams, a piece on the Harding scandals by Samuel Hopkins Adams, and a moving account of the Klan in Indiana by Robert Coughlan.

The 1920's have proved irresistible to social historians. Among the books which deal wholly or in part with this period are Charles Merz, *The Great American Band Wagon* (1928); Henry Morton Robinson, *Fantastic Interim* (1943), Laurence Greene, *The Era of Wonderful Nonsense* (1939); and the last two volumes of Mark Sullivan, *Our Times, 1900–1925* (6 vols., 1926–35). Preston Slosson, *The Great Crusade and After, 1914–1928* (1930), is the final volume in "The History of American Life" series. Paul Sann, *The Lawless Decade* (1957) presents an entertaining pictorial record of the 1920's. Fred Ringel (ed.), *America as Americans See It* (1932), surveys the early years of the depression.

The most substantial study of American society in this period is The President's Research Committee on Social Trends, *Recent Social Trends in the United States* (1933). Arthur Link, *American Epoch* (1955), a history of the United States since 1890, achieves a synthesis of materials far more stimulating than the usual "text-book." In particular, his chapter on the "Survival of Progressivism" presents a fresh view of the politics of the 1920's, although he over-states his case. Harold Faulkner, *From Versailles to the New Deal* (1950), and Harvey Wish, *Society and Thought in Modern America* (1952), are also useful. Arthur Schlesinger, Jr., *The Crisis of the Old Order, 1919–1933* (1957), the first volume of "The Age of Roosevelt," is a well-written account of the period by a liberal partisan. Henry May, "Shifting Perspectives on the 1920's," *Mississippi Valley Historical Review*, XLIII (December, 1956), 405–27, stresses the manner in which changes in intellectual fashion have altered interpretations of the period. John Montgomery, *The Twenties* (1957), surveys British society in the same era.

David Riesman, *The Lonely Crowd* (1950), presents a stimulating study of American character. Although Riesman does not fix precise dates himself, his "other-directed" man moved onto the national stage for the first time in the 1920's. So did the "new" middle class which is the subject of C. Wright Mills, *White Collar* (1951). Supporting evidence for both Riesman and Mills can be found in Richard Walsh, "The Doom of the Self-Made Man," *Century*, CIX (December, 1924), 253–58, and Irvin Wyllie, *The Self-Made Man in America* (1954). Robert and Helen Lynd, *Middletown* (1929), dissect a "typical" American town, Muncie, Indiana.

Reports on America by European travelers have usually been a prime source for American historians. In this period, they are, for the most part, unrewarding. Of the British accounts, one of the best is J. A. Spender, *Through English Eyes* (1928). W. L. George, *Hail Columbia! Random Impressions of a Conservative English Radical* (1921), and Sisley Huddleston, *What's Right with America* (1930), are amiable essays which add little. Huddleston's "America's New Industrial Doctrines," *The New Statesman*, XXXIV (December 28, 1929), 385–86, reveals that even the crash did not diminish his admiration for New Era economics. Ford Madox Ford, *New York Is Not America* (1927), is disappointing. A. G. Gardiner, *Portraits and Portents* (1926), contains essays on Coolidge and Ford. Stephen Graham, "The Spirit of America After the War," *Fortnightly Review*, CXIII (June, 1920), 874–85, and James Muirhead, "America Revisited After Ten Years," *The Land-*

Suggested Reading

mark, III (February, 1921), 107–13, are vivid sketches of the United States after Versailles. Eric Linklater, *Juan in America* (1931), is an engaging satire; at times, it is uproariously funny.

Most British accounts are either embarrassingly laudatory or savagely hostile. Colonel J. F. C. Fuller, *Atlantis* (1926), is a tedious diatribe which revives the nineteenth-century tradition of contempt for America. Colonel Fuller observes: "Spiritually, the country is a corpse, physically, a terrific machine." C. E. M. Joad, professor of philosophy at the University of London, preserves his objectivity by writing about the United States without ever visiting it. America, Joad is convinced, is *The Babbitt Warren* (1926). British critiques of American civilization are summed up in George Knoles, *The Jazz Age Revisited* (1955).

Continental accounts are generally more discerning, although André Siegfried, *America Comes of Age* (1927), is overrated. Moritz Bonn, "The American Way," *Atlantic Monthly*, CXLII (September, 1928), 300–308, is a searching German interpretation of the United States as a "man-made, not time-made commonwealth." Richard Müller-Freienfels, *Mysteries of the Soul* (1929), discusses with considerable understanding the impact of mechanization on American culture, a subject which fascinated the Germans.

Richard Watson, Jr., "Woodrow Wilson and His Interpreters, 1947–1957," *Mississippi Valley Historical Review*, XLIV (September, 1957), 207–36, is a good guide to the recent Wilson literature. Ray Stannard Baker, *Woodrow Wilson: Life and Letters* (8 vols., 1927–39), is the standard biography. Arthur Link is now writing a new multi-volume biography; the two volumes which have thus far appeared, both of high quality, cover Wilson's life through 1914. Link gives the most lucid account of the first Wilson administration in *Woodrow Wilson and the Progressive Era, 1910–1917* (1954). Herbert Bell, *Woodrow Wilson and the People* (1945), is a good one-volume work by a Wilson admirer. John Blum, *Woodrow Wilson and the Politics of Morality* (1956), and John Garraty, *Woodrow Wilson* (1956), are masterful brief biographies. Joseph Tumulty, *Woodrow Wilson As I Know Him* (1921), must be used with caution.

The most judicious biographies of the men around Wilson are John Blum, *Joe Tumulty and the Wilson Era* (1951), Frank

The Perils of Prosperity, 1914–32

Freidel, *Franklin D. Roosevelt: The Apprenticeship* (1952), and Charles Seymour (ed.), *The Intimate Papers of Colonel House* (4 vols., 1926–28). William McAdoo left a memoir of the period in *Crowded Years* (1931). Henry Pringle, *Theodore Roosevelt* (1931), is the best biography of Teddy, although a less caustic study would be welcome. Howard Beale and John Blum have written perspicacious studies of Roosevelt, but they do not cover this period. George Mowry, *Theodore Roosevelt and the Progressive Movement* (1947) concludes with a superb analysis of the strangulation of the Progressive party.

The literature on the causes of American entrance into World War I is so mountainous that there is now an impressive literature of bibliographies of literature of the topic. The more important of these are Bernadotte Schmitt, "American Neutrality, 1914–1917," *Journal of Modern History*, VIII (June, 1936), 200–211; D. F. Fleming, "Our Entry into the World War in 1917," *Journal of Politics*, II (February, 1940), 75–86; and Richard Leopold, "The Problem of American Intervention in 1917: An Historical Prospect," *World Politics*, II (April, 1950), 404–25. Harley Notter, *The Origins of the Foreign Policy of Woodrow Wilson* (1937), is a substantial work. The standard account of the foreign relations of the period is Charles Seymour, *American Diplomacy during the World War* (1934); his *American Neutrality, 1914–1917* (1935) is more polemical. Both Walter Millis, *Road to War* (1935), a popular account written in a beguiling manner, and Charles Tansill, *America Goes to War* (1938), reflect the pacifism of the 1930's, but both volumes have reputations as one-dimensional studies which they do not deserve. Millis' article, "Will We Stay Out of the Next War?: How We Entered the Last One," *New Republic*, LXXXIII (July 31, 1935), 323–27, is one of the most level-headed pieces written in the 1930's.

Although economic interpretations are not fashionable today, no historian can neglect Paul Birdsall, "Neutrality and Economic Pressures, 1914–1917," *Science and Society*, III (Spring, 1939), 217–28. Alice Morrissey, *The American Defense of Neutral Rights, 1914–1917* (1939), is a solid monograph. For public opinion, a subject which Seymour largely neglected, see Edwin Costrell, *How Maine Viewed the War, 1914–1917* ("*University of Maine Studies*," Second Series, No. 49 [1940]), one of a number of state studies;

Suggested Reading

H. Schuyler Foster, Jr., "How America Became Belligerent," *American Journal of Sociology*, XL (January, 1935), 464–75; and Harold Syrett, "The Business Press and American Neutrality, 1914–1917," *Mississippi Valley Historical Review*, XXXII (September, 1945), 215–30. Marion Siney, *The Allied Blockade of Germany 1914–1916* (1957), an impressive study based on the archives of several European countries, and Daniel Smith, "Robert Lansing and the Formulation of American Neutrality Policies, 1914–1915," *Mississippi Valley Historical Review*, XLIII (June, 1956), 59–81, examine the development of neutrality in the early part of the war.

Since World War II, historians have been more concerned with examining American foreign policy from the vantage point of power relations. Robert Osgood, *Ideals and Self-Interest in America's Foreign Relations* (1953), is the best historical work to come out of this school. Edward Buehrig, *Woodrow Wilson and the Balance of Power* (1955), also concentrates on power considerations. Buehrig has edited *Wilson's Foreign Policy in Perspective* (1957). He presents his viewpoint more briefly in "Wilson's Neutrality Re-Examined," *World Politics*, III (October, 1950), 1–19. Of all the studies of American entrance into the war, probably the most judicious is Arthur Link, *Wilson the Diplomatist* (1957); Link follows Seymour, for the most part, but modifies Seymour in the light of recent scholarship.

Frederick Paxson, *American Democracy and the World War* (3 vols., 1936–48), is the standard work on America's participation in World War I. Paxson treats one phase of it in "The American War Government, 1917–1918," *American Historical Review*, XXVI (October, 1920), 54–76. John Bach McMaster, *The United States in the World War* (2 vols., 1918–20), is pedantic. Benedict Crowell and R. F. Wilson (eds.), *How America Went to War* (6 vols., 1921), Grosvenor Clarkson, *Industrial America in the World War* (1923), and Bernard Baruch, *American Industry in War* (1941), are the chief sources for studying industrial mobilization. George Mowry, "The First World War and American Democracy," in Jesse Clarkson and Thomas Cochran (eds.), *War as a Social Institution* (1941), discusses the baleful effect of the war; in a commentary on Mowry's article, Max Lerner dissents. Sidney Kaplan, "Social Engineers as Saviors: Effects of World War I on

The Perils of Prosperity, 1914–32

Some American Liberals," *Journal of the History of Ideas,* XVII (June, 1956), 347–69, is illuminating. William Waller (ed.), *War in the Twentieth Century* (1940), assembles a number of essays on World War I and its aftermath.

Among the many works on the military and naval phases of the war, the more important include: Elting Morison, *Admiral Sims and the Modern American Navy* (1942); J. G. Harbord, *The American Army in France, 1917–1918* (1936); John J. Pershing, *Final Report* (1919); Leonard Ayres, *The War with Germany* (1919); and George Davis, *A Navy Second to None* (1940). George Sylvester Viereck (ed.), *As They Saw Us* (1929), is a fascinating volume in which Foch, Ludendorff, and others give their impressions of American troops in France; Ludendorff's essay is a pre-Hitlerian sample of his bizarre political views. Emerson Hough, *The Web* (1919), offers a frightening example of wartime chauvinism. For suppression of civil liberties, see H. C. Peterson and Gilbert Fite, *Opponents of War* (1957), and Charles Stewart, "Prussianizing Wisconsin," *Atlantic Monthly,* CXXIII (January, 1919), 99–105. Randolph Bourne, *The History of a Literary Radical and Other Papers* (1956), is a new edition of Bourne's disturbing essays, long out of print.

The best introductions to the literature of Versailles are R. C. Binkley, "Ten Years of Peace Conference History," *Journal of Modern History,* I (December, 1929), 607–29, and Paul Birdsall, "The Second Decade of Peace Conference History," *Journal of Modern History,* XI (September, 1939), 362–78. H. W. V. Temperley *et al., A History of the Peace Conference of Paris* (6 vols., 1920–24), is the standard work on that subject, but Thomas Bailey, *Woodrow Wilson and the Lost Peace* (1944), is often more rewarding. For Wilson's role, the chief source is R. S. Baker, *Woodrow Wilson and World Settlement* (3 vols., 1922). John Maynard Keynes, *The Economic Consequences of the Peace* (1920), had an enormous impact on thinking about the conference; Keynes's sparkling wit concealed the weakness of his thought. Étienne Mantoux, *The Carthaginian Peace, or The Economic Consequences of Mr. Keynes* (1946), makes an eloquent reply. Paul Birdsall, *Versailles Twenty Years After* (1941) gives an important reappraisal.

The significance of the 1918 elections is explored in Selig Adler, "The Congressional Election of 1918," *South Atlantic Quarterly,*

Suggested Reading

XXXVI (October, 1937), 447–65, and Seward Livermore, "The Sectional Issue in the 1918 Congressional Election," *Mississippi Valley Historical Review*, XXXV (June, 1948), 29–60. Thomas Bailey, *Woodrow Wilson and the Great Betrayal* (1945), is the best book on the League fight, although Bailey is too critical of Wilson. Karl Schriftgiesser, *The Gentleman from Massachusetts* (1944), D. F. Fleming, *The United States and the League of Nations, 1918–1920* (1932), and H. Maurice Darling, "Who Kept the United States Out of the League of Nations?" *Canadian Historical Review*, X (September, 1929), 196–211, are all hostile to Lodge. John Garraty, *Henry Cabot Lodge* (1953) is friendlier, but Lodge's obnoxiousness manages to overcome Garraty's generosity. Dexter Perkins, "Woodrow Wilson's Tour," ·in Daniel Aaron (ed.), *America in Crisis* (1952) is an admirable account of that tragic episode.

Robert Murray, *Red Scare* (1955), is the standard work on the subject. Robert Warth, "The Palmer Raids," *South Atlantic Quarterly*, XLVIII (January, 1949), 1–23, gives a good brief account. John Blum, "Nativism, Anti-Radicalism, and the Foreign Scare, 1917–1920," *Midwest Journal*, III (Winter, 1950–51), 46–53, is penetrating. The flavor of the Red Scare is preserved in Calvin Coolidge, "Enemies of the Republic: Are the 'Reds' Stalking Our College Women?" *Delineator*, XCVIII (June, 1921), 4–5, 66–67, and Clayton Lusk, "Radicalism under Inquiry," *American Review of Reviews*, LXI (February, 1920), 167–71. Kate Holladay Claghorn, *The Immigrant's Day in Court* (1923), which contains a good chapter on the deportations, and Nelson Van Valen, "The Bolsheviki and the Orange Growers," *Pacific Historical Review*, XXII (August, 1953), 39–50, are special studies. Francis Russell, "Coolidge and the Boston Police Strike," *Antioch Review*, XVI (December, 1956), 403–15, provides a pleasant reminiscence. Zechariah Chafee, *Free Speech in the United States* (rev. ed., 1941), is the classic account of violations of civil liberties in this period.

Theodore Draper, *The Roots of American Communism* (1957), makes a superb start on his history of the Communist Party. Joseph Freeman, *An American Testament* (1936), is perhaps the best book produced by an American Marxist. The basic sources for studying American socialism are David Shannon, *The Socialist Party of America* (1955); Daniel Bell, "Marxian Socialism in the

United States," in Donald Egbert and Stow Persons, *Socialism and American Life* (1952), Vol. I; and Ray Ginger, *The Bending Cross* (1949), a biography of Debs. Granville Hicks, *John Reed* (1936), written when Hicks was a Marxist, is an important book. G. L. Joughin and E. M. Morgan, *The Legacy of Sacco and Vanzetti* (1948), is indispensable.

Historians are only beginning to dig into the political history of the 1920's. Karl Schriftgiesser, *This Was Normalcy* (1948), is a vivid political history of the years 1920–32 by an unrestrained Democratic partisan. Malcolm Moos, *The Republicans* (1956), surveys the GOP. The best political writing on the period is by newspapermen. William Allen White, *Autobiography* (1946); his *Masks in a Pageant* (1930); Walter Johnson (ed.), *Selected Letters of William Allen White, 1899–1943* (1947); and Johnson, *William Allen White's America* (1947), all place the historian in the debt of the Sage of Emporia. Clinton Gilbert wrote *The Mirrors of Washington* (1921) anonymously and *"You Takes Your Choice"* (1924) under his signature. Among the more important sources on Republican political figures are: Henry Pringle, *The Life and Times of William Howard Taft* (1939), Vol. II; William Hutchinson, *Lowden of Illinois* (2 vols., 1957); and Joel Paschal, *Mr. Justice Sutherland* (1951).

There is no good biography of Harding. The best essay on him is by Allan Nevins in Volume 8 of the *Dictionary of American Biography*. Samuel Hopkins Adams, *Incredible Era* (1939), examines the Harding administration. Wesley Bagby, "The 'Smoke Filled Room' and the Nomination of Warren G. Harding," *Mississippi Valley Historical Review*, XLI (March, 1955), 657–74, and "Woodrow Wilson, a Third Term, and the Solemn Referendum," *American Historical Review*, LX (April, 1955), 567–75, are culled from Bagby's 1954 Columbia Ph.D. dissertation, "Progressivism's Debacle: The Election of 1920." Finley Peter Dunne, "A Look at Harding from the Side Lines," *Saturday Evening Post*, CCIX (September 12, 1936), 24–25, 74–79, is a friendly vignette.

Harry Daugherty and Thomas Dixon, *The Inside Story of the Harding Tragedy* (1932), should be read *cum grano salis*. For new light on the oil scandals, see J. Leonard Bates, "Josephus Daniels and the Naval Oil Reserves," *U.S. Naval Institute Proceedings*, LXXIX (February, 1953), 171–79; his "The Teapot Dome Scandal and the Election of 1924," *American Historical Review*, LX (January, 1955), 303–22; and Burl Noggle, "The Origins of the Teapot Dome Investigation," *Mississippi Valley Historical Review*, XLIV (September, 1957), 237–66.

William Allen White, *A Puritan in Babylon: The Story of Calvin Coolidge* (1938), is one of the best political biographies in our literature. Claude Fuess, *Calvin Coolidge* (1940), is more orthodox. Fuess's point of view is presented more briefly in "Calvin Coolidge —Twenty Years After," *Proceedings of the American Antiquarian Society*, LXIII, Pt. 2 (1954), 351–69. Gamaliel Bradford, "The Genius of the Average: Calvin Coolidge," *Atlantic Monthly*, CXLV (January, 1930), 1–13, is a perceptive essay.

Thomas Bailey, *A Diplomatic History of the American People* (1950); Samuel Flagg Bemis, *A Diplomatic History of the United States* (1950); Julius Pratt, *A History of United States Foreign Policy* (1955); and Foster Rhea Dulles, *America's Rise to World Power, 1898–1954* (1955), are among the general works on foreign affairs which have chapters on this period. Frank Simonds, *American Foreign Policy in the Post-War Years* (1935), is a brilliant analysis by a foe of collective security; although his central thesis is dubious, he makes a number of shrewd observations on the foreign affairs of the period, particularly with respect to economic policy. Dexter Perkins, "The Department of State and American Public Opinion," in Gordon Craig and Felix Gilbert (eds.), *The Diplomats 1919–1939* (1953), is excellent. George Kennan, *American Diplomacy, 1900–1950* (1952), argues the now familiar thesis that American foreign policy in the twentieth century has been founded on unreasonable assumptions about morality and power.

Selig Adler, "The War-Guilt Question and American Disillusionment, 1919–1928," *Journal of Modern History*, XXIII (March, 1951), 1–28, and "Isolationism Since 1914," *American Scholar*, XXI (Summer, 1952), 335–44, both trace the process of America's retreat from world affairs. Special interpretations which should be noted are William Appleman Williams, "The Legend of Isolationism in the 1920's," *Science and Society*, XVIII (Winter, 1954), 1–20; Daniel Boorstin, "America and the Image of Europe," *Perspectives USA*, XIV (Winter, 1956), 5–19; and Charles Beard, "The American Invasion of Europe," *Harper's*, CLVIII (March, 1929), 470–79.

The Perils of Prosperity, 1914–32

Herbert Feis, *The Diplomacy of the Dollar* (1950), is one of the few studies of America's foreign economic relations in the 1920's to break through the barrier of clichés about American isolation. Simon Kuznets, *Economic Change* (1953), has an important chapter on foreign economic relations. F. W. Taussig, *The Tariff History of the United States* (1923), contains a chapter on the 1922 act by the chief scholarly critic of protectionism. Abraham Berglund, "The Tariff Act of 1922," *American Economic Review*, XIII (March, 1923), 14–33, presents another valuable review of Fordney-McCumber. The best of the standard works on economic foreign policy are James Angell, *Financial Foreign Policy of the United States* (1933); M. F. Jolliffe, *The United States as a Financial Centre 1919–1933* (1935); Benjamin Williams, *Economic Foreign Policy of the United States* (1929); and John Madden, Marcus Nadler, and Harry Sauvain, *America's Experience as a Creditor Nation* (1937).

Merlo Pusey, *Charles Evans Hughes* (1951), Vol. II, is the major biography of the most important Secretary of State of the era, but no one should overlook the brief volume by Dexter Perkins, *Charles Evans Hughes and American Democratic Statesmanship* (1956). John Chalmers Vinson, *The Parchment Peace* (1955), offers a critical view of the Senate and the Washington Conference. For other accounts of the significance of the conference, see A. Whitney Griswold, *The Far Eastern Policy of the United States* (1943), and H. H. and Margaret Sprout, *Toward a New Order of Sea Power* (1940). Robert Ferrell, *Peace in Their Time* (1952), is a good monograph on the Kellogg-Briand pact; one phase, based on the Shotwell papers, is treated by Waldo Chamberlin, "Origins of the Kellogg-Briand Pact," *Historian*, XV (Autumn, 1952), 77–92.

W. S. Myers, *The Foreign Policies of Herbert Hoover, 1929–1933* (1940), is the standard work. E. E. Schattschneider, *Politics, Pressures, and the Tariff* (1935), and J. M. Jones, *Tariff Retaliation* (1934), discuss the adoption and impact of Smoot-Hawley. Henry Stimson and M. Bundy, *On Active Service in Peace and War* (1948), is Stimson's personal account, while Richard Current, *Secretary Stimson* (1954), hauls Hoover's Secretary of State over the coals. On the Stimson doctrine, see Robert Langer, *Seizure of Territory* (1947), and Sara Smith, *The Manchurian Crisis, 1931–*

Suggested Reading

1932 (1948). Robert Ferrell, *American Diplomacy in the Great Depression* (1957), is the most systematic analysis of Hoover's foreign policy.

The fate of progressivism in the 1920's is discussed in Richard Hofstadter, *The Age of Reform* (1955); Eric Goldman, *Rendezvous with Destiny* (1952); and Arthur Ekirch, *The Decline of American Liberalism* (1955). Important regional studies of the disintegration of progressivism include C. Vann Woodward, *Tom Watson* (1938), a first-rate political biography; George Mowry, *The California Progressives* (1951), a path-breaking interpretation of progressivism; and Albert Kirwan, *Revolt of the Rednecks* (1951). The best of the memoirs of the period is *The Autobiography of Lincoln Steffens* (1931), which is in a class by itself, but Robert Morss Lovett, *All Our Years* (1948), should not be neglected. Edgar Kemler, *The Deflation of American Ideals* (1941), is provocative.

Claude Bowers, *Beveridge and the Progressive Era* (1932), emphasizes the role of nationalism in the progressive movement. David Noble, "The New Republic and the Idea of Progress, 1914–1920," *Mississippi Valley Historical Review*, XXXVIII (December, 1951), 387–402, traces the loss of confidence of the intellectual wing of the progressives. For contemporary analyses of progressivism, see Walter Weyl, *Tired Radicals and Other Essays* (1919); Herbert Croly, "The Eclipse of Progressivism," *New Republic*, XXIV (October 27, 1920), 210–16, and "The Outlook for Progressivism in Politics," *New Republic*, XLI (December 10, 1924), 60–64; and Charles Merz, "Progressivism, Old and New," *Atlantic Monthly*, CXXXII (July, 1923), 102–9.

Kenneth MacKay, *The Progressive Movement of 1924* (1947), is the standard monograph on that subject. The background of the 1924 revolt is developed in F. E. Haynes, *Social Politics in the United States* (1924); James Shideler, "The Neo-Progressives: Reform Politics in the United States, 1920–1925" (Ph.D. dissertation, University of California, Berkeley, 1945); and Robert Morlan, *Political Prairie Fire: The Nonpartisan League, 1915–1922* (1955). Alexander Harvey, "The Advantage of Senator La Follette," *American Mercury*, III (October, 1924), 208–10, is a shrewd analysis of Battle Bob. The major biography is Belle Case and Fola La Follette, *Robert M. La Follette* (2 vols., 1953), unabashedly hero-worshipping but nonetheless important. The results of the election are canvassed in Hugh Keenleyside, "The American Political Revolution of 1924," *Current History*, XXI (March, 1925), 833–40, and James Shideler, "The Disintegration of the Progressive Party Movement of 1924," *Historian* (Spring, 1951), 189–201. Paul Carter, *The Decline and Revival of the Social Gospel* (1956), is an excellent study of American Protestantism from 1920 to 1940.

Gilbert Fite, *George Peek and the Fight for Farm Parity* (1954), is the best treatment of farm politics in the 1920's. Other major sources are Theodore Saloutos and John Hicks, *Agricultural Discontent in the Middle West, 1900–1939* (1951); Grant McConnell, *Decline of Agrarian Democracy* (1953); Harold Barger and Hans Landsberg, *American Agriculture, 1899–1939* (1942); and Russell Lord, *The Wallaces of Iowa* (1947). Two of the more revealing articles are Malcolm Sillars, "Henry A. Wallace's Editorials on Agricultural Discontent, 1921–1928," *Agricultural History*, XXVI (October, 1952), 132–40, and Alice Christensen, "Agricultural Pressure and Governmental Response, 1919–1929," *Agricultural History*, XI (January, 1937), 33–42.

Selig Perlman and Philip Taft, *History of Labor in the United States, 1896–1932*, is the final volume of John Commons' monumental "History of Labour in the United States" (4 vols., 1918–35). Leo Wolman, *Growth of American Trade Unions, 1880–1923* (1924) is a standard source. For the Industrial Workers of the World, see Paul Brissenden, *The I.W.W.* (1919); J. S. Gambs, *The Decline of the I.W.W.* (1932); and Ralph Chaplin, *Wobbly* (1948). Philip Taft, *The A.F. of L. in the Time of Gompers* (1957), is the most recent study of the American Federation of Labor. J. B. S. Hardman (ed.), *American Labor Dynamics* (1928), performs an autopsy of the labor movement from 1918 to 1928. The more important articles include Sumner Slichter, "The Current Labor Policies of American Industries," *Quarterly Journal of Economics*, XLIII (May, 1929), 393–435; David Saposs, "The American Labor Movement Since the War," *Quarterly Journal of Economics*, XLIX (February, 1935), 236–54; and Lyle Cooper, "The American Labor Movement in Prosperity and Depression," *American Economic Review*, XXII (December, 1932), 641–59. Matthew Josephson, *Sidney Hillman* (1952), is essential for studying the clothing workers.

Suggested Reading

The intellectual history of the period is treated in a number of works, of varying merit: Alfred Kazin, *On Native Grounds* (1942); Frederick Hoffman, *The Twenties* (1955), and *The Modern Novel in America, 1900–1950* (1951); Maxwell Geismar, *Last of the Provincials* (1947); J. W. Beach, *American Fiction, 1920–1940* (1941); Malcolm Cowley (ed.), *After the Genteel Tradition* (1937); and Oscar Cargill, *Intellectual America* (1941). John Hutchens, *The American Twenties* (1952), is an anthology of the literature of the era, with an introductory essay. Edmund Wilson has collected two volumes of essays and occasional pieces which he wrote during these years: *The Shores of Light* (1952) and the forthcoming *The American Earthquake* (1958), which I read in galleys. Van Wyck Brooks, *The Confident Years 1885–1915* (1952), a wearily impressionistic account of the years before the war, is the fifth and final volume of his "Makers and Finders." *Days of the Phoenix* (1957) is autobiographical.

Malcolm Cowley, *Exile's Return* (1934 [new ed., 1951]) is a brilliant survey of the "lost generation." Among the more discerning articles on the period are Henry May, "The Rebellion of the Intellectuals, 1912–1917," *American Quarterly*, VIII (Summer, 1956), 114–26; W. H. Auden, "Henry James and the Artist in America," *Harper's*, CXCVII (July, 1948), 36–40; John Aldridge, "The Predicament of Today's Writer," *Sarah Lawrence Alumnae Magazine*, XXII (June, 1957), 6–7, 21–22; T. R. Fyvel, "Martin Arrowsmith and His Habitat," *New Republic*, CXXXIII (July 18, 1955), 16–18; and Arthur Mizener, "The Novel in America: 1920–1940," *Perspectives USA*, XV (Spring, 1956), 134–47. George Snyderman and William Josephs, "Bohemia: The Underworld of Art," *Social Forces*, XVIII (December, 1939), 187–99, is an unpretentious social analysis.

The bleak intellectual mood of the period is caught in Joseph Wood Krutch, *The Modern Temper* (1929), and Walter Lippmann, *A Preface to Morals* (1929). Henry Harrison, "Last Days of the Devastators," *Yale Review*, XVIII (September, 1928), 88–103, is a shrewd commentary on the cult of self-flagellation. Harold Stearns's *America and the Young Intellectual* (1921) and *Civilization in the United States* (1922) are landmarks. Mabel Dodge Luhan, *Intimate Memories* (4 vols., 1933–37), is fascinating. For H. L. Mencken, see Edgar Kemler, *The Irreverent Mr.*

The Perils of Prosperity, 1914–32

Mencken (1950), William Manchester, *Disturber of the Peace* (1951), and Charles Angoff, *H. L. Mencken* (1956).

Morton White, *Social Thought in America* (1949), is a searching study of the "revolt against formalism." Howard Mumford Jones, *The Bright Medusa* (1952), argues unconvincingly that the revolt of youth in the name of art in the 1920's was merely the culmination of a long tradition. Bernard DeVoto, *Forays and Rebuttals* (1936), includes an essay, "The Well-Informed, 1920–1930," and a hostile review of Cowley's *Exile's Return*. DeVoto's *The Literary Fallacy* (1944), a searing indictment of the writers of the 1920's, is a curious mixture of sense and nonsense. Stanley Edgar Hyman, *The Armed Vision* (1948), contains a murderous essay on Van Wyck Brooks. Lionel Trilling, *The Liberal Imagination* (1953), is a brilliant collection of essays, some of which, like the piece on Sherwood Anderson, deal directly with the 1920's, all of which provide fresh insights on the period.

Elizabeth Drew, *T. S. Eliot, The Design of His Poetry* (1949), is lucid. In the huge Eliot literature, F. O. Matthiessen, *The Achievement of T. S. Eliot* (2d ed., 1947), and the chapters in David Daiches, *Poetry and the Modern World* (1940), Stephen Spender, *The Destructive Element* (1935), and John Crowe Ransom, *The New Criticism* (1941), are noteworthy. *Hart Crane* has been the subject of studies by Philip Horton in 1937 and Brom Weber in 1948. Arthur Mizener, *The Far Side of Paradise* (1951), is a full-length biography of F. Scott Fitzgerald; Irving Howe, *Sherwood Anderson* (1951), is a good brief study. For the art of the period, see Oliver Larkin, *Art and Life in America* (1949); James Fitch, *American Building* (1948); and John Baur, *Revolution and Tradition in Modern American Art* (1951). Meyer Schapiro, "Rebellion in Art," in Daniel Aaron (ed.), *America in Crisis* (1952), is excellent on the Armory Show.

Historians have written almost nothing about the "revolution in morals"; the best source is contemporary periodicals. John Sirjamaki, *The American Family in the Twentieth Century* (1953), is written in a dehumanized sociological style. Oliver Jensen, *The Revolt of American Women* (1952), rises considerably above the level of most "picture books." Winthrop Sargeant, "Fifty Years of American Women," *Life*, XXVIII (January 2, 1950), 64–67, is a good light account by a writer who views the 1920's as a period of

Suggested Reading

disaster for American women. Inez Haynes Irwin's *Angels and Amazons* (1933) is a disorganized but useful account of the rise of women to the dominant position in American society; it is written in the style of female chauvinism that characterizes almost all the feminist literature.

The best contemporary work on the revolution in morals is Freda Kirchwey (ed.), *Our Changing Morality: A Symposium* (1924). The May, 1929, issue of *The Annals of the American Academy of Political and Social Science* and the December 1, 1926, issue of *The Survey* are devoted to women. For contemporary comments, see Katharine Fullerton Gerould, "Reflections of a Grundy Cousin," *Atlantic Monthly*, CXXVI (August, 1920), 157–63; John Carter, Jr., " 'These Wild Young People': By One of Them," *Atlantic Monthly*, CXXVI (September, 1920), 301–4; Viola Paradise, "Sex Simplex," *Forum*, LXXIV (July, 1925), 108–11; Mary Agnes Hamilton, " 'Nothing Shocks Me,' " *Harper's*, CLV (July, 1927), 150–57; Dorothy Dunbar Bromley, "Feminist, New Style," *Harper's*, CLV (October, 1927), 552–60; Eleanor Rowland Wembridge, "Petting and the Campus," *Survey*, LIV (July 1, 1925), 393–95, 412; William Bolitho, "The New Skirt Length," *Harper's*, CLX (February, 1930), 292–96; and G. Stanley Hall, "Flapper Americana Novissima," *Atlantic Monthly*, CXXIX (June, 1922), 771–80.

Ernest Jones, *The Life and Work of Sigmund Freud* (3 vols., 1953–57) is the definitive biography of Freud. Walter Lippmann, "Freud and the Layman," *New Republic*, II (April 17, 1915), Supp. 9–10, is one of the earliest appreciations of Freud. George Santayana, "A Long Way Round to Nirvana: or, Much Ado About Dying," *Dial*, LXXV (November, 1923), 435–42, comments on Freud's *Beyond the Pleasure Principle*. Joseph Jastrow, "The Freudian Temper: And Its Menace to the Lay Mind," *Century*, CXIX (Autumn, 1929), 29–38, is critical. For the reception of Freud in the United States, see A. A. Brill, "The Introduction and Development of Freud's Work in the United States," *American Journal of Sociology*, XLV (November, 1939), 318–25; Celia Stendler, "New Ideas for Old: How Freudism Was Received in the United States from 1900 to 1925," *Journal of Educational Psychology*, XXXVIII (April, 1947), 193–206; Havelock Ellis, "Freud's Influence on the Changed Attitude Toward Sex," *Ameri-*

The Perils of Prosperity, 1914-32

can *Journal of Sociology*, XLV (November, 1939), 309-17; Karl Menninger, "Pseudoanalysis: Perils of Freudian Verbalisms," *Outlook*, CLV (July 9, 1930), 363-65, 397; and Grace Adams, "The Rise and Fall of Psychology," *Atlantic Monthly*, CLIII (January, 1934), 82-92.

Frederick Hoffman, *Freudianism and the Literary Mind* (1945), is the best source for studying that subject. Maxwell Bodenheim, "Psychoanalysis and American Fiction," *The Nation*, CXIV (June 7, 1922), 683-84, takes a dim view of the "phallic exaggerations" in American literature, especially of stories "in which young men lie upon their backs in cornfields and feel depressed by their bodies." Lucille Birnbaum, "Behaviorism in the 1920's," *American Quarterly*, VII (Spring, 1955), 15-30, is admirable. O. G. Villard, "Sex, Art, Truth and Magazines," *Atlantic Monthly*, CXXXVII (March, 1926), 388-98, and Jo Swerling, "The Picture Papers Win," *The Nation*, CXXI (October 21, 1925), 455-58, are good on the tabloids. The most rewarding of the articles written from the perspective of the 1930's are F. Scott Fitzgerald, "Echoes of the Jazz Age," *Scribner's*, XC (November, 1931), 459-65; Nancy Evans, "Goodbye Bohemia," *Scribner's*, LXXXIX (June, 1931), 643-46; and Thomas Beer, "Toward Sunrise, 1920-1930," *Scribner's*, LXXXVII (May, 1930), 536-45.

While historians of the period have scarcely done even the spadework in most areas, the economy of this era has been studied to a fare-thee-well. Thanks largely to the initiative of the Brookings Institution and the National Bureau of Economic Research, the student is faced chiefly with a problem of selection. The following lists only a few of the more important monographs: Frederick Mills, *Economic Tendencies in the United States* (1932); Arthur Burns's *Production Trends in the United States since 1870* (1934); Arthur R. Burns, *The Decline of Competition* (1936); Solomon Fabricant, *The Output of Manufacturing Industries, 1899-1937* (1940); Jacob Gould, *Output and Productivity in the Electric and Gas Utilities, 1899-1942* (1946); Ralph Epstein, *Industrial Profits in the United States* (1934); Charles Bliss, *The Structure of Manufacturing Production* (1946); Harold Barger, *Outlay and Income in the United States, 1921-1938* (1942); Robert Gordon, *Business Fluctuations* (1952); Joseph Schumpeter, *Business Cycles* (1939); Edwin Nourse *et al.*, *America's Capacity to Produce* (1934); Maurice Leven

Suggested Reading

et al., *America's Capacity to Consume* (1934); George Stigler, *Trends in Output and Employment* (1947); Thomas Wilson, *Fluctuations in Income and Employment* (1948); Paul Douglas, *Real Wages in the United States, 1890–1926* (1930); and George Edwards, *The Evolution of Finance Capitalism* (1938). Simon Kuznets, one of the great innovators of the period, is the author of *National Income and Its Composition, 1919–1938* (1941) and *National Products since 1869* (1946).

President's Conference on Unemployment, *Recent Economic Changes in the United States* (2 vols., 1929), is an invaluable compendium. George Soule, *Prosperity Decade* (1947), is the best economic history of the times. James Prothro, *The Dollar Decade* (1954), is a droll recital of business thought. Charles Chapman, *The Development of American Business and Banking Thought, 1913–1936* (1936), is less useful. For contemporary appraisals, see Thomas Nixon Carver, *The Present Economic Revolution in the United States* (1925); W. Z. Ripley, *Main Street and Wall Street* (1927); J. T. Adams, *Our Business Civilization* (1929); Adolf Berle and Gardiner Means, *The Modern Corporation and Private Property* (1932); and Stuart Chase, *Prosperity—Fact or Myth* (1930). Frederick Lewis Allen, *The Lords of Creation* (1935), offers a sound secondary account. Sidney Ratner, *American Taxation* (1942), is the best treatment of that subject.

The best sources on technology are U.S. National Resources Committee, *Technological Trends and National Policy* (1937); Harry Jerome, *Mechanization in Industry* (1934); Roger Burlingame, *Engines of Democracy* (1940); Siegfried Giedion, *Mechanization Takes Command* (1948); Walter Polakov, *The Power Age* (1933); and Stuart Chase, *Men and Machines* (1929). Allan Nevins and Frank Ernest Hill, *Ford: Expansion and Challenge: 1915–1933* (1957), is the definitive biography of Ford, but Keith Sward, *The Legend of Henry Ford* (1948), a highly critical study, should not be overlooked.

For analyses of the period, see Joseph Schumpeter, "The American Economy in the Interwar Period: The Decade of the Twenties," *American Economic Review*, XXXVI (May, 1946), 1–10, with a commentary by Garfield Cox, and Sumner Slichter, "The Period 1919–1936 in the United States: Its Significance for Business-Cycle Theory," *Review of Economic Statistics*, XIX (February, 1937), 1–19. Other useful articles are Norman Buchanan, "The Origin and Development of the Public Utility Holding Company," *Journal of Political Economy*, XLIV (February, 1936), 31–55; Sumner Slichter, "The Secret of High Wages," *New Republic*, LIV (March 28, 1928), 183–85; "Swiss Family Dreyfus," *Fortune*, VIII (September, 1933), 50–55, 139–44; "A & P and the Hartfords," *Fortune*, VII (March, 1933), 52–55, 128–32; "Woolworth," *Fortune*, VIII (November, 1933), 62–70, 104–110; N. R. Danielian, "From Insull to Injury," *Atlantic Monthly*, CLI (April, 1933), 497–508; and "Fifty Years: 1888–1938," *Printers' Ink*, CLXXXIV (July 28, 1938), Sec. 2.

John Higham, *Strangers in the Land* (1955), is a magnificent study of nativism. The best brief history of the movement for immigration restriction is contained in Charles Howland (ed.), *Survey of American Foreign Relations, 1929* (1929), Sec. III. Kenneth Roberts, *Why Europe Leaves Home* (1922), is a vicious polemic. Robert DeC. Ward, "Our New Immigration Policy," *Foreign Affairs*, III (September 15, 1924), 99–111, is the most reasoned defense of the National Origins Act. Arthur Mann, "Gompers and the Irony of Racism," *Antioch Review*, XIII (Summer, 1953), 203–14, and William Bagley, "The Army Tests and the Pro-Nordic Propaganda," *Educational Review*, LXVII (April, 1924), 179–87, are pertinent articles.

Norman Furniss, *The Fundamentalist Controversy, 1918–1931* (1954), is the best treatment of that subject. It should be supplemented by H. Richard Niebuhr's succinct article on "Fundamentalism" in the *Encyclopedia of the Social Sciences*. Gail Kennedy (ed.), *Evolution and Religion* (1957), and E. C. Vanderlaan (ed.), *Fundamentalism versus Modernism* (1925), are handy compilations. William T. Doherty, "The Impact of Business on Protestantism, 1900–29," *Business History Review*, XXVIII (June, 1954), 141–53, is a whimsical account. Russell Owen, "The Significance of the Scopes Trial: Issues and Personalities," *Current History*, XXII (September, 1925), 875–83, is the best contemporary report. There is no good biography of Bryan; Paxton Hibben and C. H. Grattan, *The Peerless Leader* (1929), is the most satisfactory. Until Ray Ginger completes his projected biography of Darrow, Irving Stone, *Clarence Darrow for the Defense* (1941), and Clarence Darrow, *The Story of My Life* (1932), will have to suffice.

Suggested Reading

Charles Merz, *The Dry Decade* (1931), is the standard work on prohibition. For other appraisals, see Herbert Asbury, *The Great Illusion* (1950), and the April, 1928, issue of *Current History*. Virginius Dabney, *Dry Messiah: The Life of Bishop Cannon* (1949), is an acid portrait which is also useful for studying the 1928 campaign.

We have no adequate history of the Ku Klux Klan. Emerson Loucks, *The Ku Klux Klan in Pennsylvania* (1936), is a sound regional study, and Frank Tannenbaum, *Darker Phases of the South* (1924), has a perceptive chapter on the origins of the Klan spirit. The best articles on the subject are Morton Harrison, "Gentlemen from Indiana," *Atlantic Monthly*, CXLI (May, 1928), 676–86; R. A. Patton, "A Ku Klux Klan Reign of Terror," *Current History*, XXVIII (April, 1928), 51–55; Waldo Roberts, "The Ku-Kluxing of Oregon," *Outlook*, CXXXIII (March 14, 1923), 490–91; Ben Lindsey, "My Fight with the Ku Klux Klan," *Survey*, LIV (June 1, 1925), 271–74, 319–21; Frank Bohn, "The Ku Klux Klan Interpreted," *American Journal of Sociology*, XXX (January, 1925), 385–407; and Robert Moats Miller, "A Note on the Relationship between the Protestant Churches and the Revived Ku Klux Klan," *Journal of Social History*, XXII (August, 1956), 355–68.

There is no good life of Al Smith. Until Oscar Handlin's biography appears, the most useful volume is Henry Pringle, *Alfred E. Smith* (1927). Samuel Lubell, *The Future of American Politics* (1952), demonstrates, in a lively fashion, the importance of the "revolt of the city" in the 1928 campaign. Lubell relies heavily on Samuel Eldersveld, "Influence of Metropolitan Party Pluralities in Presidential Elections since 1920," *American Political Science Review*, XLIII (December, 1949), 1189–1206. Roy Peel and Thomas Donnelly, *The 1928 Campaign: An Analysis* (1931), is a sound, brief account. Edmund Moore, *A Catholic Runs for President* (1956), is excellent on the religious issue. V. O. Key, Jr., *Southern Politics* (1949), contains an important chapter comparing the Hoovercrats of 1928 with the Dixiecrats of 1948. Frank Freidel, *Franklin D. Roosevelt: The Ordeal* (1954), is an invaluable source of Democratic party history in the 1920's. Gene Fowler, *Beau James* (1949), gives a sentimental and superficial view of Jimmy Walker. For statements by Smith's most redoubtable foe, see James Cannon, Jr., "Al Smith—Catholic, Tammany, Wet," *The Nation*,

The Perils of Prosperity, 1914–32

CXXVII (July 4, 1928), 9–10, and "Causes of Governor Smith's Defeat," *Current History*, XXIX (December, 1928), 373–77. Washington Pezet, "The Temporal Power of Evangelism," *Forum*, LXXVI (October, 1926), 481–91, and Robert Moats Miller, "A Footnote to the Role of the Protestant Churches in the Election of 1928," *Church History*, XXV (June, 1956), 145–59, offer contrasting views of the role of the Protestant church in politics.

Charles Merz, "Bull Market," *Harper's*, CLVII (April, 1929), 640–46, presents a lively account of the speculative fervor. Joe Alex Morris, *What a Year!* (1956), gives a once-over-lightly view of 1929. John Kenneth Galbraith, *The Great Crash* (1955), is written with a marvellously dry wit. Most of the books listed on economics are applicable to the crash and the depression. Special studies include Lionel Robbins, *The Great Depression* (1934), and Francis Hirst, *Wall Street and Lombard Street* (1931). Broadus Mitchell, *Depression Decade* (1947), is the best economic history. E. Jay Howenstine, Jr., "World War I Production Dislocations as a Causal Factor of the Great Depression in the United States," *American Journal of Economics and Sociology*, XIII (January, 1954), 129–47, minimizes the importance of World War I. Gilbert Seldes, *Years of the Locust* (1933), Mauritz Hallgren, *Seeds of Revolt* (1933), and Jonathan Leonard, *Three Years Down* (1939), are social histories of the depression.

The chief sources on Hoover are his *Memoirs* (3 vols., 1951–52), W. S. Myers and W. H. Newton, *The Hoover Administration* (1936), and Ray Lyman Wilbur and Arthur Hyde, *The Hoover Policies* (1937). Hoover emphasizes his rural origins in "Boyhood in Iowa," *Palimpsest*, IX (July, 1928), 269–76; and "In Praise of Izaak Walton," *Atlantic Monthly*, CXXXIX (June, 1927), 813–19. T. G. Joslin, *Hoover—Off the Record* (1934), is a warm defense; R. G. Tugwell, *Mr. Hoover's Economic Policy* (1932), is critical. Walter Lippmann, "The Peculiar Weakness of Mr. Hoover," *Harper's*, CLXI (June, 1930), 1–7; Allan Nevins, "President Hoover's Record," *Current History*, XXXVI (July, 1932), 385–94; William Allen White, "Herbert Hoover—the Last of the Old Presidents or the First of the New," *Saturday Evening Post*, CCV (March 4, 1933), 6–7, 53–56; and Mark Sullivan, "The Case for the Administration," *Fortune*, VI (July, 1932), 35–39, 83–88, offer contrasting views.

Suggested Reading

Two of the best accounts of the suffering caused by the depression are " 'No One Has Starved,' " *Fortune*, VI (September, 1932), 19–28, 80–88, and "New York in Third Winter," *Fortune*, V (January, 1932), 41–48, 109, 121. John Maynard Keynes, "The World's Economic Outlook," *Atlantic Monthly*, CXLIX (May, 1932), 521–26; Elmer Davis, "Confidence in Whom?" *Forum*, LXXXIX (January, 1933), 31–33; Paul Sifton, "Going, Going, Gone!" *Forum*, LXXXIX (March, 1933), 161–68; J. Russell Smith, "The End of an Epoch," *Survey*, LXVI (July 1, 1931), 333–36, 364–66; James Truslow Adams, "Shadow of the Man on Horseback," *Atlantic Monthly*, CXLIX (January, 1932), 1–10; and Reinhold Niebuhr, "Catastrophe or Social Control?" *Harper's*, CLXV (June, 1932), 114–18, all view with alarm. David Salmon, *Confessions of a Former Customers' Man* (1932), is typical of the *mea culpa* literature produced by the crash. The book opens: "For almost fifteen years I was a financial parasite and procurer. . . ." R. V. Peel and T. C. Donnelly, *The 1932 Campaign* (1935), Rexford Tugwell, *The Democratic Roosevelt* (1957), and Frank Freidel, *Franklin D. Roosevelt: The Triumph* (1956), present good descriptions of the 1932 campaign.

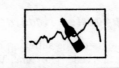

Acknowledgments

My friends Daniel Aaron, Richard Hofstadter, and Arthur Link and my wife Jean McIntire Leuchtenburg have read this manuscript in its entirety and have made invaluable suggestions on both style and content. The staff of the Columbia University Library has been invariably helpful. Miss Ermine Stone and the staff of the Sarah Lawrence College Library have gone far beyond the hospitality due a neighbor. Many of the ideas in this volume were first threshed out with students in my graduate seminars at Columbia.

WILLIAM E. LEUCHTENBURG

Index

Index

300

Index

Butler, William, 96
Byrnes, James, 66

Cabell, James Branch, 167
Canada, 15, 108, 114, 215, 223–24
Canfield, Dorothy. *See* Fisher,
   Dorothy Canfield
Cannon, Jr., James, 171, 234–36
Čapek, Karel, 152
Capitalism, 7, 13, 67, 145–46, 187,
   202, 231, 233, 237, 256, 261. *See
   also* Economy, American; Wel-
   fare capitalism
Capone, Al, 216, 270
Caporetto, 36
Capper, Arthur, 101
Capper-Volstead Act, 102
Carnegie, Andrew, 199
Carpenters and Joiners, United
   Brotherhood of, 135
Carpentier, Georges, 195
Carver, George Washington, 182
Casement, Sir Roger, 22
Castle, William, 117
Cather, Willa, 156, 273
Catholics, 10, 127, 188, 209–12, 224,
   230–37, 239
Cavell, Edith, 15, 264
Central Powers. *See* Austria-Hun-
   gary; Germany
Chains. *See* Monopoly
Chamberlain, Joseph, 122
Chaplin, Charles, 70, 196
Character, American, 9, 11, 198–
   200, 250, 252
Charleston, 170
Chase, Stuart, 137
Chase National Bank, 192
Chateau-Thierry, 36
Chautauqua, 1–2
Chicago Black Sox, 81, 169
Chicago Civic Opera, 191
Chicago and North Western Rail-
   road, 248
Child labor, 77, 99–100, 123, 254
Child Labor Act of 1916, 99
Child-rearing, 162–63
Child Study Association, 164

Children's Bureau, 5
China, 29, 114–16. *See also* Shan-
   tung
Chrysler Building, 183
Chrysler Corporation, 193, 252
Churchill, Winston, 35, 56, 250
Cities, 2, 4–5, 7–10, 96, 132, 137–39,
   141, 158, 204, 208–9, 213–16, 219,
   221–25, 227–32, 236–40, 252–53,
   271–73
Civil Liberties, 44–45. *See also* Red
   Scare
Civil War, American, 1, 12, 42, 152
Civilian Conservation Corps, 267
Civilization in the United States,
   151
Clark, Champ, 42
Clarke, Edward Y., 210
Class stratification, 3–7, 9, 45, 71,
   73, 75–76, 82–83, 126, 141–42, 158,
   213, 231–32, 236, 245–46, 248
Clayton Act, 99
Clemenceau, Georges, 49, 54–55
Clicquot Club Eskimos, 197
Coal strike of 1919, 75–76
Cohan, George M., 35
Collective security, 64, 106. *See
   also* Internationalism
Committee on Public Information.
   See Creel Committee
Commons, John, 122
Commonwealth and Southern
   Corporation, 191
Communism, 66–67, 72, 78, 81, 128,
   218, 261. *See also* Communist
   party, American
Communist Labor party, 68–69, 78
Communist party, American, 68–
   69, 78, 261
Comstock, Anthony, 176
Conformity, 7–8, 44–45, 129, 150,
   204, 272. *See also* Political Fun-
   damentalism; Red Scare
Congressional elections of 1918,
   50–52
Conscription, 33, 42–43
Conservatism, 67, 81, 86, 96–99,
   122–23, 126, 137–38, 149, 201, 231,

301

Index

Index

Index

Index

Index

Index

Index

Index

Index

Index

Simpson, John, 262
Sims, William, 38
Sinclair, Harry, 93
Sinclair, Upton, 83
Skyscrapers, 182–83
Slosson, Preston, 89
Small town, 2–4, 6–7, 43, 90, 96, 137, 151, 209, 213, 215, 218 19, 225–26, 228–29, 239
Smith, Alfred E., 10, 133, 212, 216–17, 229–40, 265–66, 272
Smith, Jesse, 91–92, 94
"Smolny," 68
Smuts, Jan, 55
Snappy Stories, 168
Social Democrats, 176, 207
Socialist party, American, 43–44, 66–70, 79, 124, 128, 131, 137, 141, 202. *See also* Debs, Eugene
Somme, 28, 36
Sound and the Fury, The, 167
Soviet Union. *See* Russia
Spain, 208
Spanish-American War, 5, 43
Spartacists, 67
Spending, government, 38–39, 98, 130, 137–38, 184–86, 242, 245, 250–52, 254–55, 257–58, 267
Spengler, Oswald, 227
Spoon River Anthology, 225
Sports, 81, 169, 195–97, 249, 270
Spreckels, Rudolph, 234
Stearns, Frank, 96
Stearns, Harold, 151
Steel strike of 1919, 74–75
Steffens, Lincoln, 125, 137, 202
Stein, Gertrude, 83, 175
Stephenson, David, 210–13
Stevens, Wallace, 156
Stieglitz, Alfred, 11, 145
Stoddard, Lothrop, 206
Stone, Irving, 97
Strange Interlude, 161, 166
Straus, Nathan, 231
Stravinski, Igor, 70
Streeter, John, 132
Strikes, 5, 71, 73–76, 99, 123, 179, 194, 204

Strong reservationists, 58, 63
Submarine. *See* Neutral rights; World War I
Suffrage, women's. *See* Women's suffrage
Sullivan, Mark, 84
Sumners, Hatton, 260
Sun Also Rises, The, 170
Sunday, Billy, 66
Supreme Court, 99–100, 132, 134, 210
"Sussex pledge," 21, 22, 25
Swope, Gerard, 41–42
Syndicalism, 64, 78, 129

Tabloids, 168
Taft, William Howard, 6, 85, 97, 120
Tamiami Trail, 185
Tammany Hall, 216, 227–30, 239
Tariff, 103, 109–12, 119, 122, 181, 234, 236, 246, 267
Tarkington, Booth, 11
Taxation, 98, 100, 123, 130, 138, 246, 259
Taylor, Frederick, 179
Teachers College, 2
Teapot Dome, Wyoming, 93, 145
Technology, 2, 5–6, 11, 144, 151–52, 178–82, 185, 193, 207, 260–61, 272
Tel. and Tel. *See* American Telephone and Telegraph Company
Tennessee Valley Authority, 130
Tennyson, Alfred, 14
Terminal Tower, 183
Texas Guinan's, 4
Thayer, Webster, 82
Theater, American, 140, 156
Third International, 67, 69
This Side of Paradise, 148, 155, 172
Thomas, George, 1
Three Contributions to a Theory of Sex, 163
Tidewater Power Company, 191
Tilden, Bill, 195

311

Index

Index

THE CHICAGO HISTORY OF AMERICAN CIVILIZATION

DANIEL J. BOORSTIN, EDITOR

Edmund S. Morgan, *The Birth of the Republic: 1763–89*

Marcus Cunliffe, *The Nation Takes Shape: 1789–1837*

*Elbert B. Smith, *The Death of Slavery: The United States, 1837–65*

John Hope Franklin, *Reconstruction: After the Civil War*

Samuel P. Hays, *The Response to Industrialism: 1885–1914*

William E. Leuchtenburg, *The Perils of Prosperity: 1914–32*

Dexter Perkins, *The New Age of Franklin Roosevelt: 1932–45*

Herbert Agar, *The Price of Power: America since 1945*

*　　*　　*

Robert H. Bremner, *American Philanthropy*

Harry L. Coles, *The War of 1812*

Richard M. Dorson, *American Folklore*

John Tracy Ellis, *American Catholicism*

Nathan Glazer, *American Judaism*

William T. Hagan, *American Indians*

Winthrop S. Hudson, *American Protestantism*

Maldwyn Allen Jones, *American Immigration*

Robert G. McCloskey, *The American Supreme Court*

Howard H. Peckham, *The War for Independence: A Military History*

Howard H. Peckham, *The Colonial Wars: 1689–1762*

Henry Pelling, *American Labor*

*John B. Rae, *The American Automobile: A Brief History*

Charles P. Roland, *The Confederacy*

Otis A. Singletary, *The Mexican War*

John F. Stover, *American Railroads*

*Bernard A. Weisberger, *The American Newspaperman*

* Available in cloth only. All other books published in both cloth and paperback editions.